EURIPIDES

Iphigenia among the Taurians

Bacchae

Iphigenia at Aulis

Rhesus

Euripides

Iphigenia among the Taurians
Bacchae
Iphigenia at Aulis
Rhesus

Translated with Explanatory Notes by
JAMES MORWOOD

With Introduction by
EDITH HALL

OXFORD
UNIVERSITY PRESS

OXFORD
UNIVERSITY PRESS

Great Clarendon Street, Oxford ox2 6DP

Oxford University Press is a department of the University of Oxford
It furthers the University's objective of excellence in research, scholarship,
and education by publishing worldwide in

Oxford New York

Athens Auckland Bangkok Bogotá Buenos Aires Calcutta
Cape Town Chennai Dar es Salaam Delhi Florence Hong Kong Istanbul
Karachi Kuala Lumpur Madrid Melbourne Mexico City Mumbai
Nairobi Paris São Paulo Singapore Taipei Tokyo Toronto Warsaw

with associated companies in Berlin Ibadan

Oxford is a registered trade mark of Oxford University Press
in the UK and in certain other countries

Published in the United States
by Oxford University Press Inc., New York

Introduction and Bibliography © Edith Hall 1999
Translation and Notes © James Morwood 1999

The moral rights of the author have been asserted

Database right Oxford University Press (maker)

All rights reserved. No part of this publication may be reproduced,
stored in a retrieval system, or transmitted, in any form or by any means,
without the prior permission in writing of Oxford University Press,
or as expressly permitted by law, or under terms agreed with the appropriate
reprographcs rights organisation. Enquiries concerning reproduction
outside the scope of the above should be sent to the Rights Department,
Oxford University Press, at the address above

You must not circulate this book in any other binding or cover
and you must impose this same condition on any acquiror

British Library Cataloguing in Publication Data

Data available

Library of Congress Cataloging in Publication Data

Euripides. Iphigenia among the Taurians; Bacchae; Iphigenia at Aulis;
Rhesus / translated with explanatory notes by James Morwood; with
an introduction by Edith Hall.
Includes bibliographical references.
1. Euripides—Translations into English. 2. Rhesus (Legendary
character)—Drama. 3. Iphigenia (Greek mythology)—Drama.
4. Pentheus (Greek mythology)—Drama. 5. Dionysus (Greek deity)—
Drama. 6. Bacchantes—Drama. I. Morwood, James. II. Title.
III. Title: Iphigenia among the Taurians; Bacchae; Iphigenia at
Aulis; Rhesus.
PA3975.A2   1998d   882'.01—dc21   98-37702
ISBN 0-19-815094-6
Typeset by Hope Services (Abingdon) Ltd.
Printed in Great Britain on acid-free paper by
Biddles Ltd., Guildford & King's Lynn

KINGSTON COLLEGE
LEARNING RESOURCES CE

Class No.	882 EUR
Acc. No.	0 010112
Date Rec	05/07
Order No	I 124/2012 ABC

ACKNOWLEDGEMENTS

The translator would like to acknowledge his considerable debt to Professor Christopher Collard and Professor James Diggle. Any errors or misjudgements are due to his own obstinacy or negligence.

CONTENTS

INTRODUCTION

I. EURIPIDES AND HIS TRADITION

Many of Euripides' most striking dramas have not even survived. The most scandalous, perhaps, was his *Aeolus*, notoriously portraying brother–sister incest leading to childbirth and suicide. The most bizarre may have been his *Cretans*, featuring Queen Pasiphaë's adulterous affair with a bull. But the most beautiful was held to be *Andromeda*, in which the Ethiopian princess, chained to a rock as a meal for a sea-monster, was rescued by the aerial epiphany of the winged hero Perseus.

According to the comic playwright Aristophanes, *Andromeda* was so delightful that it was the preferred recreational reading of Dionysus, the god of theatre himself (*Frogs* 53), and its fragments reveal an appealing concoction not unlike *Iphigenia among the Taurians*: it added the theatricality of exotic spectacle and song to emotive pathos and suspense, and distinctively 'novelistic' elements such as adventure, intrigue, an emotional reunion, and a barbarian setting. Yet Alexander the Great, no professional actor, is supposed to have been able to perform a whole episode of *Andromeda* off by heart, and did so at his last supper (Athenaeus, *Deipnosophists* 12.537d–e); the single most significant reason for Euripides' astonishing ancient popularity was really the accessible and memorable poetry in which his characters expressed themselves. Princesses and paupers, demi-gods and warriors, practitioners of incest, bestiality, human sacrifice and murder: he made them all 'speak like human beings' (see Aristophanes, *Frogs* 1058).

The Greeks and Romans were passionate about Euripides. A character in a comedy announced that he would be prepared to hang himself for the sake of seeing this (dead) tragedian (Philemon fr. 118).[1] Aristotle's formalist discussion of tragedy complains about Euripides' use of the *deus ex machina*, his unintegrated choruses, and the 'unnecessary' villainy of some of his characters. Yet even Aristotle conceded that Euripides was 'the most tragic of the poets',

---

[1] All fragments of comedy are cited from R. Kassel and C. Austin (eds.), *Poetae Comici Graeci* (Berlin and New York, 1983–95).

meaning that he was the best at eliciting pity and fear.[2] Besides
Euripides' impact on the literature of succeeding generations—especially Menander, Ennius, Virgil, Ovid, Seneca, and oratory—his
plays are everywhere apparent in the *visual* culture of the
Mediterranean. Homer apart, no author stimulated the arts more;
the Romans painted Euripides' scenes on their walls and carved
them on their sarcophagi; the Byzantines commissioned elaborate
mosaics keeping his pagan myths alive in the visual imagination of
Christendom. Touching scenes from the two Iphigenia plays were
popular choices.

The nineteenth-century scholar Benjamin Jowett said Euripides
was 'no Greek in the better sense of the term',[3] for after his revivi-
fication in the Renaissance Euripides often suffered by comparison
with the structural perfection, 'purity', and 'Hellenic' spirit perceived in his rival Sophocles. This is, however, to oversimplify the
complex and largely unwritten story of Euripidean reception and
performance. *Iphigenia among the Taurians* was much imitated in the
late seventeenth and eighteenth centuries, most importantly by
Goethe in his *Iphigenie* (completed in 1787). *Iphigenia at Aulis* has
always been popular. It was the first Greek tragedy to receive the
honour of a vernacular English translation, by Lady Jane Lumley
(1558). It inspired one of the most influential of all neoclassical
adaptations, Racine's *Iphigénie en Aulide* of 1674. Today it is most
widely known through Michael Cacoyannis's atmospheric cine-
matic version of 1976, often held to be the best film based on a
Greek tragedy ever made. Both Iphigenia plays have inspired
numerous operas, the best of which were Christoph Gluck's
Iphigénie en Aulide (1774) and *Iphigénie en Tauride* (1779). Gluck's
aim was to reform his medium by reflecting in continuous music an
authentic Greek dramatic style. The bloodthirsty maenads of
Bacchae, on the other hand, repelled readers until well into the nineteenth century, but once Nietzsche had reopened the question of
Dionysus' relationship to the theatre in *The Birth of Tragedy* (1872),
the play became extremely fashionable. *Bacchae* underlies Bernard
Shaw's *Major Barbara*,[4] and is now frequently performed. Its ecsta-

---

[2] *Poetics* 56ª25–7, 54ᵇ1, 61ᵇ21, 53ª30.
[3] See A. N. Michelini, *Euripides and the Tragic Tradition* (Madison and London,
1987), 11 n. 40.
[4] See Fiona Macintosh, 'The Shavian Murray and the Euripidean Shaw: *Major
Barbara* and the *Bacchae*', *Classics Ireland*, 5 (1998), 64–84.

tic choruses have also inspired several twentieth-century operas, most importantly Hans Werner Henze's *Bassarids* of 1966 (on the libretto of which W. H. Auden collaborated), and ballets choreographed by such important figures as Diaghilev (1912) and Martha Graham (1933). *Rhesus*, on the other hand, written almost certainly not by Euripides but by an unknown tragedian in the fourth century BCE, has been neglected in both academe and on the modern stage.

Yet the twentieth century has smiled on Euripides more than any era since antiquity. One reason is his approach to myth, which has been characterized as subversive, experimental, playful, and eccentric in an identifiably modern way. Although he has occasionally been seen as a formalist or mannerist, the term 'irony' dominates criticism. 'Irony' is taken to describe Euripides' polytonality—his ability to write in two simultaneous keys. This 'irony', however, is conceived in more than one way: sometimes it describes the hypocritical gap between the rhetorical postures Euripidean characters adopt and their true motives. Alternatively it defines the confrontation of archaic myths with the values of democratic Athens, a process which deglamorizes violence, casting heroic revenge narratives as sordid 'gangland killings'.[5]

Another reason for Euripides' modern popularity is that his supple and multi-faceted works easily adapt to the agendas of different interpreters. Euripides has been an existentialist, a psychoanalyst, a proto-Christian with a passionate hunger for 'righteousness', an idealist and humanist, a mystic, a rationalist, an irrationalist, and an absurdist nihilist. But perhaps the most tenacious Euripides has been the pacifist feminist.

'Radical' Euripides was born in the first decade of this century with Gilbert Murray as midwife. This famous liberal scholar, later Chairman of the League of Nations, initiated in Edwardian London a series of performances of Euripides in his own English translations. *Trojan Women* (1905) was interpreted by some as a retrospective indictment of the concentration camps in which the British had starved women and children during the Boer War: as a result of *Medea* (1907), the heroine's monologue on the plight of women (see § VIII) was recited at suffragette meetings. A prominent suffragette, Lillah McCarthy, daringly took the role of Dionysus in *Bacchae* in

---

[5] This phrase is borrowed from W. G. Arnott's excellent article, 'Double the vision: a reading of Euripides' *Electra*', *G&R* 28 (1981), 179–92.

1908, and subsequently of Iphigenia in *Iphigenia among the Taurians* (1912). Murray's political interpretations of Euripides, developed in performance, found academic expression in *Euripides and his Age* (1913). This book has fundamentally conditioned all subsequent interpretation, whether by imitation or reaction. A decade later Euripides' radicalism had become apocalyptic: 'not Ibsen, not Voltaire, not Tolstoi ever forged a keener weapon in defence of womanhood, in defiance of superstition, in denunciation of war, than the *Medea*, the *Ion*, the *Trojan Women*'.[6]

II. EURIPIDES THE ATHENIAN

What would Euripides have made of his modern incarnations? The reliable external biographical information amounts to practically nothing. No dependable account of Euripides' own views on politics, women, or war survives, unless we are arbitrarily to select speeches by characters in his plays as the cryptic 'voice of Euripides'. Aristophanes and the other contemporary Athenian comic poets, who wrote what is now known as 'Old Comedy', caricatured Euripides as a cuckolded greengrocer's son, but their portrait offers little more truth value than a scurrilous cartoon.

The problem is not any dearth of evidence but a dearth of factual veracity. The student of Euripides has access to a late antique 'Life' (*Vita*) and a fragmentary third-century biography by Satyrus. There are also the so-called 'Letters of Euripides', a collection of five dull epistles purporting to be addressed to individuals such as Archelaus (king of Macedon) and Sophocles, but actually written in the first or second century CE. Collectively these documents provide the first example in the European tradition of the portrait of an alienated artist seeking solace in solitude. This Euripides is a misogynist loner with facial blemishes who worked in a seaside cave on the island of Salamis, and retired to voluntary exile in Macedon as a result of his unpopularity. Unfortunately, however, this poignant portrait is demonstrably a fiction created out of simplistic inferences from Euripides' own works or from the jokes in Athenian comedy. Beyond what is briefly detailed below, the only aspect of the 'Euripides myth' almost certain to be true is that he possessed a large personal library (see Aristophanes, *Frogs* 943, 1049).

---

[6] F. L. Lucas, *Euripides and his Influence* (London and Sydney, 1924), 15.

Euripides' lifespan was almost exactly commensurate with that of democratic Athens's greatness. He was born in about 485 BCE, and was therefore a small boy when the city was evacuated and his compatriots defeated the second Persian invasion in 480 BCE. He spent his youth and physical prime in the thriving atmosphere of the 460s and 450s, a period which saw the consolidation of Athens's empire and position as cultural centre of the Greek-speaking world. He wrote at least eighty plays, and possibly ninety-two. Nineteen have been transmitted from antiquity under his name. Of these, *Rhesus* is probably not by Euripides himself, and *Cyclops* is a satyr play (a comic version of a heroic myth sporting a chorus of sex-starved satyrs). Euripides first competed in the drama competition in 455 BCE, was victorious in 441, won again in 428 with the group including *Hippolytus*, and posthumously (in 405?) with *Bacchae* and *Iphigenia in Aulis*.

Besides the un-Euripidean *Rhesus*, all the plays in this volume date from the last decade of his life. *Iphigenia among the Taurians* was almost certainly first performed between 415 and 412, at least sixteen years after the outbreak in 431 of the Peloponnesian War, fought between Athens and her rival Sparta over hegemony in the Aegean. If it was performed in 412, with the similar *Helen* and *Andromeda*, it dates from the year after the worst Athenian disaster ever: the fleet and many thousands of men were lost at Syracuse in Sicily after an attempt to extend Athenian imperial influence. Thucydides, near-contemporary of Euripides and author of the *History of the Peloponnesian War*, saw the significance of the calamity (7.87): it was 'the greatest action of this war, and, in my view, the greatest action that we know of in Greek history. To its victors it was the most brilliant of successes, to the vanquished the most catastrophic of defeats'. Athens never fully recovered from this blow to her morale and her resources, and in 404, the year after the probable first production of *Bacchae* and *Iphigenia in Aulis*, lost the war, her empire, and (briefly) her democracy and her pride.

It is tempting to speculate on Euripides' own reaction to these unfolding events. There are heartbreaking dramatizations of the *effects* of military conflict in *Trojan Women* (415) and *Iphigenia at Aulis* (?405), which confronts its audience with warlords justifying unspeakable atrocities under pressure in time of war. These unforgettable plays however lend no substantial support to the widely held view that Euripides, after initially supporting Athenian expansionism, despaired and retreated from the contemporary scene as the promoters of war became more powerful. It may be that truth lies behind the biographical tradition that he spent his last two years at the Macedonian court of Pella, supposedly writing plays including *Bacchae* and *Iphigenia at Aulis*; it may be that the very existence of the 'Macedonian exile' tradition reveals Euripides' antidemocratic sympathies. On the other hand the lack of evidence for a political career, in contrast with Sophocles' attested appointments to high office, may suggest a neutral emotional detachment from public affairs. But Euripides was clearly engaged with the intellectual and ethical questions which the war had asked and which underlay the policy debates in the Athenian assembly. For these appear in disguise in his tragedies: the arguments used by the characters in *Iphigenia at Aulis* for and against the plan to sacrifice the princess confront notions of patriotism, pragmatism, expediency, and *force majeure* with the ideals of loyalty, equity, justice, and clemency. This ethical conflict echoes repeatedly the chilling debates in Thucydides which decided the fates—usually death or slavery— of the citizens of rebel states on both sides in the Peloponnesian War, including Mytilene, Melos, and Plataea.

One certainty is that Euripides, intellectually, was a child of his time. Every significant field studied by the professional intellectuals ('sophists') in contemporary Athens surfaces in his tragedies: ontology, epistemology, philosophy of language, moral and political theory, medicine, psychology, and cosmology. There is thus a kind of truth in Aulus Gellius' statement that Euripides studied Physics with Anaxagoras, rhetoric with Prodicus, and moral philosophy with Socrates (*Noctes Atticae* 15.20.4); in the first version of Aristophanes' *Clouds* (fr. 401) it was even alleged that Socrates provided Euripides with the ideas for his clever tragedies! And Euripidean characters certainly adopt the new philosophical *methods*: they subtly argue from probability and relativism, and formulate their points as antilogy, proof, and refutation.

III. EURIPIDES IN PERFORMANCE

Most Euripidean tragedies were first performed at an annual festival in honour of Dionysus, the Greek god of wine, dancing, and theatrical illusion, who is the protagonist of Euripides' most obviously

'Dionysiac' tragedy, *Bacchae*. The Great Dionysia was held in the spring when sailing became feasible. It was opened by a religious procession in which a statue of Dionysus was installed in the theatre, along with sacrifices and libations. Yet the Dionysia was also a political event. It affirmed the Athenian citizenry's collective identity as a democratic body with imperial supremacy: front seats were reserved for distinguished citizens, and only Athenians could perform the prestigious benefaction of sponsorship (*chorēgia*). For the spectators included representatives from the allied states which made up the Athenian empire. They displayed their tribute in the theatre, where they also witnessed a display by the city's war orphans. The plays were expected to befit this audience: insulting Athens at the Dionysia may have been a prosecutable offence (Aristophanes, *Acharnians* 501–6). It is not certain whether women attended the drama competitions, although most scholars assume that, if women were present at all, it was in small numbers, perhaps including only important priestesses.

The tragedies were performed over three successive days in groups by three poets: each poet offered three tragedies plus one satyr play. In 431 BCE, for example, Euripides took third place with three tragedies (*Medea*, *Philoctetes*, and *Dictys*), followed by a satyr play called *Theristai*, 'Reapers': the other two competitors were Euphorion (Aeschylus' son), who won first prize, and Sophocles, the runner-up. The plays were judged by a panel of democratically selected citizens, and care was taken to avoid juror corruption, but the audience's noisy applause and heckling influenced the outcome (Plato, *Republic* 6.492b5–c1).

The plays were performed in the theatre of Dionysus on the south slope of the Athenian acropolis. Individual actors probably performed their speeches and songs most of the time on the stage (*skēnē*), while the chorus of twelve sang and danced to forgotten steps and gestures in the dancing arena (*orchēstra*). All the performers were male, and all were masked. For performance conventions we have to rely on the characters' words, since the Greeks did not use stage directions. The last two decades have produced important work on the visual dimension and its contribution to the meaning of tragedy: scholarship has focused on physical contact, and on entrances and exits. The evidence for the material resources of the theatre as early as the fifth century is slight, although the poets had access to a machine which permitted the airborne epiphanies *ex machina*, such as Athena at the end of *Iphigenia among the Taurians*. There was also the *ekkuklēma*, a contraption allowing bodies to be wheeled out of the doors of the palace or tent forming the 'backdrop' to most surviving tragedies. Vase-paintings offer a stylized reflection of the costumes, masks, and scenery, and some are directly inspired by individual tragedies.

IV. IPHIGENIA AMONG THE TAURIANS

Towards the end of his career Euripides became attracted to dramas set in faraway, exotic lands, and thus turned the theatre of Dionysus into a panoramic window onto the barbarian margins of the known world. He may have been consciously reviving one of the traditions of earlier tragedy, for the earliest extant play, Aeschylus' *Persians*, had in 472 BCE thrilled its audience with the oriental setting, costumes, and protocols of the Persian court at Susa. Exactly sixty years later Euripides transported his audience to the Ethiopian coast in his *Andromeda*, and in *Helen* to the mouth of the Egyptian Nile; in his (possibly earlier) *Iphigenia among the Taurians* his spectators could feast their eyes on a barbarian temple, running with the blood of human victims, on the craggy coast of the Crimean peninsula. This is the most remote setting of any Greek tragedy except the Aeschylean *Prometheus Bound*.

More clearly than any other tragic drama except Euripides' own *Helen*, *Iphigenia among the Taurians* reflects the popularity in Athens of the historian and ethnographer Herodotus. His prose treatise on the Persian wars, which had become familiar at Athens in the previous decade, had included a description of the Taurians of the Crimea (4.99, 103). It is this strange people, whose economy rests on cattle farming, whom Euripides brings to life in the theatre. Several details in Herodotus' account reappear in the tragedy, especially the custom of sacrificing shipwrecked sailors and the impalement of victims on stakes (38–41, 1429–30).[7] It will probably never be known whether the savage tribes of this area really worshipped, as they do in Euripides, a goddess equivalent to the Greeks' Artemis (Herodotus actually says that they called their maiden goddess 'Iphigenia'). But one of Artemis' Greek titles, *Tauropolos*

---

[7] See Edith Hall, *Inventing the Barbarian: Greek Self-Definition through Tragedy* (Oxford, 1989), 110–12.

('bull-hunting'), was aurally sufficiently similar to suggest that Artemis was connected with the Taurians.

This helps to illuminate the invention of the myth which told of Orestes' Black Sea quest for Artemis' ancient cult image, destined to come from the Taurians to Greece. But it is just as important that in his later career Euripides became increasingly interested in what happened to Orestes *after* he killed his mother; in *Electra*, in the immediate aftermath of the murder, he suffers feelings of intense self-hatred; in *Orestes*, in the grip of a nervous breakdown, he is condemned to death by the people of Argos, tries to kill Helen, but is rescued from the angry mob by Apollo. In *Iphigenia among the Taurians* the same god diverts him to the Black Sea on a quite different mission, the quest for the image of Artemis. In the land of the Taurians he is nearly sacrificed, but is reunited in time with his long-lost sister, and makes good his escape to Greece.

At times the play's atmosphere is not unlike that of 'Westerns' made in the 1950s, where white frontiersmen are taken captive by Red Indians, to face barbaric death and mutilation. Superficially Euripides seems to take every available opportunity to contrast Greek valour with barbarian cowardice, Greek cunning intelligence with barbarian gullibility, and Greek sensibility with barbarian savagery. For some of its spectators it may therefore have offered little more than an escapist romp legitimizing their patriotism and xenophobia. Yet on a deeper level the play presents a greater challenge to unthinking Greek ethnic supremacism than any other text of the fifth century. For the averted catastrophe of the tragedy—the sacrifice of Orestes—is consistently paired in the audience's imaginations with the intended sacrifice of Iphigenia by her Greek father, so long ago at Aulis. The parallelism between the fates of the siblings is repeatedly stressed, forcing the audience to question whether Greek ethics were really so superior. After all, as far as the Taurians were concerned, Orestes was only a shipwrecked sailor: the Greek Agamemnon, on the other hand, had been prepared to authorize the ritual killing of his own beloved daughter. The most explicit questioning of the 'double standard' underlying conventional Greek thinking about the inferiority of other cultures is, strikingly and appropriately, put into the mouth of the barbarian king Thoas: when told that Orestes had murdered his own mother, he exclaims, in horror, 'By Apollo, no one would have dared to do this even among barbarians!' (1174).

Scholarship has tended to focus on the play's interest in religious ritual and especially in 'aetiology'—the provision of mythical explanations for religious customs still practised in Euripides' day. For example, the play offers an original explanation for the presence of the cult image of Artemis at her sanctuary at Brauron in Attica. But it also shows how Iphigenia and Orestes, who in today's language are horrifically 'abused' children of a catastrophically dysfunctional family, are enabled by their encounter to come to terms with their psychological trauma, and to avoid re-enacting their family past by transforming it into ritual. Their acquired wisdom allows the substitution of harmless rites for actual atrocity.[8]

This deeply thoughtful, moving, atmospheric, and humane drama has nevertheless caused critics much consternation, especially during the last two hundred years. Its escapist plot, lack of a catastrophic death or suffering, and happy ending have led it to be classified as a tragicomedy, as a satyric tragedy owing much to the conventions of satyr play, as a burlesque, or as a 'romantic' tragedy. Its enigmatic status has led it to be neglected even more than *Helen*, which, although not dissimilar, is far more clearly intended to be overtly funny. But the ancients had no such problem with the play; even Aristotle, who preferred unhappy endings, admired the skilfully crafted recognition scene, which involves the fascinating device of Iphigenia's 'letter home'. Aristotle's admiration was deserved: the reunion is not only emotionally touching but in preventing the performance of human sacrifice is integral to the development of the plot. The tragedy was repeatedly performed in later antiquity, becoming familiar enough to inspire a bizarrely parodic Alexandrian mime in which the heroine is stranded among barbarians who speak an ancient dialect of India.[9] At Rome the tragedy's celebration of the friendship between Orestes and Pylades was much admired; Cicero's treatise *On Friendship* records that an audience rose to its feet and applauded spontaneously at the scene in Pacuvius' lost Latin adaptation of the play when Pylades volunteered to die in his friend's place (7.24).

Yet by far the greatest strength of the play undoubtedly lies in its articulate, expressive, brave and intelligent heroine, a charming

---

[8] David Sansone, 'The sacrifice-motif in Euripides' *IT*', *TAPA* 105 (1975), 283-311.

[9] Published and translated in Denys Page (ed.), *Select Papyri*, iii (Cambridge, Mass., and London, 1941), 336-49.

character unique amongst the remains of extant Greek tragedy. Euripides' tragedy, astonishingly, makes it easy for his audience— who were almost entirely male—to relate powerfully to the emotional plight of a childless, lonely, exiled woman in at least early middle age, who has never married and (unlike her sister Electra in other plays) certainly never will. In *Iphigenia among the Taurians* the unlikely figure of a spinsterly older sister has an extraordinary opportunity to confide her innermost thoughts and fears to the assembled citizens of Athens and beyond them to posterity.

V. BACCHAE

Although a popular play in antiquity (it was a favourite of the emperor Nero), the modern admiration for *Bacchae* is a relatively recent development. In the late eighteenth century a critic of Greek tragedy could still hardly contain his revulsion, warning his readers that 'the refined delicacy of modern manners will justly revolt against this inhuman spectacle of dramatick barbarity'.[10] But the great upsurge of interest in the connections between ancient Greek ritual and myth which developed at the end of the last century drew scholars magnetically to this extraordinary play, and it is now rightly considered one of Euripides' supreme masterpieces.

It has long been debated how far, if at all, the savage rites in *Bacchae* reflect the 'real' maenadism known to have been practised in antiquity. Yet it is certainly legitimate to see the play as staging a narrative symbiotically connected with the rituals performed in honour of Dionysus, as for Christians the narrative of the Last Supper is inextricably bound up with the ritual breaking of bread and drinking of wine, ceremonial substitutes for the flesh and blood of the sacrificed body of Jesus. The *Bacchae* includes many elements suggestive of the experience of those participating in Dionysus' mysterious cult: stories relating the birth of the god, odes describing the altered state of consciousness—the sublime state of *ekstasis* or ecstasy ('standing outside of oneself')—which his cult offers, messenger speeches recounting the Bacchants' collective worship on the mountain of Cithaeron with their ivy-twined branches and dappled fawnskins, the ritual sacrifice of a man whose flesh is

---

[10] Richard Paul Jodrell, *Illustrations of Euripides on the Ion and the Bacchae* (London, 1781), ii, 550.

torn apart, and miracles and epiphanies through which the god manifests himself to mortals.

The cult of Dionysus was regarded by the Greeks as an import from barbarian lands, and the play enacts an ancient myth narrating its problematic arrival at the mainland Greek city of Thebes. The story is one of numerous mythical illustrations of an archaic Greek imperative: those who doubt the power of the gods must be disabused of their disbelief. The royal house of Thebes must be punished because it questioned the divine paternity of Dionysus, its most illustrious offspring. Yet the work is much more than an exemplum of divine prerogative expressed through the consecutive motifs of resistance, punishment, and acceptance. Dionysus is not only the play's protagonist: his drama is a study of his own elusive personality and of his devastating power.

Most Greek tragedy did not treat myths directly involving Dionysus. His connection with the theatre expresses his function as god of altered consciousness, of appearance, and of illusion. In one of the most powerful moments in world theatre Dionysus, himself disguised as a mortal, puts the finishing touches to the Bacchanal disguise of Pentheus, his mortal cousin and adversary, and sends him to the mountains to be dismembered by the women of the city he is supposed to rule. Pentheus is in a Dionysiac trance; he can no longer distinguish between reality and illusion; he is taking on the identity of someone other than himself. This scene self-consciously forces the onlooker into contemplating the experience of watching any performance which entails the impersonation of one being by another. Drama demands that performer and spectator collude in a suspension of the empirically 'real' world, and an involvement in a world that is not really there. Pentheus dresses in a maenad's attire, just as each chorus-member had adopted the costume and mask of a maenad before actuality was forsaken and the drama began; in the original production this also required assuming the identity of the opposite sex, for all the performers would have been male. *Bacchae*, therefore, can be seen as a meditation on the very experience of theatre; a mimetic enactment of the journey into and out of illusion, the journey over which Dionysus presides in the mysterious fictive worlds he conjures up in his theatre.[11]

---

[11] See Helene Foley, *Ritual Irony: Poetry and Sacrifice in Euripides* (Ithaca, NY, and London, 1985), 205-58.

The Greek mind was trained to think in polarities; to categorize, distinguish, and oppose. If the divine personality of Dionysus can be reduced to any one principle, it is the demonstration that conventional logic is an inadequate tool with which to apprehend the universe as a whole. Dionysus confounds reason, defies categorization, dissolves polarities, and inverts hierarchies. He is a youthful god and yet as an immortal, respected by the elderly Cadmus and Teiresias, cannot be defined as young. He is a male god and yet in his perceived effeminacy and special relationship with women cannot be defined as conventionally masculine. Conceived in Thebes yet worshipped abroad he is neither wholly Greek nor barbarian. He conflates the tragic and comic views of life, as the patron deity of both genres. Similarly, his worship can bring both transcendental serenity and repulsive violence: the slaughter of Pentheus, followed by his mother's invitation to the Bacchants to share in the feast, entails three crimes considered by the ancient Greeks to be among the most abominable: human sacrifice, infanticide, and cannibalism. Dionysus may be worshipped illicitly on the wild hillsides of Thebes, but he is also the recipient in Euripides' Athens of a respectable cult at the heart of the city-state: as such, he cannot be defined as the representative of nature in opposition to culture and civilization.[12] And in using illusion to reveal the truth he confounds all conventional distinctions between fiction and fact, madness and sanity, falsehood and reality. In *Bacchae* Dionysus causes the imprisoned to be liberated, the 'rational' to become demented, humans to behave like animals, men to dress as women, women to act like men, and an earthquake physically to force the untamed natural world into the 'safe', controlled, interior world of the household and the city.

Until the last minute, when the deluded Agave appears, Thebes is represented exclusively by males; the beliefs of the 'other', dangerous culture which the disguised Dionysus threatens to introduce have been articulated in the mouths of women. But with the arrival of Agave and her gradual return to 'normal' consciousness, even this binary, gendered opposition is exploded. Here is a Theban woman who once doubted the existence of the god, but who comes to know as she emerges from her Dionysiac mania that in the severed head of her son she bears the physical proof that Dionysus

---

[12] C. Segal, *Dionysiac Poetics and Euripides' Bacchae* (Princeton, 1982).

is a living reality in Thebes. The revealed truth is that the denied god, the outsider, the alien, has belonged inside all along.

The transhistorical appeal of *Bacchae* is partly due to its insusceptibility—appropriate for a Dionysiac text—to any single interpretation. Its portrayal of the unrestrained emotionalism which can lead human crowds into inhuman conduct spoke loud to scholars at the time of the rise of fascism;[13] its portrayal of the conflict within Pentheus' psyche has also fascinated psychoanalytical critics. But ultimately the tragedy frustrates all attempts to impose upon it a unitary central 'meaning'. It neither endorses nor repudiates the cult whose arrival in Thebes it narrates. It never did prescribe for its audience a cognitive programme by which to understand an inexplicable universe. It simply enacts one occasion on which the denial, repression, and exclusion of difference—psychological, ethnic, and religious—led to utter catastrophe.

VI. IPHIGENIA AT AULIS

From pious Abraham and his son Isaac to the tale of Jephthah's sacrifice of his only daughter in the *Book of Judges*, the motif of the child sacrificed to please divinity has taken various forms in Judaeo-Hellenic tradition. *Iphigenia at Aulis* is the most detailed and developed literary version of this archetypal myth, but also the one which most calls into question the motives and integrity of the sacrificing parent. One of the most shocking moments in Greek tragedy occurs at the point in *Iphigenia at Aulis* where Clytemnestra, the heroine's mother, is desperately trying to prevent her husband Agamemnon from carrying out the intended sacrifice. Clytemnestra opens her appeal with the information that Iphigenia is not the first child of hers whom Agamemnon has killed. Clytemnestra says that she married him against her will, after he murdered her first husband, Tantalus, and tore her baby from her breast to dash him to the ground.

In no other tragedian does this information appear: the effect of the nasty little secret which proves that Agamemnon has always been capable of slaughtering innocents in his own self-interest is therefore quite devastating. Euripides has turned a tragedy about Agamemnon's famous dilemma over Iphigenia into one incident in

[13] R. P. Winnington-Ingram, *Euripides and Dionysus: an interpretation of the Bacchae* (first published 1946, second edition with foreword by P. E. Easterling (Bristol, 1997)).

the life of a self-serving warlord guilty of previous atrocity. But Clytemnestra, in the past and currently a blameless victim of her husband's callousness, goes on in the same speech to imply that if Agamemnon kills Iphigenia he may himself be killed on his return from Troy—that is, she threatens Agamemnon with the plot of Aeschylus' *Agamemnon*. Even a virtuous and forgiving woman, it is suggested, can be transformed into a vindictive murderess under sufficient pressure. Indeed, almost all the characters are portrayed as strangely wedded to the past, from which they provide narratives to justify a present attitude or action or decision. Yet they also seem curiously conscious of their futures, or at least of the characters they later became according to the mythical and dramatic tradition—an 'intertextual' feature which lends this tragedy a distinctively 'modern' tone. The inclusion in the drama of the tiny baby Orestes, it could be argued, forces the audience to 'remember the future' even as it recalls these characters' past.[14]

Clytemnestra's future is suggested by her characterization in earlier tragedy, but for the male characters the text against which *Iphigenia at Aulis* works is, above all, the *Iliad*. The youthful and naive Achilles of Euripides, for example, is given a trial run at conceiving a great grudge against Agamemnon, a precursor of the 'wrath' which determines the plot of the *Iliad*, and the Argive king himself is shown vulnerable to the moral weakness and inconsistency which in epic mars his generalship at Troy. The psychological depth with which Euripides treats the familiar story thus makes *Iphigenia at Aulis* one of his most profound and tragic plays.

Euripides was fascinated by the factors which condition the moral choices made by individuals, and in his tragedies repeatedly explored the dangers inherent in precipitate and unconsidered decision-making. In *Hippolytus*, for example, the hero's death is caused by his father's hasty decision to curse and exile him without proper deliberation or due legal process. Athenian history provides several examples of similar decisions, especially in time of war: a notorious incident was the Athenian assembly's furious decision in 427 BCE summarily to execute all the male inhabitants of Mytilene, a decision they revoked the very next day after a 'sudden change of heart' (Thucydides 3.36). This resulted in a desperate race against time as one trireme chased another across the Aegean sea. *Iphigenia at Aulis*

---

[14] C. A. E. Luschnig, 'Time and Memory in Euripides' *Iphigenia at Aulis*', *Ramus*, 11 (1982), 99–104.

uses myth to stage a not dissimilar occasion during a military crisis when several members of the same family took and rescinded hasty decisions about the life of an innocent girl.

Aristotle notoriously complained about the 'inconsistent' characterization of Iphigenia, whose understandable rejection of the plan to sacrifice her is subsequently replaced by a passionate death-wish (*Poetics* 1454ª26). It has occasionally been proposed, in defence of Euripides, that Iphigenia's predicament has virtually driven her mad.[15] But Iphigenia is only imitating the male characters in her own play. Agamemnon has summoned her to be sacrificed, changes his mind at the beginning of the play, but is incapable of sticking to the better moral course when Iphigenia's arrival forces his hand: fear of his own army's reaction prevents him from rescinding the authorization of the sacrifice. Menelaus changes his mind no less dramatically, emotionally rejecting his earlier 'rational' view that Iphigenia's sacrifice was an unfortunate necessity when he sees his brother's distress. Even Achilles, who longs to prove his heroic stature and defend Iphigenia against the army, allows her to persuade him that she really wants to die. Is it so surprising that a young girl should be swayed by the militaristic ideology of the community in which she finds herself, when the strongest warriors in Greece are incapable of real moral reflection or maintaining a consistent moral position?

One school of interpretation used to insist that the tragedy offered an uncomplicated patriotic celebration of a Greek heroine's selfless heroism in offering herself for immolation on the altar of her country. It is of course true that women were regarded as inferior to men in Euripides' day, and that war against the barbarians of Asia would not have been seen in itself as morally problematic. There might well have been a warm glow in the theatre when Iphigenia declares that she is happy to die because 'it is right that the Greeks should rule barbarians, mother, and not barbarians Greeks' (1400–1). Yet the overall impression made by the play is of a community in absolute moral crisis. The prospect of Iphigenia's death is unbearably moving, but it is inseparable from the tragedy's portrayal of the volatile, unreflective Greek mob, manipulated by the sinister, unseen Odysseus, and above all the hypocrisy, self-justification, self-delusion, and cynical duplicity (underscored by the motif

---

[15] See e.g. H. Siegel, 'Self-delusion and the *volte-face* of Iphigenia in Euripides' *Iphigenia at Aulis*', *Hermes*, 108 (1980), 300–21.

of the fraudulent letter) practised by its leaders. Iphigenia's real problem is how to die nobly in an ignoble cause for the sake of thoroughly ignoble men.

Euripides did not write the whole text of the play as it stands. It may be relevant that it was produced posthumously by his son, who possibly completed or rewrote it. There is a question mark over Agamemnon's 'delayed' prologue, positioned after the opening dialogue; there are also several spurious passages scattered throughout the play, probably interpolated by actors after the fifth century. But by far the most significant interpolation begins with the appearance of the second messenger, or at least at that part of his speech which reports the disappearance of Iphigenia, whisked away by Artemis, and the substitution of a deer. This comforting alternative ending to the tragedy—perhaps inserted by an ancient theatrical company familiar with *Iphigenia among the Taurians*— radically affects both its theological meaning and its emotional impact, and modern directors often prefer, quite legitimately, to conclude performances with Iphigenia's unrelievedly tragic walk to her death at line 1531.

VII. RHESUS

This colourful and unusual tragedy has been direly neglected for the simple reason that it is probably not by Euripides himself, although it has been preserved in the manuscripts of his works, and he did almost certainly write a (lost) play entitled *Rhesus*. But the emotional, intellectual, aesthetic, and theatrical impact made by the play is so unlike that produced even by Euripides' least distinguished tragedies that in the ancient world some ancient literary critics already claimed that it was spurious. The modern reader will be struck in particular by the un-Euripidean lack of interest in women, and absence of the intellectual bravura which marks every one of his surviving plays.

In the 1960s one respectable scholar published a spirited defence of the Euripidean authorship of *Rhesus*, arguing that its distinctive qualities are signs that it dated from early in his career.[16] But most experts now agree that the ancient written record somehow substituted the text we possess for Euripides' tragedy of the same name.

---

[16] William Ritchie, *The Authenticity of The Rhesus of Euripides* (Cambridge, 1964).

There are several possible explanations for such a substitution: Euripides was widely imitated by other tragedians, and others bore his name, including his own youngest son, who was responsible for the posthumous production of *Iphigenia at Aulis* and *Bacchae*. The prevalent scholarly view holds therefore that *Rhesus* is the work of an unidentifiable playwright active in the fourth century BCE (when there was a revival of interest in dramatizing themes from the *Iliad*), and as such it is a unique document, since all the other Greek tragedies date from the century before.

The activities in the military camps of the Trojan war had provided the Greek tragedians with the plots of numerous tragedies, such as Sophocles' *Ajax*, inaugurating a western theatrical tradition still evident in the camp scenes of Shakespeare's *Troilus and Cressida*. *Rhesus* dramatizes the exciting and bloody story of Rhesus and Dolon, familiar to the Athenian audience from the tenth book of the *Iliad* (which just so happens to be the book of that epic whose own authenticity is most suspected).[17] It is the only Greek tragedy whose entire action takes place at night. Its setting is military—the temporary sleeping quarters of the Trojan army, between their city and the camp of the Greeks. The tragic action consists of the arrival of the Trojans' great ally, King Rhesus of Thrace, and his murder by two Greeks, Odysseus and Diomedes, who have been sent on a secret mission into the enemy camp. They also kill Dolon, the Trojan spy sent to discover the plans being made by the Greeks. The occasion is the night after Hector has nearly succeeded in setting fire to their ships and routing them. Hector seems invincible, and the Greek campaign doomed to failure. But by the end of the play the situation has been reversed: although Hector concludes the piece by resolutely ordering the army to prepare for action, for the dawn brings him confidence that the Trojans can fire the enemy ships, and 'herald the day of freedom for the Trojans', his audience, who knew the *Iliad* intimately, will have heard the tragic irony in his totally misguided optimism.

The ethical interest centres on the virtues and vices of military leaders, by providing a gallery of fighting men with different approaches to the war. Hector is a brilliant warrior, but hasty and impetuous, just as he is in Homer. Aeneas' presence in the play is largely to point a contrast with his imprudent leader, to urge cau-

---

[17] See Bernard Fenik, *Iliad X and the Rhesus: The Myth* (= *Latomus* 73, Brussels, 1964).

tion and to suggest that espionage should precede any major military decision (86-130); further contrasts are drawn between Hector and his sexually obsessed brother Paris, and between Hector and his late-arriving ally Rhesus of Thrace. Rhesus' reputation seems to rest on nothing but a frontier war, and his bombastic boasts and ambitions know no limits: he is a prototype of the *miles gloriosus*, or braggart soldier, of the incipient genre of New Comedy. Rhesus is completely incompetent: he neglects even the most elementary precautions, letting his contingent fall asleep without posting a single sentry to keep watch, or even laying out arms and chariot gear in preparation for combat.[18] It is probably relevant that Athenian history of the late fifth and early fourth centuries includes some extremely hostile relationships with the kings of Thrace, who were believed to be unreliable and disloyal military allies; the figure of Rhesus as portrayed in this tragedy may well have been consonant with the audience's real historical views of his countrymen. The play certainly endorses the notion that Greeks were better warriors: both the Trojan and Thracian fighters are contrasted with the cunning Greek Odysseus and his companion Diomedes, who lay their plans carefully, secure Athena's goodwill, and complete their assignment with ruthless efficiency.

Yet despite the tragedy's emphasis on its aristocratic heroes, it is a curiously democratic rewriting of the epic story. Two of the minor characters—the shepherd and Rhesus' charioteer—are vocal and independent-minded men, whose scenes greatly enliven the effect of the drama. Moreover, the convention of the chorus allows a much fuller development of the lower-class perspective on the action than the aristocratic focus of epic ever could. The chorus of sentries provide an interesting commentary on the activities of their superiors, and offer an unusual amount of interventionist advice, criticism, and support.

Rhesus certainly does not deserve the relegation to the margins of literary history that it has suffered. Perhaps more than any play by Euripides, it needs to be read as a theatrical script for enactment by expert actors. It is not particularly great literature (although some passages, particularly in the choral odes, are not inconsiderable poetry). But it is likely to have been highly successful theatre. The nocturnal, masculine, military atmosphere, with its passwords

---

[18] G. M. A. Grube, *The Drama of Euripides* (London, 1941), 443.

and watch fires, disguises, scouts and reconnaissance, will have enthralled the male spectators for whom it was designed, many of whom will have seen military action themselves. The play also offered them a series of flamboyant visual effects. It opens on a lively note, with the sleeping Hector being wakened by the noisy entrance of the chorus of Trojan sentries, bursting with the news that the enemy have convened a meeting. Rhesus' arrival, with jangling bells on his shield, golden armour, twin spears, and Thracian entourage, must have provided a splendid spectacle. At the heart of the play the goddess Athena appears on stage to offer help to the Greek spies Odysseus and Diomedes, and then, in a theatrical stunt without equivalent in extant tragedy, pretends to be Aphrodite in order to divert Paris' attention: Dionysus in *Bacchae* also assumes a disguise, but not that of another immortal.

Yet the theatrical climax of the play is postponed until the end, with the surprise appearance of a second female immortal, rising above the all-male plane of the human action. Rhesus' corpse is carried on in the arms of his mother, a Muse borne aloft in the theatrical machine. The Muse, an epic rather than a tragic figure, provides a link with the Homeric archetype, reminding the audience of the poem from which the tragedy takes its inspiration, and also underlining the imminence of the Trojan defeat. In a musical moment without parallel in the other plays, this divine embodiment of song sings a solo lyric lament over her son's body, announces that she will consecrate him at a mysterious oracle of Dionysus in Thrace, and predicts the deaths of both Hector and Achilles. The play, which deftly telescopes within a single night of military subterfuge the story of the whole Trojan war, constitutes a fast-paced, action-packed, theatrical *Iliad* in miniature.

VIII. ATHENIAN SOCIETY

Euripides' plays were first performed in Athens at a festival celebrating Athenian group identity, and consequently reveal an 'Athenocentrism' manifested in the famous praise in *Medea* of the beauty of Athens's environment, the grace of its citizens, and its cultural distinction (824-45). In this volume the clearest example is the appearance of Athena (rather than Artemis) at the conclusion of *Iphigenia among the Taurians*, who gives instructions for the foundation of cults on Attic soil, and promises Orestes that his trial at

Athens will ensure that tied verdicts at the court of the Areopagus will forever secure acquittal for defendants (1435–72).

Yet the social fabric of the city which Euripides inhabited was heterogeneous. In 431 BCE an estimated 300,000 human beings lived in the city state of Attica. But at least 25,000 were resident non-Athenians ('metics'), including businessmen and professionals; a third were slaves, the majority of whom came from beyond Hellenic lands—from the Balkans, the Black Sea, Asia, or Africa. This ethnic pluralism perhaps finds expression in the 'multi-ethnic' casts of tragedy: the present volume alone introduces Crimean Taurians in *Iphigenia among the Taurians*, maenads from Asia Minor in *Bacchae*, and Trojans and their allies from Balkan Thrace in *Rhesus*.

Slavery was fundamental to the Athenian economy and society, and tragedy reminds us of this unfortunate portion of the population (e.g. *Electra* 632–3). In *Acharnians* Aristophanes commented on the intelligence Euripides imputed to his slaves (400–1), and his plays include slaves with important roles as well as mute attendants: *Iphigenia at Aulis* opens with a powerful exchange between Agamemnon and a voluble old slave belonging to his wife, Clytemnestra. The institution of slavery is itself much discussed: a character in a lost play affirmed that a noble slave is not dishonoured by the title, because 'many slaves are superior to the free' (fr. 511).[19] The old slave in *Iphigenia at Aulis* is certainly a strong moral presence: articulate, unblinkingly opposed (unlike his supposed superiors) to the barbarous plan to slaughter Iphigenia, prepared to fight Menelaus for what he believes is right, and profoundly loyal to Clytemnestra, on whose behalf he intervenes independently in the action (855–96).

The ethical dilemmas and emotional traumas in Euripides are never wholly inseparable from the decidedly unheroic pressures of finance and economics. It is not just that the metaphorical fields draw colour from monetary transactions (Clytemnestra in *Iphigenia at Aulis* speaks of Agamemnon 'paying for' Helen at the price of Iphigenia's life, 1168–70). Money or lack of it colours the characters' experiences. Euripidean characters express anxiety about maintaining the means to live, especially in exile; Orestes recounts how he was spurned by his friends, and forced to receive meals as charity, sitting alone at a separate table (*Iphigenia among the Taurians* 949–54). Others express lucid insights into the economic

---

[19] All references to fragments of Euripides are cited from A. Nauck, *Tragicorum Graecorum Fragmenta*, 2nd edn., with supplement by B. Snell (Hildesheim, 1964).

basis of society: the most striking example by far is Medea's first monologue in *Medea*, which clarifies the socio-economic imperatives underlying her own and other women's predicament:

Of everything that is alive and has a mind, we women are the most wretched creatures. First of all, we have to buy a husband with a vast outlay of money—we have to take a master for our body . . . divorce brings shame on a woman's reputation and we cannot refuse a husband his rights . . . I would rather stand three times in the battle line than bear one child (*Medea* 230-51).

She trenchantly exposes the jeopardy in which marriage placed women: besides the insulting dowry system, women were subject to legalized rape in marriage, a hypocritical double standard in divorce, and agonizing mortal danger in childbirth.

This kind of speech outraged the Christian writer Origen, who criticized Euripides for inappropriately making women express argumentative opinions (*Contra Celsum* 7.36.34-6); in *Frogs* Euripides claimed to have made tragedy 'more democratic' by keeping his women— young ones and old ones—talking alongside their masters (948-50). It is indeed a remarkable feature of Euripidean tragedy that most of his best thinkers and talkers are women: Medea is a superior rhetorician to any man in her play; Iphigenia in *Iphigenia among the Taurians* is more lucid and expressive than her brother, and extemporizes brilliantly in the scene where she dupes the barbarian king Thoas; in *Iphigenia at Aulis* Clytemnestra's appeals to both Achilles and Agamemnon are masterpieces of emotive and cogent persuasion.

Women are of course prominent in tragedy generally: patriarchal cultures often use symbolic females to help them imagine abstractions and think about their social order. It is also relevant that women performed the laments at funerals, that Dionysus' cult in reality as well as in *Bacchae* involved maenadism and transvestism, and that women were perceived as more emotionally expressive and susceptible, like the women of Thebes in *Bacchae*, to divine possession. They were also regarded as lacking moral autonomy: Athenian men were obsessed with what happened in their households behind their backs, and all the transgressive women in tragedy—like Agave and her sisters—are temporarily or permanently husbandless. The plays are products of an age where huge sexual, financial, and affective tensions surrounded the transfer of women between the households that made up the city state.

Clytemnestra's appeal to Agamemnon in *Iphigenia at Aulis* describes the vulnerability of women in such a society with pungent accuracy (1146–65). There was certainly a feeling in antiquity that Euripides' focus on women was sharper than that of either Aeschylus or Sophocles; until recently critics were debating whether Euripides was a misogynist or a feminist. Yet the only certainties are that he repeatedly chose to create strong and memorable female characters, and that as a dramatist he had a relativist rhetorical capacity for putting both sides of the argument in the sex war.

The position of women in the real world of Athens has itself long been a contentious issue, especially the degree of confinement to which citizen women were subject. But it is clear that most men would have preferred their wives and daughters to stay indoors, to be little discussed in public, to practise thrift, to possess unimpeachable sexual fidelity, and to produce several healthy sons. They certainly regarded women as inferior, and would probably have approved of Iphigenia's statement that 'it is better that one man should see the light of day than any number of women' (*Iphigenia at Aulis* 1394). Women could not vote, or participate in the assembly; nor could they speak for themselves in the courts of law or normally conduct financial transactions except through the agency of their male 'guardian' (*kyrios*)—father, husband, or nearest male relative. But women did, of course, negotiate with the existing power structures (we hear hints in the orators of the need for men to seek their womenfolk's approval), and were prominent in the central arena of public life constituted by official religion. This illuminates Iphigenia's present role in *Iphigenia among the Taurians* as priestess of a Taurian cult of Artemis, and in her future role, prescribed by Athena, as keeper of the keys of Artemis' shrine in Attica (1462–3). Another dignified priestess appears in Euripides' *Ion* (the 'Pythia' of Apollo at Delphi), and in *Helen* the Egyptian priestess Theonoe plays an important part. In a lost play the wise woman Melanippe defended women against practitioners of misogynist rhetoric like Hippolytus (*Hippolytus* 616–68);[20] one of her strategies was to list the Panhellenic cults which women administered (fr. 499):[21]

---

[20] Practising generalized invective against women seems to have been a favoured pastime: an example of the behaviour of Theophrastus' 'tactless man' is not that he inveighs against womankind, but that he does it *at weddings* (12.6)!

[21] Translation taken from M. R. Lefkowitz and M. B. Fant, *Women's Life in Greece and Rome: A Source Book in Translation*, 2nd edn. (London, 1992), 14.

Men's criticism of women is worthless twanging of a bowstring and evil talk. Women are better than men, as I will show . . . Consider their role in religion, for that, in my opinion, comes first. We women play the most important part, because women prophesy the will of Zeus in the oracles of Phoebus. And at the holy site of Dodona near the sacred oak, females convey the will of Zeus to inquirers from Greece. As for the sacred rituals for the Fates and the Nameless Ones, all these would not be holy if performed by men, but prosper in women's hands. In this way women have a rightful share in the service of the gods. Why is it, then, that women must have a bad reputation?

IX. EURIPIDES AND RELIGION

Melanippe's words are a fitting introduction to the category of *dramatis personae* constituted by the gods. What is to be deduced about Euripides' religion from his on-stage divinities in these plays (Athena in *Iphigenia among the Taurians*, Dionysus in *Bacchae*), and the Apollo, Death, Aphrodite, Artemis, Dioscuri, Thetis, Madness, Hermes, and Poseidon who physically appear in others? One function of Euripides' gods from the machine, for example in *Iphigenia among the Taurians*, is certainly to act as a metatheatrical 'alienation' device drawing attention to the author's power over the narrative. But does this mean that he was an atheist?

Allegations that Euripides was a religious radical began in his lifetime. Aristophanes' caricature includes the charge that Euripides' tragedies had persuaded people 'that the gods do not exist' (*Thesmophoriazusae* 450-1), and portrays him praying to the air ('Ether') and 'Intelligence' (*Frogs* 890-2). By later antiquity it was believed that it was at Euripides' house that Protagoras, the great relativist and agnostic thinker, read out his famous treatise on the gods, beginning 'Man is the measure of all things' (fr. 80 B 1 Diels–Kranz).

Some characters in Euripides undoubtedly articulate views which must have appeared advanced or sceptical to his audience. Cadmus in *Bacchae* tells the vindictive Dionysus that gods *ought* to be less susceptible to anger than humans (1348), and Iphigenia stoutly denies the tradition that the goddess Artemis could favour human sacrifice (*Iphigenia among the Taurians* 380-91). Orestes thinks that even the supposedly omniscient gods are as blind, confused, and ignorant as humans, and that sensible people must rely upon their own judgement (570–5). Other characters express views that will have sounded modern and 'scientific'. They depart from traditional theology by attributing the workings of the universe either to physical causes or to the power of the human mind. In *Trojan Women* Hecuba wonders whether Zeus should be addressed as 'Necessity of nature or the mind of man' (884–6). In one lost play a character asserted that 'the mind that is in each of us is god'; in another that the first principle of the cosmos was Air, which 'sends forth the summer's light, and makes the winter marked with cloud, makes life and death'; in a third Air was explicitly equated with Zeus (frr. 1018, 330.3–5, 941).

Consequently there has always been a critical tendency to see Euripides as seeking to overturn or challenge traditional religion, especially belief in the arbitrary, partisan, and often malevolent anthropomorphic Olympian gods of the Homeric epics. It has been argued that in figures like the vengeful Dionysus of *Bacchae* and the bloodthirsty Artemis of *Iphigenia at Aulis* he included the most uncompromisingly 'archaic' and self-interested of all Greek tragic gods precisely to undermine them. Thus his theatrical divinities are a literary throwback to the old anthropomorphism, constituting a consciously reductive enactment of the commonly accepted personalities of the Olympians. Alternatively, Euripides is interpreted as a humanist who denies any but human motivation to human action and whose works operate on a similar principle to Thucydides' rationalist and atheological determination that it is human nature, *to anthrōpinon* (3.82.2), which drives and conditions history. Critics have even seen Theonoe in *Helen* as a proselyte advocating a new Euripidean doctrine: her striking statement that Justice has a great shrine in her heart (*Helen* 1002–3, see also *Trojan Women* 886) offers, allegedly, a completely new religion of peace and justice, which Euripides is urging should replace the old Olympian cults.

Yet it is mistaken to confuse Euripidean characters' more innovative theological opinions with his own (unknown) personal views. Moreover, many of the expressions of scepticism are more complicated than they seem. One rhetorical function of scepticism is to *affirm* the belief being doubted simply by raising it to consciousness. Orestes may doubt that the gods know what they are doing, but his scepticism brings his tense relationship with Apollo into sharp focus. This helps the audience to appreciate the play's underlying argument, which emphatically reaffirms the infallibility of the Delphic oracle.[22]

For the overall impact of Euripidean tragedy does nothing to disrupt the three fundamental tenets of Athenian religion as practised by its citizens: that gods exist, that they pay attention (welcome or unwelcome) to the affairs of mortals, and that some kind of reciprocal allegiance between gods and humans was in operation, most visibly instantiated in ritual. The tragic performances were framed by the rituals of the Dionysia, and ritual fundamentally informs tragedy's imagery, plots, and songs: a study of wedding and funeral motifs, for example, has shown how they become conflated into sinister variations of the figure of the 'bride of death',[23] a particularly important poetic figure in *Iphigenia at Aulis*.

The plays themselves frame accounts of ritual: in *Iphigenia among the Taurians* Iphigenia pours out a funeral libation to the brother she believes to be dead (157–77) and orchestrates a purificatory procession from the temple of Artemis to the sea (1222–33). In *Bacchae* Pentheus is prepared on stage (912–70) for participation in the mountain rites of Dionysus, which are also described repeatedly in the songs of the chorus. The history of religion, moreover, seems to have fascinated Euripides, who includes in his tragedies numerous 'aetiological' explanations of the origin of cults. This is a conspicuous feature of *Iphigenia among the Taurians*, which provides mythical explanations for several aspects of the cult of Artemis both in and beyond Attica, and the whole of *Bacchae* is an aetiological explanation for the origin of Dionysus' cult in Greece.

It is true that Artemis in the Iphigenia plays and Dionysus in *Bacchae* are unusually brutal and demanding, even by the standards of ancient Greek gods. But Artemis still provides a shrine where families can dedicate the clothing of their women who died in childbirth (*Iphigenia among the Taurians* 1466–7), Dionysus brings joy as well as terror, and the songs concluding *Iphigenia at Aulis* help to prepare Iphigenia for death and the community for losing her. Ritual brings group consolidation and profound consolation, as a human response in the face of catastrophe.

[22] T. C. W. Stinton ('"Si credere dignum est": Some Expressions of Disbelief in Euripides and Others', *PCPS* 22 (1976), 60–89) discusses the complicated impact of apparently sceptical remarks in both *Helen* and *Electra* (74–82).

[23] See Rush Rehm, *Marriage to Death: the Conflation of Wedding and Funeral Rituals in Greek Tragedy* (Princeton, 1994).

Euripidean plots are also repeatedly driven by violations of the great taboos and imperatives constituting popular Greek ethics, the boundaries defining unacceptable behaviour which Sophocles' *Antigone* calls the 'unwritten and unshakeable laws of the gods' (*Antigone* 454–5), and which Euripidean characters are more likely to call 'the laws common to the Greeks' (e.g. *Heraclidae* 1010). These regulated human relationships at every level. In the family they proscribed incest, kin-killing, and failure to bury the dead: kin-killing, for example, is absolutely central to both *Iphigenia* plays and to *Bacchae*. At the level of relationships between members of different households and cities these 'common laws' ascribed to Zeus the protection of three vulnerable groups: suppliants, recipients of oaths, and parties engaged in the compact of reciprocal trust required by the guest/host relationship.

Supplication is a formal entreaty, accompanied by ritualized touching of knees, hand, and chin, which puts the recipient under a religious obligation to accede to the suppliant's requests. Supplication in Euripides characterizes numerous crucial scenes. In *Iphigenia among the Taurians* Iphigenia supplicates Orestes (1067–71), but also recalls desperately supplicating her father as she begged him to spare her (361–4); this terrible scene is actually enacted in *Iphigenia at Aulis*, shortly after Clytemnestra has supplicated Achilles (1216–17, 908–10). Oaths are also frequent: in *Iphigenia among the Taurians* the heroine makes Pylades swear to deliver her letter to Orestes, when she still believes him to be in Greece (744–58). The regulation of hospitality is also apparent in these plays: in *Iphigenia among the Taurians* Thoas demonstrates the wrong way of receiving strangers by slaughtering visitors to his country, and in *Iphigenia at Aulis* one reason the Greeks want to punish Troy is because Paris violated his relationship with his host Menelaus.

X. MUSIC, CHORUS, SONG

We have lost the melodies to which the lyrics of tragedy were sung to the accompaniment of pipes (*auloi*). But it is possible partially to decipher what John Gould has called 'strategies of poetic sensibility'[24] within the formal, conventional media open to the tragedian:

---

[24] J. Gould, 'Dramatic Character and "Human Intelligibility" in Greek Tragedy', *PCPS* 24 (1978), 43–67, esp. 54–8.

besides the choral passages, which were danced and sung, the tragedian had several modes of delivery to choose from for his individual actors. In addition to set-piece speeches and line-by-line spoken dialogue (*stichomythia*), they included solo song, duet, sung interchange with the chorus, and an intermediate mode of delivery, probably chanting to pipe accompaniment, signalled by the anapaestic rhythm ($\cup\cup-$). Euripides' songs were extremely popular: the ancients believed that some Athenians in Sicily saved themselves after the disaster at Syracuse in 413 BCE by singing some of his songs to their captors (Plutarch, *Life of Nicias* 29). In a lost comedy named *Euripides-Lover* (Axionicus fr. 3) a character discusses people who hate all lyrics but those by Euripides.

In this edition the sung and chanted sections have been labelled and laid out in shorter lines so that the reader can appreciate the shifts between speech and musical passages. This matters because it mattered in antiquity. The musicologist Aristoxenus said that speech begins to sound like song *when we are emotional* (*Elements of Harmony* 1.9-10). It certainly affects our appreciation of Iphigenia's desolate state of mind, for example, that Euripides chose to make her *sing* about her plight in the first scene of *Iphigenia among the Taurians*; Pentheus never sings in *Bacchae*, a sign, perhaps, of his emotional repression, while his mother Agave moves from song in her madness to speech as she recovers sanity; for much of *Iphigenia at Aulis* male spoken rhetoric contrasts sharply with the songs of the female chorus and Iphigenia's own funeral lament, performed before her weeping mother.

The chorus can also speak, and even function as an 'umpire' between warring parties in a debate (*Iphigenia at Aulis* 376-7, 402-3). Sometimes it is sworn to collusive silence (*Iphigenia among the Taurians* 1056-77), although the chorus of *Bacchae* is partisan in that tragedy to an unusual degree. Sometimes its songs 'fill in' time while actors change roles, or 'telescope' time while events happen offstage (e.g. *Iphigenia among the Taurians* 1234-82). Often the chorus sings forms of lyric song derived from the world of collective ritual. A choral song may be a hymn of praise, like the hymns to Dionysus sung by his followers in *Bacchae* (e.g. 64-166, 370-431). At the climax of *Iphigenia among the Taurians* the chorus sing an exquisite hymn to Apollo, relating how as a baby he took away the Delphic Oracle from Earth, its previous owner (134-82): it was the Delphic oracle which sent Orestes on his mission to Tauris. But the ritual reflected in choral odes is often of a darker character; in *Iphigenia at Aulis* the trick played on the heroine is macabrely reflected in the sad ode which evolves from a marriage-song into a funerary lament (1036-97).

Some choral odes present a mythical narrative functioning as a form of memory; early in *Iphigenia among the Taurians* the Greek chorus trace the curse on the heroine's family back to her ancestor Pelops (179-202), and in a lovely later ode recall the sacking of their city (1088-152). Other choral songs may be more firmly rooted in the time of the action taking place, but likewise offer valuable contextualizing material. In the unusual first song of *Iphigenia at Aulis*, the chorus of women breathlessly catalogue the famous heroes they have been lucky enough to see assembling at Aulis for the expedition against Troy (164-302). The bellicose, brooding Greek army is a forceful unseen presence in the tragedy, and it was a brilliant stroke to present the audience with a description of the famous leaders—Ajax, Diomedes, Achilles, and so on—seen from the admiring and slightly eroticized perspective of a group of ordinary women. Yet some choral odes are more philosophical or contemplative in orientation, and meditate in general terms on the issues which have been explored in the concrete situation of the play's previous episode. Thus the chorus of *Iphigenia among the Taurians* are prompted by the arrival of Greek men they assume to be merchants to reflect on the excitement and danger inherent in overseas trade (392-438).

XI. SPEECH

In Aristophanes' *Frogs* a prominent feature of Euripidean tragedy is the spoken 'programmatic' prologue of the kind which opens *Iphigenia among the Taurians* and *Bacchae*; it is characterized as predictable in both metrical form and in 'scene-setting' function. But this is reductive: the prologue typically establishes expectations, themes, and images which will subsequently become central to the drama. Euripides, moreover, varied the impact by his choice of speaker: he opens *Iphigenia among the Taurians* with its sad, reflective heroine, thus allowing her to charm the audience with her deeply personal story and intrigue them with her account of her mysterious dream; in contrast, he alienates the audience of *Bacchae* from Pentheus partly by letting his deadly enemy, Dionysus, have the first word. The chanted opening of *Iphigenia at Aulis*, moreover, suggests that Euripides was quite capable of experimenting with opening scenes in which the speakers are locked in urgent, agitated, dialogue.

The Roman rhetorician Quintilian (10.1.67) judged Euripides of more use than Sophocles to the trainee orator. The modern reader will undoubtedly be struck by the highly formal debates in Euripides, for example in the confrontation of Medea and Jason in *Medea* or Helen and Hecuba in *Trojan Women*. The plays in this volume are some of the least rhetorical in Euripides, but important debates take place in which Pentheus confronts the disguised Dionysus in *Bacchae* and Menelaus quarrels terribly with Agamemnon in *Iphigenia at Aulis*. The debate (*agōn*) is one of the features which Athenian tragedy assimilated from the oral performances which characterized two other great institutions of the democracy: the law courts and the assembly. To meet the increasing need for polished public speaking and its assessment under the widened franchise, the study of the science of persuasion, or the art of rhetoric, developed rapidly around the middle of the fifth century; this is reflected in tragedy's increased use of formal rhetorical figures, tropes, 'common topics' such as pragmatism and expediency, and hypothetical arguments from probability. One form of exercise available to the trainee orator was the 'double argument'—the construction or study of twin speeches for and against a particular proposition, or for the defence and prosecution in a hypothetical trial. As a character in Euripides' lost *Antiope* averred, 'If one were clever at speaking, one could have a competition between two arguments in every single case' (fr. 189). In assessing Euripidean rhetoric it must be remembered that his audience had become accustomed to startling displays by litigants in lawsuits (Aristophanes, *Wasps* 562–86); by the 420s political oratory sometimes descended into competitive exhibitionism in which the medium had superseded the message (Thucydides 3.38).

Euripides' gift for narrative is perhaps clearest in his 'messenger speeches', vivid mini-epics of exciting action, whether it is the herdsman's bemused description of Orestes' fit of madness near the beginning of *Iphigenia among the Taurians* (260–339), the hair-raising account of the Greeks' escape to their ship at its end (1327–419), or the gruesome picture of Pentheus' death and dismemberment at the hands of the crazed maenads in *Bacchae*

(1043–52). All Euripides' poetry is marked by exquisite simile and metaphor, often traced thematically, as in Shakespeare, through a play (in *Iphigenia among the Taurians* images of the sea and voyaging; in *Bacchae* hunting and wild animals): his 'picturesque' style was much admired in antiquity ('Longinus', *On the Sublime*, 15.1–4).

Euripides showed infinite versatility of register, and was capable of selecting rare poetic words for special effect (Aristotle, *Poetics* 58^{b}19–24). Yet he still revolutionized the diction of tragedy by making his characters speak in his distinctively 'human way': Aristotle affirms that it was not until Euripides wrote roles using language drawn from everyday conversation that tragedy discovered natural dialogue (*Rhetoric* 3.2.5). This ordinary quality to his characters' language attracted emulation by able poets even within his lifetime, yet in Aristophanes' *Frogs* Dionysus dismisses them as insignificant 'chatterers' in comparison (89–95). For Euripides was really doing something extremely difficult in making his unforgettable characters speak 'like human beings'. Thus the author of an encomium to Euripides in the *Palatine Anthology* justifiably discourages the aspiring imitator (7.50):[25]

> Poet, do not attempt to go down Euripides' road;
> It is hard for men to tread.
> It seems easy, but the man who tries to walk it
> Finds it rougher than if it were set with cruel stakes.
> If you even try to scratch the surface of Medea, daughter of Aeetes,
> You shall die forgotten. Leave Euripides' crowns alone.

[25] I would like to thank both Paul Cartledge and James Morwood for helpful comments on a previous draft.

NOTE ON THE TRANSLATION

This is a prose translation. However, lyrical and choric passages—intended for sung or chanted performance—have been laid out on shorter lines. These will inevitably have the appearance of free verse, but the translator's aim has been simply to denote the distinction between the spoken and sung or chanted areas of the play.

The translations are from James Diggle's Oxford Classical Text. Quite apart from the question of the authorship of *Rhesus*, there are serious problems of authenticity in these plays, especially in *Iphigenia at Aulis*. I have put square brackets round passages of any serious significance which Professor Diggle believes are not by Euripides or are highly unlikely to be by him. Corrupt passages where the meaning is seriously in doubt are placed between † signs. I have kept discussion of both kinds of passage to an absolute minimum in the notes.

I have followed Professor Diggle where he has put the lines in a different order from that of the standard text. However, it is traditional to refer to the line numbers of the standard text. This has led to an anomaly on p. 202 of the Notes, where it appears that the numerical sequence of the lines has been violated. I have adopted this proceedure so that the notes occur in the order appropriate to the text of my translation.

Asterisks (*) signify that there is a note on the words or passages so marked.

I have used the Latinized spellings of the Greek names.

Line numbers refer to the Greek text.

SELECT BIBLIOGRAPHY

GENERAL BOOKS ON GREEK TRAGEDY

P. E. Easterling (ed.), *The Cambridge Companion to Greek Tragedy* (Cambridge, 1987) (henceforth *Cambridge Companion*); Simon Goldhill, *Reading Greek Tragedy* (Cambridge, 1986); Rush Rehm, *Greek Tragic Theatre* (London, 1992); Charles Segal, *Interpreting Greek Tragedy: Myth, Poetry, Text* (Ithaca, NY, and London, 1986); Oliver Taplin, *Greek Tragedy in Action* (London, 1978); J. P. Vernant and P. Vidal-Naquet, *Tragedy and Myth in Ancient Greece* (English trans., Brighton, 1981); John J. Winkler and F. I. Zeitlin (eds.), *Nothing to do with Dionysos? Athenian Drama in its Social Context* (Princeton, 1990).

GENERAL BOOKS ON EURIPIDES

P. Burian (ed.), *New Directions in Euripidean Criticism* (Durham, NC, 1985); Christopher Collard, *Euripides* (Greece & Rome New Surveys in the Classics 24; Oxford, 1981); D. J. Conacher, *Euripidean Drama* (Toronto, 1967); *Euripide* (Entretiens sur l'antiquité classique 6, Fondation Hardt, Geneva, 1960); Helene P. Foley, *Ritual Irony: Poetry and Sacrifice in Euripides* (Ithaca, NY, 1985); G. M. Grube, *The Drama of Euripides*, 2nd edn. (London, 1962); M. Halleran, *Stagecraft in Euripides* (London, 1985); A. N. Michelini, *Euripides and the Tragic Tradition* (Madison, Wis., 1987); Judith Mossman (ed.), *Oxford Readings in Euripides* (Oxford, 1999); E. Segal (ed.), *Euripides: A Collection of Critical Essays* (Englewood Cliffs, 1968); P. Vellacott, *Ironic Drama: A Study of Euripides' Method and Meaning* (Cambridge, 1976); C. H. Whitman, *Euripides and the Full circle of Myth* (Harvard, 1974).

EURIPIDES' LIFE AND BIOGRAPHIES

Hans-Ulrich Gösswein, *Die Briefe des Euripides* (Meisenheim am Glan, 1975); J. Gregory, *Euripides and the Instruction of the Athenians* (Ann Arbor, 1991); P. T. Stevens, 'Euripides and the Athenians', *JHS* 76 (1956), 87–94; M. R. Lefkowitz, *The Lives of the Greek Poets*

(London, 1981), 88-104, 163-9; R. E. Wycherley, 'Aristophanes and Euripides', *G&R* 15 (1946), 98-107.

OPINIONS AND INTERPRETATIONS

R. B. Appleton, *Euripides the Idealist* (London, Toronto, and New York, 1927); Robert Eisner, 'Euripides' use of Myth', *Arethusa*, 12 (1979), 153-74; for 'historicist' approaches see E. Delebecque, *Euripide et la guerre du Péloponnèse* (Paris, 1951), and V. di Benedetto, *Euripide: teatro e societa* (Turin, 1971); E. R. Dodds, 'Euripides the Irrationalist', *CR* 43 (1929), 97-104; H. Reich, 'Euripides, der Mystiker', in *Festschrift zu C. F. Lehmann-Haupts sechzigsten Geburtstage* (Vienna, 1921), 89-93; K. Reinhardt, 'Die Sinneskrise bei Euripides', *Eranos*, 26 (1957), 279-317—Euripides as a nihilist; in his *Existentialism and Euripides* (Victoria 1977) William Sale draws on both Heidegger and Freud; A. W. Verrall, *Euripides The Rationalist* (Cambridge, 1895).

RECEPTION OF EURIPIDEAN TRAGEDY

Peter Burian, 'Tragedy Adapted for Stages and Screens: The Renaissance to the Present', in Easterling (ed.), *Cambridge Companion*, 228-83; Stuart Gillespie, *The Poets on the Classics* (London and New York, 1988), 90-4; K. Mackinnon, *Greek Tragedy into Film* (London and Sydney, 1986); Martin Mueller, *Children of Oedipus and other Essays on the Imitation of Greek Tragedy 1550-1800* (Toronto, 1980), 46-63; Helga Geyer-Ryan, 'Prefigurative Racism in Goethe's *Iphigenie auf Tauris*', in Francis Barber *et al.* (eds.), *Europe and its Others* (Colchester, 1985), 112-19; Robert Heitner, 'The Iphigenia in Tauris Theme in Drama of the Eighteenth Century', *Comparative Literature*, 16 (1964), 289-309; F. L. Lucas, *Euripides and his Influence* (New York, 1928); Sally MacEwen (ed.), *Views of Clytemnestra, Ancient and Modern* (Lewiston, Queenston, and Lampeter, 1990); Fiona Macinstosh, 'Tragedy in Performance: Nineteenth and Twentieth-Century Productions', in Easterling (ed.), *Cambridge Companion*, 284-323; Diane Purkiss (ed.), *Three Tragedies by Renaissance Women* (Harmondsworth, 1998), which includes Jane Lumley's *The Tragedie of Iphigenia*.

VISUAL ARTS

Vase-paintings illustrating scenes from Euripides are collected in
A. D. Trendall and T. B. L. Webster, *Illustrations of Greek Drama*
(London, 1971), 72–105, and supplemented in the articles under
the names of each important character (e.g. 'Iphigenia') in the
multi-volume ongoing *Lexicon Iconographicum Mythologiae Classicae*
(Zurich/Munich 1984–?). See also Oliver Taplin, 'The Pictorial
Record', in Easterling, *Cambridge Companion*, 69–90; Kurt
Weitzmann, 'Euripides scenes in Byzantine art', *Hesperia*, 18
(1949), 159–210.

PRODUCTION AND PERFORMANCE CONTEXTS

Giovanni Comotti, *Music in Greek and Roman Culture* (Eng. trans.,
Baltimore and London 1989), 32–41; E. Csapo and W. J. Slater, *The
Context of Ancient Drama* (Ann Arbor, 1995), 79–101; S. Goldhill,
'The Great Dionysia and Civic Ideology', in J. Winkler and F. I.
Zeitlin (eds.), *Nothing to do with Dionysos? Athenian Drama in its
Social Context* (Princeton, 1990), 97–129; John Gould, 'Tragedy in
Performance', in B. Knox and P. E. Easterling (eds.), *The Cambridge
History of Classical Literature*, i (Cambridge, 1985), 258–81; E. Hall,
'Actor's Song in Tragedy', in S. Goldhill and R. Osborne (eds.),
Performance and Democracy (Cambridge, 1998); Nicolaos C.
Hourmouziades, *Production and Imagination in Euripides: Form and
Function of the Scenic Space* (Athens, 1965); Maarit Kaimio, *Physical
Contact in Greek Tragedy* (Helsinki, 1988); Solon Michaelides, *The
Music of Ancient Greece: An Encyclopaedia* (London, 1978), 117–19;
A. Pickard-Cambridge, *The Dramatic Festivals of Athens*, 3rd edn. rev.
J. Gould and D. M. Lewis (Oxford, 1988); Erika Simon, *The Ancient
Theater* (London and New York, 1982); Oliver Taplin, *The Stagecraft
of Aeschylus* (Oxford, 1977), and 'Did Greek Dramatists write Stage
instructions?', *Proceedings of the Cambridge Philological Society*, 23
(1977), 121–32.

On satyr drama see P. E. Easterling, 'A Show for Dionysos', in
Easterling (ed.), *Cambridge Companion*, 36–53; Richard Seaford (ed.),
Euripides' Cyclops (Oxford, 1984), 1–45; E. Hall, 'Ithyphallic Males
Behaving Badly: Satyr Drama as Gendered Tragic Ending'; in
M. Wyke (ed.), *Parchments of Gender: Reading Ancient Bodies* (Oxford,
1998).

SOCIAL AND HISTORICAL CONTEXT

See J. K. Davies, *Democracy and Classical Greece* (Glasgow, 1978), 63–128, and 'Athenian Citizenship: The Descent Group and the Alternatives', *CJ* 73 (1977–8), 105–21; Anton Powell, *Athens and Sparta: Constructing Greek Political and Social History from 478 BC* (London, 1988); Paul Cartledge, *The Greeks* (Oxford, 1996) and (ed.), *The Cambridge Illustrated History of Ancient Greece* (Cambridge, 1997).

For an overview of the problems in reconstructing Athenian women's lives, see Josine Blok's survey in J. Blok and H. Mason (eds.), *Sexual Asymmetry: Studies in Ancient Society* (Amsterdam, 1987), 1–57. For a recent range of views on gender issues see D. Cohen, *Law, Sexuality, and Society: The Enforcement of Morals in Classical Athens* (Cambridge, 1991); John Gould, 'Law, Custom, and Myth: Aspects of the Social Position of Women in Classical Athens', *JHS* 100 (1980), 38–59; Virginia Hunter, *Policing Athens* (Princeton, 1994), 9–42; R. Just, *Women in Athenian Law and Life* (London and New York, 1989); Elaine Fantham *et al.* (eds.), *Women in the Classical World* (New York and Oxford, 1994).

SPECIFIC ASPECTS OF EURIPIDEAN DRAMA

Rachel Aélion, *Euripide. Héritier d'Eschyle*, 2 vols. (Paris, 1983); W. G. Arnott, 'Euripides and the Unexpected', *G&R* 20 (1973), 49–63; Francis M. Dunn, *Tragedy's End: Closure and Innovation in Euripidean Drama* (New York and Oxford, 1996); H. Erbse, *Studien zum Prolog der euripideischen Tragödie* (Berlin, 1984); M. Fusillo, 'Was ist eine romanhafte Tragödie? Überlegungen zu Euripides' Experimentalismus', *Poetica*, 24 (1992), 270–99; Richard Hamilton, 'Prologue, Prophecy and Plot in Four Plays of Euripides', *AJP* 99 (1978), 277–302, and 'Euripidean Priests', *HSCP* 89 (1985), 53–73; Martin Hose, *Studien zum Chor bei Euripides* (Berlin, 1990–1); E. O'Connor-Visser, *Aspects of Human Sacrifice in the Tragedies of Euripides* (Amsterdam, 1987); Bernd Seidensticker, 'Tragic Dialectic in Euripidean Tragedy', in M. S. Silk (ed.), *Tragedy and the Tragic: Greek Theatre and Beyond* (Oxford, 1996), 377–96; Sophie Trenkner, *The Greek Novella in the Classical Period* (Cambridge, 1958), 31–78; R. P. Winnington-Ingram, 'Euripides: *poiētēs sophos*', *Arethusa*, 2 (1969), 127–42.

For the lost plays of Euripides see C. Collard, M. J. Cropp, and K. H. Lee (eds.), *Euripides: Selected Fragmentary Plays*, i–ii (Warminster, 1995, 1999); T. B. L. Webster, *The Tragedies of Euripides* (London, 1967).

On slaves in Euripides see K. Synodinou, *On the Concept of Slavery in Euripides* (Eng. trans., Ioannina, 1977); E. Hall, 'The Sociology of Athenian Tragedy', in Easterling (ed.), *Cambridge Companion*, 93–126; D. P. Stanley-Porter, 'Mute Actors in the Tragedies of Euripides', *BICS* 20 (1973), 68–93. On children see G. Sifakis, 'Children in Greek Tragedy', *BICS* 26 (1979), 67–80. On women see H. Foley, 'The Conception of Women in Athenian Drama', in H. P. Foley (ed.), *Reflections of Women in Antiquity* (London and New York, 1981), 127–67; Ruth Herder, *Die Frauenrolle bei Euripides* (Stuttgart, 1993); Nicole Loraux, *Tragic Ways of Killing a Woman* (Eng. trans., Cambridge, Mass., 1987); Richard Seaford, 'The Structural Problems of Marriage in Euripides', in A. Powell (ed.), *Euripides, Women and Sexuality* (London and New York, 1990), 151–76; Nancy Sorkin Rabinowitz, *Anxiety Veiled : Euripides and the Traffic in Women* (Ithaca, NY, and London, 1993); Froma Zeitlin, *Playing the Other: Gender and Society in Classical Greek Literature* (Chicago and London, 1996).

For religion in Euripides see C. Sourvinou-Inwood, 'Tragedy and Religion: Constructs and Meanings', in Christopher Pelling (ed.), *Greek Tragedy and the Historian* (Oxford, 1997), 161–86. For sceptical discussions see M. R. Lefkowitz, 'Was Euripides an Atheist?', *Studi Italiani*, 5 (1987), 149–65, and ' "Atheism" and "impiety" in Euripides' dramas', *CQ* 39 (1989), 70–82; G. E. Dimock, '*God or Not God, or between the Two*': *Euripides' Helen* (Northampton, Mass., 1977—Euripides' evangelism); Harvey Yunis, *A New Creed: Fundamental Religious Beliefs in the Athenian Polis and Euripidean Drama* (= Hypomnemata 91, Göttingen, 1988). On supplication scenes, see J. Gould, 'Hiketeia', *JHS* 93 (1973), 74–103.

On the sophists, philosophy, and the intellectual background see J. H. Finley, 'Euripides and Thucydides', in *Three Essays on Thucydides* (Cambridge, Mass., 1967), 1–24; S. Goldhill, *Reading Greek Tragedy* (Cambridge, 1986), 222–43; G. B. Kerferd, *The Sophistic Movement* (Cambridge, 1981); W. Nestle, *Untersuchungen über die philosophischen Quellen des Euripides* (*Philologus* suppl. 8.4 (1901), 557–655, and *Euripides: der Dichter der griechischen Aufklärung* (Stuttgart, 1901); F. Solmsen, *Intellectual Experiments of the Greek Enlightenment* (Princeton, 1975), 24–31, 132–41.

On rhetoric see V. Bers, 'Tragedy and Rhetoric', in
I. Worthington (ed.), *Greek Rhetoric in Action* (London and New
York, 1994), 176–95; Richard Buxton, *Persuasion in Greek Tragedy*
(Cambridge, 1982); C. Collard, 'Formal Debates in Euripidean
Drama', *G&R* 22 (1975); D. J. Conacher, 'Rhetoric and relevance
in Euripidean drama', *AJP* 102 (1981), 3–25; E. Hall, 'Lawcourt
Dramas: The Power of Performance in Greek Forensic Oratory',
BICS 40 (1995), 39–58; M. Lloyd, *The Agon in Euripides* (Oxford,
1992).

On characterization, see H. P. Stahl, 'On "Extra-Dramatic"
Communication in Euripides', *YCS* 25 (1977), 159–76; J. Griffin,
'Characterization in Euripides', in C. Pelling (ed.), *Characterization
and Individuality in Greek Literature* (Oxford, 1990), 128–49.

On speech, language, style, and imagery, see Shirley Barlow, *The
Imagery of Euripides* (London, 1971); I. J. F. de Jong, *Narrative in
Drama: The Art of the Euripidean Messenger-Speech* (Leiden, 1991);
P. T. Stevens, *Colloquial Expressions in Euripides* (Wiesbaden, 1976);
Ernst Schwinge, *Die Verwendung der Stichomythie in den Dramen des
Euripides* (Heidelberg, 1968).

INDIVIDUAL PLAYS

Iphigenia among the Taurians

Editions: M. Platnauer (ed.), *Euripides: Iphigenia at Tauris* (Oxford,
1938); Martin Cropp (ed.), *Euripides' Iphigenia in Tauris* (forthcoming, Warminster, 1999).

Studies: R. Caldwell, 'Tragedy Romanticized: The *Iphigenia Taurica*',
CJ 70 (1974–5), 23–40; Dietrich Ebener, 'Der humane Gehalt der
Taurischen Iphigenie', *Altertum*, 12 (1966), 97–103; Karelisa
Hartigan, 'Salvation via Deceit: A New Look at the *Iphigenia at
Tauris*', *Eranos*, 84 (1986), 119–25; A. O. Hutton, 'Euripides and
the Iphigenia Legend', *Mnemosyne*, 15 (1962), 364–8; David
Sansone, 'The Sacrifice-Motif in Euripides' *Iphigenia among the
Taurians*', *TAPA* 105 (1975), 283–311; D. F. Sutton, 'Satyric
Qualities in Euripides' *Iphigenia at Tauris* and *Helen*', *RSC* 20 (1972),
321–30; J. T. Svendsej, 'The Letter Device in Euripides and
Shakespeare', in K. Hartigan (ed.), *Legacy of Thespis* (University of
Florida Comparative Drama Papers), iv (1984), 75–88; C. Wolff,
'Euripides' *Iphigenia among the Taurians*: Aetiology, Ritual, and

Myth', *Classical Antiquity*, 11 (1992), 308-34; Froma Zeitlin, 'Figures of Dreams, Figures of Doubles: Mortals and Immortals in Euripides' *Iphigenia in Tauris*', in her *Vision, Figuration, and Image: From Theater to Romance* (Berkeley and Los Angeles, 1999).

Bacchae

Commentaries: E. R. Dodds (ed.), *Euripides' Bacchae*, 2nd edn. (Oxford, 1960); Richard Seaford (ed.), *Euripides' Bacchae* (Warminster, 1996).

Studies: M. Arthur, 'The Choral Odes of the *Bacchae* of Euripides', *YCS* 22 (1972), 145-79; S. des Bouvrie, 'Euripides' *Bacchae* and Maenadism', *Classica et Medievalia*, 48 (1997), 75-114; A. P. Burnett, 'Pentheus and Dionysus: host and guest', *CP* 65 (1970), 15-29; R. Buxton, 'News from Cithaeron: Narrators and Narratives in the *Bacchae*', *Pallas*, 90 (1970), 39-48; G. Devereux, 'The Psychotherapy Scene in Euripides' *Bacchae*', *JHS* 90 (1970), 35-48; H. Foley, 'The Masque of Dionysus', *TAPA* 110 (1980), 107-33; H. Oranje, *Euripides' Bacchae: The Play and its Audience* (Leiden, 1984); W. C. Scott, 'Two Suns over Thebes: Imagery and Stage Effects in the *Bacchae*', *TAPA* 105 (1975), 333-46; R. Seaford, 'Dionysiac Drama and the Dionysiac Mysteries', *CQ* 31 (1981), 252-75; B. Seidensticker, 'Comic Elements in Euripides' *Bacchae*', *AJP* 99 (1978), 303-20, and 'Sacrificial Ritual in the *Bacchae*', in G. W. Bowersock *et al.* (eds.), *Arktouros: Hellenic Studies Presented to Bernard M. W. Knox* (Berlin and New York, 1979), 181-90; John Whitehouse, 'The Dead as Spectacle in Euripides' *Bacchae* and *Supplices*', *Hermes*, 114 (1986), 59-72.

Iphigenia at Aulis

Commentaries: C. Collard (ed.), *Euripides' Iphigenia in Aulis* (Warminster, forthcoming).

Studies: Dale Chant, 'Role Inversion and its Function in the *Iphigenia at Aulis*', *Ramus*, 15 (1986), 83-92; H. Foley, 'Marriage and Sacrifice in Euripides' *Iphigenia in Aulis*', *Arethusa*, 15 (1982), 159-80; J. Ferguson, 'Iphigenia at Aulis', *TAPA* 99 (1968), 157-63; Bernard Knox, 'Euripides' *Iphigenia in Aulide* 1-163 (in that order)', *YCS* 22 (1972), 239-62; C. A. E. Luschnig, 'Time and Memory in Euripides' *Iphigenia at Aulis*', *Ramus*, 11 (1982),

99–104, and *Tragic Aporia: A Study of Euripides' Iphigenia at Aulis* (=
Ramus Monographs 3, 1988); Gudrun Mellert-Hoffman, *Unter-
suchungen zur 'Iphigenie in Aulis' des Euripides* (Heidelberg, 1969);
Herbert Siegel, 'Self-delusion and the *volte-face* of Iphigenia in
Euripides' *Iphigenia at Aulis'*, *Hermes*, 108 (1980), 300–21; Herbert
Siegel, 'Agamemnon in Euripides' *Iphigenia at Aulis'*, *Hermes*, 109
(1981), 257–65; Wesley D. Smith, 'Iphigenia in Love', in
Arktouros (see above under *Bacchae*), 173–80; F. Wassermann,
'Agamemnon in the *Iphigenia at Aulis'*, *TAPA* 80 (1949), 117–86;
F. I. Zeitlin, 'Art Memory, and *kleos* in Euripides' *Iphigenia in Aulis'*,
in B. Goff (ed.), *History, Tragedy, Theory: Dialogues on Athenian
Drama* (Austin, Tex., 1995), 174–201.

Rhesus

Commentaries: W. H. Porter, *The Rhesus of Euripides*, 2nd edn.
(Cambridge, 1929); Edith Hall (ed.), *The Rhesus attributed to
Euripides* (Warminster, forthcoming).

Studies: Francesca Bernacchia, '*Il Reso*: eredità rituali ed elabo-
razione drammaturgica', *Dioniso*, 60 (1990), 40–53; Anne
Burnett, '*Rhesus*: Are Smiles Allowed?', in P. Burian (ed.),
Directions in Euripidean Criticism (Durham, 1985), 13–51; Dietrich
Ebener, *Rhesos: Tragödie eines unbekannten Dichters* (Berlin, 1966);
B. Fenik, *Iliad X and the Rhesus: The Myth* (= *Latomus* 73, Brussels,
1964); H. D. F. Kitto, 'The *Rhesus* and Related Matters', *YCS* 25
(1977), 317–50; Grace Macurdy, 'The Dawn Songs in *Rhesus*
(525–556) and in the Parodos of *Phaethon*', *AJP* 64 (1943),
406–18; Guido Paduano, 'Funzioni drammatiche nella struttura
del *Reso*', *Maia*, 25 (1973), 3–29; G. Pagani, 'Il Reso di Euripide:
il dramma di un eroe', *Dioniso*, 44 (1970), 30–43; Hugh Parry,
'The Approach of Dawn in the *Rhesus*', *The Phoenix*, 18 (1964),
283–93; W. Ritchie, *The Authenticity of the Rhesus of Euripides*
(Cambridge, 1964); V. J. Rosivach, 'Hector in the Rhesus', *Hermes*,
104 (1978), 54–73; H. Strohm, 'Beobachtungen zum *Rhesus*',
Hermes, 87 (1959), 257–74.

CHRONOLOGY

Euripides was born in Attica, the country whose main city is Athens, in about 484 BCE. He died in 406 in Macedonia, where he had gone probably in 408. He wrote some sixty-six tragedies which were performed at the Great Dionysia festival in Athens. Seventeen of these survive complete. In addition, he must have written twenty-two satyr plays (comic and obscene dramas on mythological subjects), only one of which (*Cyclops*) survives. He won the first prize at the festival on five occasions, one of them after his death. In the ancient *Life* it is said that he was indifferent to theatrical success.

Dates of productions of extant plays (adapted from C. Collard, *Euripides* (Oxford, 1981), 2)		Dates in the history of Athens	
		462	Radical democracy established in Athens
455	first production		
		448	Building of Parthenon begun
441	first prize (play unknown)		
438	*Alcestis*—second prize		
431	*Medea*—third prize	431	Outbreak of Peloponnesian War between Athens and Sparta
430–428	*Heraclidae*	430	Outbreak of plague in Athens
428	*Hippolytus* (revised from earlier production)—first prize		
?425	*Andromache*		
before 423	*Hecuba*		
?423	*Supplices*		
?before 415	*Hercules Furens*		

before 415 *Electra*

	416 Slaughter by the Athenians of the men of the island of Melos and the enslavement of its women and children
415 *Troades*—second prize	415 Disastrous Athenian -413 expedition to Sicily
before 412 *Iphigenia at Tauris*	
?before 412 *Ion*	
412 *Helen*	
?412 *Cyclops* (satyr play)	
411-408, ?409 *Phoenissae*—second prize	411 Oligarchic revolution in Athens
408 *Orestes*	
after 406 *Iphigenia at Aulis* and *Bacchae*—first prize	
	404 Defeat of Athens by Sparta in the Peloponnesian War

ABBREVIATIONS

AJP	*American Journal of Philosophy*
BICS	*Bulletin of the Institute of Classical Studies*
CA	*Classical Antiquity*
CJ	*Classical Journal*
CP	*Classical Philology*
CQ	*Classical Quarterly*
CR	*Classical Review*
G&R	*Greece & Rome*
GRBS	*Greek, Roman, and Byzantine Studies*
HSCP	*Harvard Studies in Classical Philology*
JHS	*Journal of Hellenistic Studies*
PCPS	*Proceedings of the Cambridge Philological Society*
RSC	*Revista di Studi Classici*
SO	*Symbolai Osloensis*
TAPA	*Transactions and Proceedings of the American Philological Association*
YCS	*Yale Classical Studies*
s.d.	*stage direction*

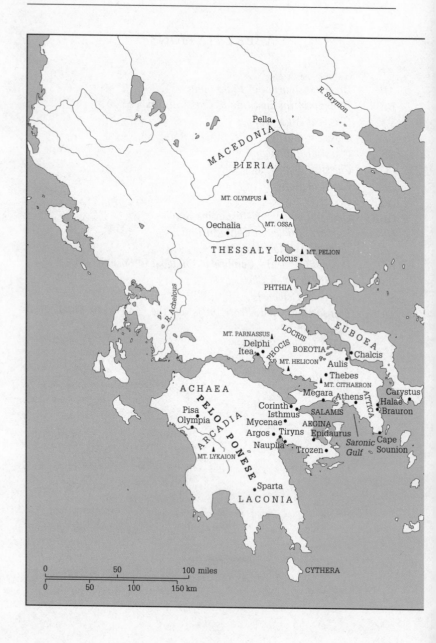

Pella

MACEDONIA

R. Strymon

PIERIA

MT. OLYMPUS ▲

Oechalia   ▲ MT. OSSA

THESSALY   ▲ MT. PELION

Iolcus

PHTHIA

R. Achelous

MT. PARNASSUS ▲   LOCRIS   EUBOEA
Delphi   PHOCIS
Itea   BOEOTIA   Chalcis
          MT. HELICON ▲   Aulis

          Thebes
ACHAEA   MT. CITHAERON ▲
PELO   Megara   Athens   Carystus
Pisa   Corinth   ATTICA   Halae
Olympia   Isthmus   SALAMIS   Brauron
ARCADIA   Mycenae   AEGINA
PONESE   Argos ● Tiryns   Epidaurus
          Nauplia   Saronic   Cape
▲   Trozen   Gulf   Sounion
MT. LYKAION

          Sparta

          LACONIA

0   50   100 miles
0   50   100   150 km

          CYTHERA

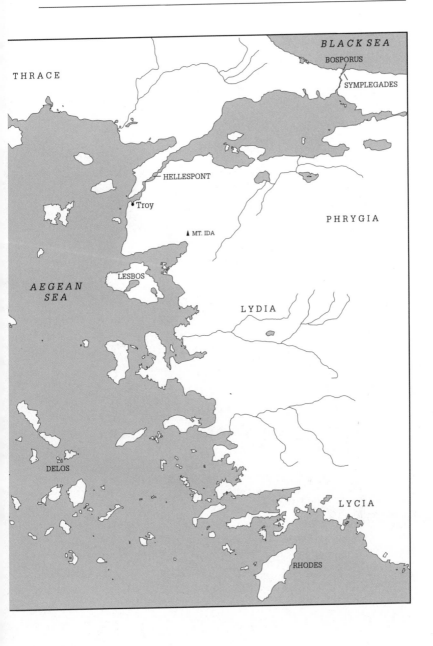

IPHIGENIA AMONG THE TAURIANS

Characters

IPHIGENIA, *daughter of Agamemnon and priestess of Artemis*
ORESTES, *brother of Iphigenia*
PYLADES, *friend of Orestes*
HERDSMAN
THOAS, *king of Thrace*
MESSENGER
ATHENA

CHORUS *of captured Greek women from Delos, the handmaidens of*
Iphigenia

The action is set in front of the Temple of Artemis in the country
of the Taurians.* IPHIGENIA enters from the temple.

IPHIGENIA. Pelops, the son of Tantalus, arrived with his swift
mares at Pisa and married the daughter of Oenomaus.* She
bore Atreus to him. And Atreus' sons were Menelaus and
Agamemnon. I am Agamemnon's daughter Iphigenia, the
child of Clytemnestra whose father was Tyndareus. My
father slaughtered me, or so he thought, in sacrifice to
Artemis for Helen's sake in the famous bays of Aulis beside
the eddies which Euripus whirls round and round with frequent gusts of wind as it ruffles the dark-blue sea.* For it was
there that King Agamemnon assembled a Greek sea-force of   10
a thousand ships,* wishing to win the crown of glorious victory over Troy for the Achaeans* and to do Menelaus the
favour of avenging the outrage to Helen's marriage.

However, he could get no winds and that made sailing
impossible. Faced with this crisis, he resorted to divination
from burnt offerings, and Calchas* spoke these words: 'O
Agamemnon, commander of this army of Greece, you shall
not unmoor your ships from the land before Artemis receives
your girl Iphigenia as her slaughtered victim. For you vowed   20
that you would sacrifice to the goddess of the moon the most
beautiful thing that the year produced.* Well, Clytemnestra

your wife bore a child in the house'—said Calchas, applying
the title of most beautiful to me—'which you must sacrifice.'

And in a scheme instigated by Odysseus, they said that I
was to marry Achilles and took me away from my mother.
I, poor girl, came to Aulis. They lifted me up above the altar
and were on the point of killing me with the sword. But
Artemis stole me away and gave the Achaeans a deer in my
place. She sent me through the bright air and brought me   30
to live in this land of the Taurians where Thoas rules, a barbarian among barbarians. He got this name thanks to his
speed, for he runs as if his swift feet are wings.* She made
me her priestess in this temple. In that office, by the customs
in which the goddess rejoices, I begin the holy rites of her
festival. Only its name is fair: I keep silent about the rest in
fear of the goddess [for by the city's ancient custom I sacrifice any Greek man who puts to shore in this land.] I begin   40
the ritual of his slaughter* [but the unspeakable deed is for
others to perform inside this temple of the goddess].

I shall tell to the air the strange visions which the night
time brought me, and see if that brings any healing.* In my
sleep I seemed to have escaped from this land and to be living in Argos and sleeping in the middle of my girls in our
maiden quarters. An earthquake shook the surface of the
ground. I ran out, and as I stood outside I seemed to see the
cornice tumbling from on high and the whole roof thrown
down in ruin from its topmost column. Only one supporting   50
pillar of my father's house was left standing—so it appeared
in my dream—and from its capital it let fall locks of golden
hair and spoke with a human voice. Then I, in due obser-
vance of this art of killing strangers that I practise, sprinkled
it with water as a victim doomed to death, weeping as I did
so. For this is how I interpret my dream. Orestes is dead—
he was the victim that I sprinkled in preparation for sacrifice. The pillars of a house are its male children, and those
on whom my holy water falls are killed. [And I cannot apply
my dream to any other relatives, for Strophius had no son   60
on my death-day.]*

So now I wish to pour libations for my brother, separated
though we are,—that at least I can do—in company with
my handmaidens, the Greek women whom the king gave to

me. But for some reason they are not here yet. I shall go inside this temple of the goddess where I live.

IPHIGENIA *goes into the temple.* ORESTES *and* PYLADES *enter.*

ORESTES. Take care, watch out that there's nobody on the path.
PYLADES. I am keeping my eyes open and looking around everywhere.
ORESTES. Pylades, do you think that this is the goddess's dwelling to which we steered our ship over the sea from 70 Argos?
PYLADES. I do, Orestes,* and you must think so too.
ORESTES. And this is the altar* where drips Greek blood?
PYLADES. Its coping is certainly red with blood.
ORESTES. And do you see the heads* hung up under the coping?
PYLADES. Yes, these are the trophies of foreigners that they have killed. But we must stay on our guard and look around us everywhere.
ORESTES. O Phoebus, into what new snare have you led me now by your oracle, after I have avenged my father's blood by killing my mother? Troop upon troop of Furies drove me 80 as I fled, an outcast from my land, and I have completed many a race as I doubled back on my track.* So I came to you and asked how I could find an end of spinning madness, an end to the troubles which I endured as I wandered Greece. You told me to go to the shores of the Taurian land where Artemis your sister has her altars, and to take the image of the goddess which they say fell from the sky here into this temple. And after I had taken it, whether by stratagem or good luck, and braved all the danger, I should give 90 it to the land of the Athenians. (As for the sequel, nothing further was said.) That done, I could breathe again after my labours.

In obedience to your orders I have come here to an unknown, inhospitable land. And I ask you, Pylades—for you have shouldered this labour with me—what should we do? For you see the lofty walls which encircle the temple. Shall we climb up ladders? How could we avoid being seen? Or should we use crowbars to break open the bronze doors †though we know nothing about their bolts†? But if we plan 100 to enter by the doors and are caught opening them, we shall be killed. No, rather than die, let us flee on the ship on which we sailed here.

PYLADES. To run away is intolerable, and we are not accustomed to behave in that manner. We must not hold the oracle of the god in dishonour. Let us slip off from the temple and hide ourselves in the caves which the dark sea swills with its waters—at a distance from our ship in case anyone spots our vessel and tells the king, and then we are seized by force.

But when the eye of gloomy night has come, we must   110
summon up the courage to take the carved image from the temple with all the cunning we can bring to the task. †Look there—where there is space between the triglyphs to let ourselves down.*† Brave men do not flinch from ordeals but cowards never amount to anything. We have not rowed so far on our voyage only to turn back from our goal.

ORESTES. Your advice is good and I must follow it. We must find some place where the two of us can hide ourselves without being seen. I shall not be to blame for the failure of the   120
god's oracle. We must not flinch. For the young, there is no excuse for shirking a task, however hard.

ORESTES and PYLADES go out. The CHORUS of captured Greek
women enter and IPHIGENIA comes out of the temple.

IPHIGENIA (*sings*). Keep reverent silence,
  you who dwell by the two Clashing Rocks
  of the inhospitable sea.*
CHORUS (*sings*). O daughter of Leto,
  Dictynna, goddess of the mountains,*
  to your halls, the golden cornices
  of your temple with its lovely columns,*
  I make my way, a pure virgin,   130
  slave of the pure priestess who holds your key.
  I have left the towers and the walls
  of Greece famed for its horses
  and Europe with its wooded pastures
  where my father and his father lived.
  Here I am.* What news is there? What do you have in
    mind?

Why have you brought me, brought me to the temple,
o daughter of the king who went to the towers of Troy
with his famous fleet, 140
master of a thousand ships, of numberless men in arms,
†the elder of the famous sons of Atreus.†
IPHIGENIA (*sings*). O you captive women,
how deep sunk I am in lamentation, bitter lamentation,
in my songs of mourning, ill-suited to the joyful lyre,
with their music that is no music—alas!—
my piteous elegy for my brother.
Disaster is my companion, disaster,
as I bewail my brother's lost life—
such a vision, 150
such a dream I saw
in the darkness of this last night.
I am lost, utterly lost,
The house of my fathers is no more.
Cry sorrow for me—my family is all gone.
Alas, alas for the woes in Argos.
O you evil spirit
who despoiled me of my only brother
sending him to Hades! To him
I am about to sprinkle these libations 160
on the ground's surface
from the mixing bowl devoted to the dead,
streams of milk from mountain heifers, the wine of
Bacchus,
and the produce of the toil of the buzzing bee,
which are poured to soothe the spirits of the dead.*
Give me the urn of gold
which holds the libation for the god of the Underworld.
O son of Agamemnon beneath the ground,
I send these offerings to you as a dead man.
Accept them. For I shall not bring my golden hair* 170
to your tomb, nor my tears.
I have been sundered
far from your fatherland and mine where, as men suppose,
I, wretched Iphigenia, lie slaughtered.
CHORUS (*sings*). I shall answer you, mistress,
in songs to echo yours,

crying out the barbarian dirge of Asian women,*   180
keening the wretched music for the dead
which Hades sings in his songs
where no triumphal chants resound.
Alas for the house of Atreus' sons.
The sceptred brilliance of your ancestral home—o
    sorrow—is no more.
†Who of Argos' prosperous kings
holds the sovereignty now?†   190
One trouble after another darts
⟨upon the house, causing the Sun's⟩ winged mares to veer
    round.*
Yes, the Sun god altered his fixed course,
†shifting the brightness of his holy face.
Different distresses have fallen upon the family's different
    branches
because of the golden-fleeced lamb,*
murder has followed murder, griefs have been piled on
    griefs.†
From this source, from the children murdered long ago,
springs vengeance on the house of Tantalus' descendants,*   200
and its evil spirit speeds with disastrous haste
against you.
IPHIGENIA (*sings*). From the start the spirit that pursues me
has been a spirit of bad fortune—
from that marriage night when my father untied my
    mother's girdle.
From the start, those goddesses, the Fates presiding at my
    birth,
tightened the thread of destiny round my childhood and
    made it bite.
†The unhappy daughter of Leda*   210
gave birth to me, the first-born child of the marriage,
and brought me up, but I was promised by a vow,
destined to be slaughtered in a grim sacrifice,
the outrage committed on me by my father.†
The Greeks set me down from a horse-drawn chariot
on the sands of Aulis,
a bride—o sorrow! I was no bride—
for the son of the daughter of Nereus*—alas!

But now I dwell a stranger
in a barren land by an inhospitable sea.
I have no husband, no child, no city, no friend—   220
yet I was wooed by Greeks.
I sing no song to Hera, the goddess of Argos,*
I do not embroider with my shuttle
on the soft-voiced loom
an image of Athenian Pallas
and the Titans,*
†but I stain the altars as, to the hideous music of their
   screams,
I send blood-boltered strangers to their doom.†*
Pitiful are the cries they pour forth
and pitiful the tears they shed.   230
And now I have forgotten all that,
and I weep for my brother who has died in Argos.
I left him still a baby,
still young, still a child
in his mother's arms and at her breast,
Orestes, heir to the sceptre of Argos.

CHORUS. But look, here is a herdsman who has come from the
sea shore to tell us some news.

Enter HERDSMAN.

HERDSMAN. Daughter of Agamemnon and Clytemnestra, listen to the strange events which I shall report to you.
IPHIGENIA. What is there so alarming about your news?   240
HERDSMAN. Two young men have rowed safely through the
dark-blue Clashing Rocks* and come to our land—a welcome sacrifice to slaughter to the goddess Artemis. Lose no
time in preparing the holy water and the first offerings.
IPHIGENIA. Where are they from?* What country's clothes do
the strangers wear?
HERDSMAN. They are Greeks. That is the one thing I know,
nothing more.
IPHIGENIA. Can't you tell me the strangers' names? Didn't
you hear them?
HERDSMAN. One of them called the other Pylades.
IPHIGENIA. And what was the name of the stranger's com-   250
panion?

HERDSMAN. No one knows this. We didn't hear.

IPHIGENIA. Where did you see them? And where did you meet and capture them?

HERDSMAN. By the shore of our inhospitable sea where the waves break.

IPHIGENIA. Tell me, what have herdsmen to do with the sea?

HERDSMAN. We went there to wash our cattle in the sea water.

IPHIGENIA. To return to my previous question, how did you capture them—by what stratagem? I would like to know this. [It is strange that no Greeks have come here until now. The altar of the goddess has not yet been dyed with streams of Greek blood.]

HERDSMAN. When we were driving our cattle from their 260 woodland pastures to the sea which flows out through the Clashing Rocks, there was a broken cliff, hollowed out by the constant erosion of the rolling waves, where the purple-fishers shelter.* There one of us herdsmen saw two young fellows and he crept back to us on tiptoe. 'Don't you see them?' he said. 'These are gods sitting here.' And one of our number, a pious man, held up his hands and looked at them and prayed: 'O son of the sea-goddess Leucothea, lord 270 Palaemon, guardian of ships, be gracious to us. Is it you, the two Dioscuri, who sit on the shore, or are you the darlings of Nereus who fathered the noble company of fifty dancing Nereids?'*

But someone else, an irreverent man with a rash, anarchic spirit, laughed at his prayers. He said that they were shipwrecked sailors sitting in the cleft in fear of our custom, for they must have heard that we sacrifice strangers here. He seemed to most of us to be talking sense, and we thought 280 it a good idea to hunt down sacrificial victims for the goddess in accordance with our local rites.

Meanwhile one of the strangers left the rock cleft, and stood there jerking his head violently up and down. He groaned aloud as his hands shook and he rushed about in a frenzy of madness. And he shouted like a hunter:* 'Pylades, do you see this one? Can you not see how that one, a she-dragon from Hell, wants to kill me and turns her weapons, the fearful vipers of her hair, against me? This one nearby wings her way breathing fire and murder, holding my

mother in her arms, now a massive stone, so that she can   290
throw her on me. O horror! She will kill me. Where can I
take refuge?'

We could see no such forms as he described, but he mis-
interpreted the lowing of cattle and the barking of dogs as
the similar sounds which they say the Furies make.
Thinking he was going to die, we cowered together in fright
and sat there silently. Then he drew his sword in his hand
and, rushing into the middle of the heifers like a lion, struck
them with his blade, plunging it into their flanks and ribs—
he believed that he was keeping off the goddesses, the Furies,
in this way—until the sea bloomed red with blood.   300

Meanwhile each one of us, as we saw our cattle falling to
the ground amid this carnage, began to arm ourselves and
blew on spiral shells to summon the local inhabitants. For
we thought that herdsmen would be no match for the
strangers who were fit, well-built and young. Soon a large
number of us had gathered. The stranger's pulse of madness
was stilled and he fell down, his chin dripping with foam.
And when we saw that he had collapsed so conveniently,
everybody energetically threw weapons and struck blows.   310
But the second stranger wiped off the foam from his friend's
face and protected his body by screening it with the sturdy
material of his cloak. He was dodging the missiles which
threatened to hit him and looking after his dear friend with
dutiful attention. The stranger then regained consciousness
and, leaping up from where he lay, he realized that a surge
of enemies was rolling against them and that imminent danger stared them in the face. He cried out in anguish.
However, we didn't slacken our efforts as we pelted them
with stones and pressed hard on them from every direction.

At this moment we heard that terrible cry to arms: 320
'Pylades, we shall die. See that we die with honour. Draw
your sword in your hand and follow me!' When we saw
both of our enemies brandishing their swords, we all ran to
take refuge in the woods on the cliffs. But every time that
some of us fled, the others would move to the attack and
hurl missiles at our enemies. However, if the strangers drove
them back, those who had just now been giving way began
to pelt the enemy in their turn. But it was incredible.

Though missiles were flying from innumerable hands, no
one had the good fortune to hit the victims destined for the
goddess. It was with difficulty that we managed to over-   330
power them and it was not through any courage on our part
that we did so. What happened was that we surrounded
them and knocked the swords out of their hands with
stones, and they sank to their knees in utter exhaustion.

We took them to the king of this land. When he saw them
he sent them with all speed to you for lustral purification
and sacrifice. You have often prayed for such strangers as
victims, maiden, and if you kill strangers like this, Greece
will make atonement for your death and pay the penalty for
your slaughter at Aulis.

CHORUS. You have told an amazing tale about this madman,   340
whoever he is, who has come from the land of Greece to this
inhospitable sea.

IPHIGENIA. Well then. You go off and bring the strangers
while we shall see that the holy rites here are duly prepared.

> *The* HERDSMAN *goes out.*

O my unhappy heart, in the past you were always gentle to
strangers, always full of pity, paying the tribute of a tear to
one of your own race when you took Greek men in your
grasp.* Now, however, because of the dream that has put me
in a frenzy [as I think that Orestes no longer looks upon the
sun], you shall find me hard of heart, whoever you are who   350
have come here.* [And this saying is true to nature, as I now
perceive, my friends: when things go badly for them, the
unfortunate feel no warmth towards the more fortunate.]*
But not a breath of wind from Zeus* has yet blown to waft a
ship carrying Helen—the woman who destroyed me—here
through the Clashing Rocks, and Menelaus too. Then I could
have taken revenge on them, paying back with an Aulis here
that Aulis there where the Greeks held me down and slaughtered me like a calf, and the priest of the sacrifice was my own   360
father. O misery—for I cannot forget my agonies then—how
many times I reached out for my father's chin and his knees
and clung to them, saying words like these: 'O my father,
what a shameful wedding you have prepared for me. Now,
while you are killing me, my mother and the women of Argos
are singing songs for my marriage and the whole palace is

resounding with the music of the pipe. But I am dying, slain
by you. So Achilles has proved to be the god of Death, not the
son of Peleus whom you falsely promised me as my husband   370
when you brought me in a royal chariot through trickery to
a blood-stained marriage.' And as I looked out modestly from
behind my fine-spun bridal veil,* I did not take up my brother
in my arms, my brother who now is dead, and I did not kiss
my sister on the lips, as I thought I was going to Peleus' halls.
I saved up many loving embraces for later since I imagined I
would come back to Argos again.

     Wretched Orestes, if you are dead, from what fair fortunes
you have fallen, from what an enviable heritage!

     I hold to blame the goddess's sophistries. If someone   380
stains his hand with human blood or touches a corpse or
even a woman giving birth, she bars him from her altars
since she considers him polluted. However, she herself takes
pleasure in human sacrifices. It is impossible that Zeus and
Leto could have produced so perverse a child. This reason-
ing leads me to regard the feast which Tantalus gave to the
gods as incredible—as though the gods could delight in a
boy's flesh!* My view is that the people here, murderers of
men themselves, impute their own bad deeds to the goddess.   390
For I think that none of the gods is evil.*

                                   IPHIGENIA *goes out.*

CHORUS (*sings*). Dark, dark blue are the straits of the sea
     where the horsefly flew from Argos
     and crossed to the inhospitable surging waves,
     exchanging Europe
     for Asia's soil.*
     Whoever are these who have left the fair waters
     of the Eurotas, the river green with reeds,   400
     or the holy streams of Dirce,* and have come,
     come to this unfriendly land
     where, in honour of the maiden goddess,
     human blood wets her altars
     and her columned temple?

     Why did they sail their ship-chariot with pine-wood oars
     which dashed the surge to right and left,
     over the waves of the sea, the breezes speeding its sails?   410

Are they eagerly competing
to increase their houses' wealth?*
For hope is a fond delusion
which brings disaster to mortals. It can never satisfy men
who seek to win a heavy freight of wealth
as they wander over the sea and cross to barbarian
    cities,
all drawn by the same hope.
To some the thought of wealth comes out of season,   420
for others it is the centre of their lives.

How did they make their way
through the Clashing Rocks
and past the unsleeping coast of Phineus,*
scudding by the shore
amid the surge of Amphitrite,* goddess of the sea,
where the fifty daughters of Nereus
swirl in circles
as they dance and sing—
the sails billowing in the winds,   430
the rudder creaking in its socket
at the stern,
before the winds from the South
or the West wind's breath,
speeding to the land of many birds
with its white coast,
where the fine race-course of Achilles runs,*
over the inhospitable sea?

If only in answer to my mistress's prayer
Leda's beloved daughter Helen   440
would leave the city of Troy
and come here*
so that, her hair wreathed with a circlet of lustral water-
    drops
soon to become blood,
she might die, her throat cut by my mistress's hand,
in payment of the penalty that is due!
But the most welcome news I could receive
would be that a sailor
had arrived from the land of Greece

to put an end to the labours   450
of my wretched slavery.
For if only in dreams
may I be at my home in the city of my fathers,
finding joy in sweet sleep,
that pleasure †for rich and poor alike†!

ORESTES *and* PYLADES *are led on by guards.*

(*chants*)
Here come the pair,
their hands bound fast,
new victims for the goddess. Quiet, dear friends.
For these are choicest specimens of Greeks
that are approaching the temple,   460
and the herdsman did not give us
false information.
O mistress Artemis, if you take pleasure
in the rites which this city performs,
accept the sacrifice
†which our Greek custom
plainly declares unholy†.

IPHIGENIA enters.

IPHIGENIA. Well then, my first consideration must be to
see that the goddess's rituals are duly performed. (*to the
guards*) Untie the strangers' hands so that, as holy victims,
they may be bound no longer. Go inside the temple and   470
prepare what custom dictates as proper for the present
occasion.
                                                The GUARDS *go out.*

(*with a sigh*) Who is the mother who once gave you birth?
Who is your father? And your sister if you have one? How
fine are the two young men that she will lose, a sister no
more. Who knows on whom such shifting fortunes will fall?
Everything that the gods dispense is clouded in obscurity. No
one knows what ill may come. For fortune leads men into a
mist of doubt. Wherever have you come from, you sad
strangers? What a long voyage you have sailed to reach this   480
land! What a long time you will be away from home as you
lie in the Underworld!

ORESTES. Why do you lament like this and bring sadness on yourself, whoever you are, lady, at the thought of sorrows which belong to us? Indeed I hold a man a fool if on the point of killing he is willing to let pity conquer his fear of committing the act—a fool too the man who bewails his imminent doom when he has no hope of safety. To multiply one evil and make it two is to invite the accusation of folly, and to die all the same. We should let fortune take its course. Do not weep for us. We know the sacrificial rites of this place 490 only too well.

IPHIGENIA. Which of you is called Pylades, that name by which he was addressed on the shore? I want to know that first.

ORESTES. This man*—if to know that gives you any pleasure.

IPHIGENIA. Of what Greek country is he a citizen?

ORESTES. What good would it do you to learn this, lady?

IPHIGENIA. Are the two of you brothers, born from the same mother?

ORESTES. We are brothers in love, lady, not in blood.

IPHIGENIA. And you, what name were you given by *your* father?*

ORESTES. By rights I should be called Unfortunate. 500

IPHIGENIA. That is not what I am asking. You must put that down to fortune.

ORESTES. If I were to die without a name, no one could mock me.*

IPHIGENIA. Why do you grudge me this? Are you really so proud?

ORESTES. Your business is to sacrifice my body, not my name.

IPHIGENIA. Will you not tell me what your city is?

ORESTES. No, for what you are asking will not profit me. I am about to die.

IPHIGENIA. But what prevents your doing me this favour?

ORESTES. I boast that my country is the famous land of Argos.

IPHIGENIA. In the gods' name, stranger, are you really from there?

ORESTES. Yes, from Mycenae,* which was happy once. 510

IPHIGENIA. You left Argos, yet your arrival here is welcome to me.

ORESTES. Not to me though. If it is so to you, that's your affair.

IPHIGENIA. Did you set sail from your country as an exile? Or
was it something else?
ORESTES. In a way it was exile. But I both wanted and did not
want to go.*
IPHIGENIA. Will you tell me something that I am eager to know?
ORESTES. Yes, for to do that is nothing when set beside my
misfortune.
IPHIGENIA. Perhaps you have heard of Troy, a city famous the
whole world over?
ORESTES. How I wish I'd never heard of it—not even seen it
in a dream!
IPHIGENIA. They say it no longer exists. War has destroyed it.
ORESTES. That is so. What you have heard has come to pass. 520
IPHIGENIA. And has Helen gone back to Menelaus' house?
ORESTES. She has. And her return has brought no good to one
member of my family.*
IPHIGENIA. Where is she now? I too nurse a grudge against her.
ORESTES. She lives in Sparta with her former bed-fellow.
IPHIGENIA. O hateful Helen—hated by all the Greeks, not me
alone.
ORESTES. I too won some joy from her marriage to Paris!
IPHIGENIA. And the Achaeans came back home, as I was told?
ORESTES. How short your question is, yet how comprehensive!
IPHIGENIA. Yes. I want to get this information from you
before you die.
ORESTES. Question me closely then, since that is what you 530
desire. I shall answer you.
IPHIGENIA. Did someone called Calchas, a seer, return from
Troy?
ORESTES. He died,* as the report goes among the Mycenaeans.
IPHIGENIA. O lady Artemis, how just that is.* What then
about Laertes' son, Odysseus?
ORESTES. He has not yet returned home, but he is alive, as the
report goes.
IPHIGENIA. May he perish! May he never return to his father-
land!
ORESTES. Do not curse him. He and all his fortunes are
plagued by disaster.
IPHIGENIA. And is the son of Thetis, Nereus' grandson, still
alive?

ORESTES. No, he is not. His marriage at Aulis was no use to
him.

IPHIGENIA. Yes, that marriage was a trick, as those who suffered from it know.

ORESTES. Whoever are you? How well you question me about   540
the news from Greece!

IPHIGENIA. I am from there. I was lost to Greece while I was
still a child.

ORESTES. It is right then that you should want to know what
has happened there, lady.

IPHIGENIA. What of the general who they say has good fortune?

ORESTES. What general? The one I know cannot be numbered
among the fortunate.

IPHIGENIA. They talked of a king Agamemnon, son of Atreus.

ORESTES. I know nothing of this. Ask about something else,
lady.

IPHIGENIA. In the gods' name do not say that, but tell me,
stranger. Make me happy.

ORESTES. The wretched man is dead, and in addition he
destroyed another.*

IPHIGENIA. Dead? By what stroke of fate? What tears for me!

ORESTES. Why do you cry out so sadly? Surely he was no rela-   550
tion of yours?

IPHIGENIA. I grieve for his former prosperity.

ORESTES. Yes, for he died terribly, at a woman's hand.

IPHIGENIA. How pitiful—killer and victim alike!

ORESTES. Stop now and do not ask any further questions.

IPHIGENIA. Let me ask just this. Is the wife of the unhappy
man still alive?

ORESTES. She is not. The son she bore killed her with his own
hand.

IPHIGENIA. O house of troubles! Why did he kill her?

ORESTES. He was taking revenge on her for the murder of his
father.

IPHIGENIA. Alas! How right he was to exact this wrongful
justice.

ORESTES. Right he may have been, but the gods do not let him   560
prosper.

IPHIGENIA. Has Agamemnon left any other child in his home?

ORESTES. Yes, he has left one girl, Electra.

IPHIGENIA. Well now, is there any word of the daughter who was killed?

ORESTES. No, none, except that she is dead and looks upon the light of day no more.

IPHIGENIA. She was a pitiable girl—and pitiable too the father who killed her.

ORESTES. She was slaughtered for the worthless sake of a worthless woman.

IPHIGENIA. And is the dead father's son alive in Argos?

ORESTES. He lives, poor creature, everywhere and nowhere.*

IPHIGENIA. False dreams, farewell. So you were nothing then.

ORESTES. Yes, fleeting dreams are false, but not more false 570 than the gods we men call wise. In what the gods dispense, in how men live, there is utter confusion. †One thing alone brings grief to a man,† and that is when someone who is no fool is influenced by the words of seers and meets the death he meets, as only those who have experienced it know.*

CHORUS. Alas! Alas! What about us and our parents? Are they alive or dead? Who could tell us?

IPHIGENIA. Listen. In my eagerness to benefit both you, strangers, and myself, I have thought of a plan. Success is 580 most easily won if the same scheme pleases everybody. If I spared you, would you be willing to go to Argos and take a message for me to my friends there, carrying a letter which a prisoner wrote out of pity for me,* since he considered that it was not my hand that would murder him and that he was the victim †of the law which the goddess sanctioned†. For I had no one whom I could keep alive* to go back to Argos with my news and hand over my letter to one of my friends. 590 But you—for you seem to be of good birth and you know Mycenae and those I love—you must be kept alive and go there. Your payment is one you need not be ashamed to take. It is your life, for the delivery of a simple letter. But you must part company with this man. Since the city forces us to follow this rite, he must be sacrificed to the goddess.

ORESTES. You have spoken well in all respects but one, stranger. The slaughter of this man would lie heavily on my soul. I am the captain of this ship of sorrows and he sails with me in pity for my troubles. It is not right for me to do 600 you a favour at the cost of his murder and to escape disaster myself. No, let this be what happens. Give *him* the letter. For he will deliver it to Argos and thus things will work out well for you. As for me, let whoever wishes to kill me do so. It is most shameful when a man plunges others into calamity while he finds safety himself. Here stands my friend. I hold his life as dear as my own.

IPHIGENIA. O admirable spirit, what a noble family you have   610
sprung from! You are a true friend to your friend. I pray that
the brother I have left to me may be such a man. For I have
a brother too, strangers, it is simply that I cannot see him.*
Since this is what you wish, I shall send this man with the
letter and you shall die. You must have conceived a great
desire for death.

ORESTES. Who will sacrifice me* and steel himself to the dreadful deed?

IPHIGENIA. I shall. I hold this sacred office of the goddess.

ORESTES. An unenviable office, maiden, and a far from happy one.

IPHIGENIA. I have no choice. There is a set of rules I must   620
observe.

ORESTES. Do you make the sacrifice with the sword yourself—
a woman killing men?

IPHIGENIA. No, but I shall pour the water of purification on
your hair.

ORESTES. Who does the killing, if I may ask you this?

IPHIGENIA. The men who see to that are inside this temple.

ORESTES. What grave will receive me when I die?

IPHIGENIA. A gaping chasm in the rock, full of holy fire.*

ORESTES. Alas! If only a sister's hand could lay out my corpse
for burial!

IPHIGENIA. Unhappy man, whoever you are, you pray that
prayer in vain. For your sister lives far from this barbarian
land. However, since you happen to be an Argive, I shall not   630
fail to perform whatever sister's service lies within my
power. I shall place many an ornament upon your grave, I
shall †quench† your body's smouldering ashes with golden
olive oil, and I shall pour upon your pyre gleaming streams
of honey which the buzzing bee culls from the mountain
flowers.

But now I shall go to bring the letter from the goddess's
temple. As a token of good will, I give these instructions.
Guard these men, attendants, but without tying them up.
Perhaps I shall send undreamt of news to a friend in Argos,   640
the man I love the best, and the letter will announce to him
that one whom he thinks dead is still alive, and bring him
unbelievable joy.   IPHIGENIA *goes into the temple.*

CHORUS (*chants to* ORESTES).
  I lament for you, consigned to the care
  of drops of holy water, drops of blood.
ORESTES. No, this is no cause for pity. You must rejoice,
  strangers.
CHORUS (*chants to* PYLADES).
  We count you happy for your blessed fate, young man,
  for you will walk upon your native soil again.
PYLADES. It is wrong to envy friends when their friends are   650
  dying.
CHORUS (*chants*).
  O cruel return—alas, alas!—
  which destroys these two—o sorrow!
  †Which of the pair will be truly destroyed?†
  For still my mind moves this way and that, doubtfully
    debating
  whether I should lament rather for you or for you.

ORESTES. By the gods, Pylades, has the same thought struck
  you as has struck me?
PYLADES. I don't know. I cannot answer your question.
ORESTES. Who is the maiden? How like a true Greek she was   660
  as she questioned us about the sufferings at Troy and the
  return of the Achaeans, about Calchas, that expert in bird-
  auguries, and famous Achilles, and how she pitied wretched
  Agamemnon and asked me about his wife and children. This
  stranger must have been born there in Argos. Otherwise, she
  would not be sending a letter there or cross-questioning me
  about these things like someone who shares Greece's good
  fortunes personally.
PYLADES. I had almost reached that conclusion myself. There
  is just one thing I do not agree with you on. All who have   670
  had dealings with the world know about the tragedies of

kings. However, I have been considering another point as
well.

ORESTES. What is that? You will clarify your own ideas by
sharing them.

PYLADES. It brings me shame to look upon the light of day if
you are dead. I sailed here in your company and in your
company I must die. For I shall win a reputation for base
cowardice in Argos and the Phocians' many valleys,* and I
shall be thought by most men—since most men are malicious—to have come back safely home, a sole survivor, by
betraying you, or even to have killed you while the fortunes   680
of your house were sick, contriving death for you to win
your throne. After all, your sister, and your heiress, is my
wife. These things fill me with fear and shame, and my mind
is made up. I am determined to breathe my last with you, to
be sacrificed with you and have my body burnt with yours.
I am your friend and I fear slander.

ORESTES. Don't say that. I must endure my own misfortunes.
If it is possible for me to bear just one man's woes, I shall
not shoulder a double burden. What you call painful and
shaming applies equally to me if I cause your death while   690
you share my labours. For my part, I hold it no misfortune
if, suffering what I suffer from the gods, I lose my life. You
are blessed and your house is pure, not sick, while mine is
unholy and dogged by misfortune. If you could get away
safely and have children with my sister whom I have given
you in marriage, my family's name would live and my
father's house would be blest with children. It would never
be erased.* Go and live. Dwell in my father's house. And
when you come to Greece and Argos, that land famed for   700
her horses,* by this right hand I lay this charge upon you.
Heap up a tomb and place mementoes of me on it, and let
my sister give the grave her tears and a lock of her hair. Tell
her that I was killed by an Argive woman who purified me
at the altar for my sacrifice. And do not ever abandon my
sister when you see my father's house, now also yours by
marriage, made desolate by another death.

And fare thee well. I found in you the dearest of my
friends, o fellow-huntsman, my foster-brother,* you who
have borne the heavy burden of my many woes. But   710

Phoebus has misled us, prophet though he is. He set his cunning to work and drove me unimaginably far from Greece in his shame over his first prophecies to me. I gave my all to him and obeyed his words. I killed my mother and now myself die in return.

PYLADES. You shall have a grave, and I shall not abandon your sister's bed, unhappy man, when I find you a dearer friend in death than in your life. However, the oracle of the god has not destroyed you yet. Even so, you stand very close 720 to death. But lay this truth to heart. Sometimes the tide of fortune shifts. The blackest night heralds the brightest dawn.

ORESTES. Quiet. The words of Phoebus are no help to me. The woman is coming here out of the temple.

IPHIGENIA enters from the temple with attendant guards.

IPHIGENIA (*to guards*). Away with you. Go inside and prepare everything there for those who have charge of the sacrificial slaughter.   *The guards go back into the temple.*
   Strangers, here are the many folding leaves of my tablets.*
Listen to what I want in addition to this. A man in trouble is one thing. But he may not stay the same if fear prompts 730 him to boldness. I am frightened that when the man who is going to take my letter to Argos has got safely away from this land, he will simply forget about it.

ORESTES. What do you want then?* What is the problem?

IPHIGENIA. Let him give me an oath that he will carry this letter to Argos, to the friends I wish to send it to.

ORESTES. And will you in return swear an oath to him as valid as his own?

IPHIGENIA. What do you want me to swear? Tell me.

ORESTES. To send him away from this barbarian land alive.

IPHIGENIA. I cannot object to that. For how else could he 740 deliver my message?

ORESTES. Will the king allow this?

IPHIGENIA. Yes. I shall persuade him, and I myself shall put the stranger on board his ship.

ORESTES (*to Pylades*). Swear. (*to Iphigenia*) And you, speak out the sacred oath for him to repeat.

IPHIGENIA. He must say, 'I shall give this letter to your friends.'

PYLADES. 'I shall give this letter to your friends.'

IPHIGENIA. And I shall bring you safely beyond the dark-blue rocks.

ORESTES. What god will you swear by to bind you to your promise?

IPHIGENIA. By Artemis, in whose house I hold my holy office.

PYLADES. And I shall swear by the king of heaven, almighty Zeus.

IPHIGENIA. And if you were to break my oath and wrong me? 750

PYLADES. May I never return to Greece! And what penalty for you if you do not send me away safely?

IPHIGENIA. May I never set foot in Argos! May I die!

PYLADES. Now let me tell you something which we have overlooked.

IPHIGENIA. Share it with us at once if it is helpful.

PYLADES. Allow me this exception. If the ship is wrecked and the letter disappears along with the cargo in the surging waters while I save myself alone, grant that this oath of mine will no longer be binding.

IPHIGENIA. Here is what I propose. For it pays to have more than one string to one's bow. I shall tell you in words all that is written inside the folding tablets so that you can 760 repeat it to my friends. That way we shall be safe. If you do not lose the letter, though silent itself, it will speak what has been written. But if this writing disappears in the sea, by saving your body you will save my words for me.

PYLADES. An excellent suggestion which benefits both yourself and me. But let me know who I must carry this letter to at Argos and what I must say in your name.

IPHIGENIA. Take this message to Orestes, the son of Agamemnon: 'Iphigenia, who was slaughtered at Aulis, sends this 770 letter. She is alive, though people there think that she lives no longer.'

ORESTES. Where is she? Has she come back from the dead?

IPHIGENIA. It is the woman you see before you now. Don't break my flow of words. 'Bring me to Argos, brother, before I die. Take me away from this barbarian land and from the sacrifices of the goddess at which my office is to slaughter strangers.'

ORESTES. Pylades, what can I say? Can we be dreaming?

IPHIGENIA. 'If you don't, I shall become a curse to your

house, Orestes.' I repeat the name a second time so that you
can memorize it.

ORESTES. O gods!

IPHIGENIA. Why do you call on the gods in matters that are   780
my concern?

ORESTES. It is nothing. Finish your message. My thoughts
were wandering.

IPHIGENIA. Perhaps as he questions you Orestes will begin to
find what you say incredible. In that case say: 'The goddess
Artemis kept me alive by putting in my place a deer, which
my father sacrificed, believing that he drove his sharp sword
into me. She brought me to live in this land.' Here is the letter and that is what the writing in the tablets says.

PYLADES. O maiden, how easily I can fulfil the oath with
which you bind me! How nobly you have sworn! I shall lose
no time in making good the oath that I have taken. Look, I   790
am carrying and delivering the letter to you, Orestes, from
your sister here.*

ORESTES. I accept it. But I shall set aside the folding tablets and
lay hold on my joy without words. O my dearest sister,
though I am out of my mind with amazement, I shall clasp
you in my unbelieving arms. I have made a wondrous discovery and shall not suppress my joy.

IPHIGENIA (*recoiling*). Stranger, it is not right that you should
defile the attendant of the goddess by embracing her holy
robes.

ORESTES. O sister, sister, daughter of Agamemnon, my father   800
and yours, do not turn away from me. You have your
brother though you never thought that you would have him
again.

IPHIGENIA. I . . . you . . . my brother. Stop. He lives in Argos
and in Nauplia.

ORESTES. Your brother is not there,* poor woman.

IPHIGENIA. But did the Spartan daughter of Tyndareus really
give you birth?

ORESTES. Yes, and her husband was the grandson of Pelops.
He was my father.

IPHIGENIA. What are you saying? Do you have some proof of
this to offer me?

ORESTES. I do. Ask me some questions about my father's house.

IPHIGENIA. No, you must speak and I shall listen.*   810

ORESTES. First I shall tell you something that I heard from
   Electra.* You know that a feud arose between Atreus and
   Thyestes?*

IPHIGENIA. Yes, I heard about that. The quarrel was about a
   golden lamb.

ORESTES. Do you remember weaving this feud in your fine-
   textured web?*

IPHIGENIA. Dearest man, you touch a chord in my memory.

ORESTES. And you pictured in your woven work the sun turning back its course?

IPHIGENIA. I wove that picture too in the web's delicate thread.

ORESTES. And do you remember the nuptial water* which you
   received from your mother for your marriage at Aulis?

IPHIGENIA. I do. My splendid marriage did not take *that* away
   from me.

ORESTES. Another thing. Do you remember giving someone a   820
   lock of hair to take to your mother?

IPHIGENIA. Yes—as a grave-token in place of my body for my
   cenotaph at Argos.

ORESTES. I shall mention these further proofs, ones which I
   saw myself. In our father's house there was an ancient spear
   of Pelops. This he brandished in his hand when he killed
   Oenomaus* and won Hippodameia, the maiden from Pisa. It
   was hidden in your maiden's quarters.

IPHIGENIA (*sings*).
   Orestes, dearest—I can call you nothing else for dearest
       you are—
   I hold you †far from our native land†
   of Argos, o my friend.   830

ORESTES. And I hold you, the girl men thought dead.*

IPHIGENIA (*sings*).
   Tears and weeping mixed with joy
   make your eyes wet, wet mine.
   You are the child I left at home,
   just a baby
   in your nurse's arms.
   O my soul, happier than words can express,
   what can I say? Beyond wonder,
   beyond speech is what has come to pass.   840

ORESTES. May we be happy with each other for all time to
  come!
IPHIGENIA (*sings*).
  The joy I now feel is strange, my friends.
  I am afraid that Orestes may fly out of my arms
  into the sky above.
  O hearth of the Cyclops-built palace, o fatherland,
  beloved Mycenae,*
  I give you thanks for Orestes' life, thanks for his nurture,
  for you have brought up this brother of my blood
  to be a light to save our house.
ORESTES. Our birth may be glorious, sister, but when you look   850
  at what we have suffered, we were born to lives of misery.
IPHIGENIA (*sings*).
  I remember, I, Iphigenia the wretched, remember the day
  when my father, wretched at heart, thrust his sword into
      my neck.
ORESTES. Alas! I was not at Aulis but I see you there in my
  mind's eye.
IPHIGENIA (*sings*).
  Without the wedding song, my brother, I was led
  to a marriage bed, a fraud of a marriage to Achilles.
  And beside the altar there was weeping and groaning.   860
  Alas, alas for that lustral water! O my sorrow!
ORESTES. I too lament the deed my father dared.
IPHIGENIA (*sings*).
  Fate doomed me to a father who was no father.
  One woe treads on another's heels
  by some god's dispensation.
ORESTES. Woe indeed, wretched girl, if you had killed your
  brother.
IPHIGENIA (*sings*).
  O my terrible cruelty, how miserable you make me! I
      steeled myself,
  steeled myself to do a terrible deed, alas, my brother,   870
  and you barely escaped
  unholy destruction at my hands.
  What will be the end of it all?
  What fortune will befall me?
  What way can I find, what way

to send you back from death in this city
to your fatherland of Argos
before the sword comes near to shed your blood?   880
It is your task, my wretched heart,
to invent one.
Should he go by land, not on a ship
but on storm-swift feet? Then you will make your way
through barbarian tribes along pathless tracks,
a hair's breadth from death. No, you must go the long
     journey
through the dark-blue rocks that guard the narrow strait   890
in flight on your ship.
Unhappy, unhappy Iphigenia!
†What god or mortal
or what unlooked for chance
could find a way where there is no way†
and bring the two of us, the last of Atreus' descendants,*
release from our troubles?

CHORUS. I saw this with my own eyes. I did not hear it from   900
     a messenger. It is truly wonderful, beyond what words can
     express.*
PYLADES. Orestes, it is natural that loved ones should embrace
     when they see each other. But you must stop these laments
     and tackle the problem of how we can seize the glorious light
     of safety and leave this barbarian land. [For when wise men
     find an opportunity given to them by chance, they must
     seize it and not allow themselves to be pleasantly diverted.]
ORESTES. Your words show good judgement. Indeed I think
     that fortune is working with us to secure our escape. When
     a man shows eagerness, it is fitting that the gods should help 910
     him more.
IPHIGENIA. You won't stop me asking my questions.* First, I
     want to know what kind of life fate has given Electra. For
     everything I can learn about her will be precious to me.
ORESTES. She lives with my friend here.* Her life is happy.
IPHIGENIA. And where is he from? Whose son is he?
ORESTES. Strophius the Phocian is his father.
IPHIGENIA. Is he the son of Atreus' daughter,* and thus my
     kinsman?

ORESTES. Yes, he is your cousin, and my one true friend.

IPHIGENIA. He was not born at the time my father tried to kill 920
me.

ORESTES. No, Strophius was childless for some time.

IPHIGENIA. I give you greetings, o husband of my sister.

ORESTES. Yes, and my saviour too, not just a relative.

IPHIGENIA (*to Orestes*). How did you dare to do that terrible
deed? She was your mother.

ORESTES. Let us say nothing about that. I was taking revenge
for my father.

IPHIGENIA. And what was the reason that she killed her husband?

ORESTES. Let our mother be. It is not good for you to hear
about her.

IPHIGENIA. I say no more. Does Argos look to you for protection?

ORESTES. Menelaus is ruling there. I am a fugitive from my
fatherland.

IPHIGENIA. Surely our uncle has not done outrage on our 930
house in its sickness?

ORESTES. No, but I fled the land in terror of the Furies.

IPHIGENIA. I understand. The goddesses drove you out
because of our mother.

ORESTES. Yes, they forced a blood-stained bit into my mouth.*

IPHIGENIA. That was the madness then they said possessed
you here on our shore too.

ORESTES. Yes, and this is not the first time that I have been
visibly affected by it.

IPHIGENIA. Why did you make your way to this land?

ORESTES. I came here because the oracles of Phoebus commanded me to.

IPHIGENIA. To do what? Is it something you may tell us, or
must you keep silence?

ORESTES. I shall tell you. This was how my many woes began.
As soon as it fell to me to punish my mother's crimes—of 940
which we do not speak—I was driven into exile by the pur-
suing Furies. Next Loxias directed my steps at last to Athens
to stand defendant against the nameless ones.* For there is
a holy tribunal which Zeus established long ago for Ares
after some criminal act of pollution.* However, when I came

there, at first no host received me willingly because I was
hated by the gods, and those who did have a sense of duty
to their guest gave me their hospitality but made me sit at a
separate table although we were under the same roof, and   950
by their own silence they contrived to exclude me from conversation so that I would enjoy my drink and food apart
from them. In fact, they had an individual cup for everyone,
which they filled with an equal measure of wine and took
their pleasure thus.* And I did not think it right to protest
about this to my hosts. No, I grieved in silence and pretended
not to notice, though often sighing deeply because I was my
mother's murderer. I hear that my sad experience has been
established as an Athenian ritual and it is still the custom
for the people of Pallas to observe the Wine-jug feast.   960

When I came to the hill of Ares I faced my trial, myself
standing on one platform, the eldest of the Furies on the
other.* I heard the charge and answered in my defence
about the shedding of my mother's blood. Phoebus saved me
by his evidence and when Pallas' hand counted up the votes,
they proved to be equal.* Thus I emerged victorious from my
murder trial. All of the Furies who were contented with the
judgement kept their seats and ordained a holy place for
themselves to live in by the very scene of the voting.*
But those who were not persuaded by the verdict ran after   970
me in unresting, unremitting pursuit until I came in turn
to Phoebus' holy ground,* lay down fasting before his
shrine, and swore that I would break my life's thread in that
very place unless Phoebus, he who had destroyed me,
should save me. Then Phoebus echoed forth his oracle from
the golden tripod* and sent me here to take the image of
Artemis which fell from the sky, and set it up in the land of
Athens.

So help me win this salvation which he ordained for me.
For if we get hold of the wooden image of the goddess, I shall 980
find an end to my madness and I shall put you on board a
ship with many oars and take you back to Mycenae. O my
beloved, o my sister, save the house of our fathers and get
me safely away. For it is all over for me and Pelops' line if
we do not take the image of the goddess which fell from
heaven.

CHORUS. A terrible rage of the gods has boiled up against the seed of Tantalus and drives it on through torment.

IPHIGENIA. I *am* eager—and was eager even before you came here—to stand in Argos and look on you there, my brother. 990 What you want I want—to set you free from torment and to cure the sickness of our father's house, nursing no anger against the one who did his best to kill me. Not only would I keep my hands free from pollution by your slaughter but I would also save our house. However, I am anxious about how I may elude the goddess and the king—when he finds the stone pedestal empty of its statue. How shall I avoid execution? What excuse can I offer? But if †we do succeed in our two objectives at one and the same time,† and you both carry off the statue and take me away on your fair-prowed 1000 ship, it will be a noble venture. If I do not sail away with the statue in your ship, I shall be killed for losing it, but you may meet with success yourself and win a happy return. I do not flinch at death if die I must, provided I have saved you. My own death does not trouble me since women do not matter, but when a man dies he leaves a void in the house.

ORESTES. I will not be my mother's murderer *and* yours. Her blood is enough. My wish would be to share my life and thoughts with you and join you in your death. I shall take 1010 you with me if I myself sail home from here, or I shall remain here with you if I die.

But hear how I view the matter. If the carrying off of her statue is displeasing to Artemis, why would Loxias have declared that I should take it to the city of Pallas?* ⟨The gods must be on our side since they have let me reach my goal among the Taurians⟩ and look upon your face. Putting this evidence together, I expect to succeed in returning to Argos.

IPHIGENIA. How could we arrange it that we can take what we want without being killed? There lies the difficulty for our return back home. This is what we have to discuss.

ORESTES. Would we be able to kill the king?*   1020

IPHIGENIA. This is a fearful thing you have suggested—that visitors should kill their host.*

ORESTES. If it will save us both, we must find the courage to do it.

IPHIGENIA. I could not. But I admire your boldness.

ORESTES. What if you were to smuggle me into this temple and
hide me there?

[IPHIGENIA. Do you mean that we should make our escape
under cover of darkness?

ORESTES. Yes. Night is the time for deception, the day for
truth.]

IPHIGENIA. There are temple guards inside and they would
see us.

ORESTES. Alas, it is all over for us. How could we find safety?

IPHIGENIA. I think I have found a new solution.

ORESTES. What's that? Share your thoughts with me so that 1030
I may know them too.

IPHIGENIA. I shall use your troubles as a trick.

ORESTES. Clearly women are clever at improvising schemes.

IPHIGENIA. I shall say that you have come from Argos with
your mother's blood on your hands.

ORESTES. Make use of my woes if you will gain by it.

IPHIGENIA. We shall say that it is not right in the eyes of
heaven to sacrifice you to the goddess.

ORESTES. What reason have you to offer? I think I know what
you have in mind.

IPHIGENIA. That you are not pure. I shall say that I can
devote to sacrifice only what is holy.

ORESTES. How does this make it easier to take the goddess's
statue, then?

IPHIGENIA. I shall require that you be purified in the waters
of the sea.

ORESTES. But even so, the statue for which we sailed here is 1040
still in the temple.

IPHIGENIA. I shall say that I must wash it as well, on the pretext that you have touched it.

ORESTES. Where? Will you go to the spray-swept inlet of the
sea?

IPHIGENIA. Yes, where your ship lies moored by its flaxen
cable.

ORESTES. Will you or someone else carry the image there?

IPHIGENIA. I shall. It is unholy for any hands but mine to
touch it.

ORESTES. And what part shall our friend Pylades have played
in the enterprise?

IPHIGENIA. I shall say that he has the same pollution on his
hands as you.
ORESTES. Will you do this with or without the king's knowledge?
IPHIGENIA. I must tell him and win him over, since I couldn't
do it without his finding out. It is your job to see to everything else* and ensure that it goes smoothly.
ORESTES. Well, at least the ship is there with its oars ready. 1050
Only one thing remains—that the handmaidens should keep
this secret. Entreat them and find persuasive words. A
woman's tongue has the power to move pity. As for everything else, perhaps it may turn out well.
IPHIGENIA. O my dear women, I look to you. All of my fortunes lie in your hands. You can determine whether I shall
find success or utter ruin, losing my fatherland, my dear
brother and my dearest sister. Let me begin my appeal like 1060
this. We are women, and, as women, sympathetic to each
other and totally reliable in keeping matters which concern
all of us to ourselves. Remain silent, we beg you, and help
us in our efforts to escape. It is a fine thing to have a loyal
tongue. See how a single fortune unites this trio of dear
friends. Are we to return to our native land, or are we to
die? If I escape, I shall bring you safely to Greece so that you
too may share in my good fortune.
   You I beseech by your right hand, and you, and you, and
you by your dear face and knees* and all that is most pre- 1070
cious in your homes, your mother, father, children if you
have them. What do you say? Which of you says yes?
Which says no, you will not help in this? Tell me plainly. If
you do not grant me what I ask, all is over for me and my
unhappy brother.
CHORUS. Take heart, dear mistress. Save yourself. That is all
that matters. May great Zeus be my witness, I shall keep
silent about everything as you bid me.
IPHIGENIA. Bless you for those words. I wish you happiness.
(*to Orestes and Pylades*) Both of you must play your part now
and go into the temple. For the ruler of this land will arrive 1080
at any moment to see if the sacrifice of the strangers has
been performed.
   O Artemis my mistress, who saved me from a father's mur-
dering hand by the bays of dreadful Aulis, save me now—and

these men too. If you do not, you will cause mankind no more
to hold the words of Loxias true. But be gracious to us and
come from this barbarian land to Athens.* It is not fitting for
you to dwell here when you can live in a blessed city.

IPHIGENIA, ORESTES, *and* PYLADES *go into the temple.*

CHORUS (*sings*).
You halcyon bird, who sing a lament for your fate
by the rocky cliffs of the sea,   1090
a cry which those who know sorrow well
can easily understand*
because you sing of your husband always in your songs,
I, a bird without wings,
liken my dirges to yours,
as I long for the festival gatherings of the Greeks,
long for Artemis goddess of childbirth
who dwells by Mount Cynthus
by the feathery palm tree
and the flourishing bay   1100
and the youthful sacred shoot
of the pale-green olive
dear to Leto in her travail,
and the lake that whirls its waters round in a circle
where the melodious swans
pay service to the Muses.*

O those streams upon streams of tears
which fell down my cheeks
when I was taken from my city's ruined walls
in the enemy's ships,
the plunder of oars and spears.   1110
Purchased for plentiful gold
I came to a barbarian land
where I serve the handmaiden
of the goddess who hunts and kills the deer,
the girl who is Agamemnon's daughter,
serve the altars where no sheep are sacrificed,
and envy those who have always
been unfortunate.
Those who have grown up with necessity are not dis-
    tressed by it.

Misfortune lies in change. 1120
To fall to grief from happiness—
that makes life grim for mortals.*

And you, mistress, will sail home
in an Argive ship with fifty oars,
and the wax-bound reed-pipes
of Pan the mountain god will cry out
with its piercing whistle to the rowers,
and Phoebus the seer,
singing as he summons music
from his seven-chorded lyre, 1130
will bring you triumphantly to the gleaming land of the
    Athenians.*
†You will leave me here as you voyage
on oars which whip up the foam,
and in the breeze the sails billow out against the forestays
prow-wards over the bows†
as the ship speeds you on your way.

If only I could travel along the dazzling race course
where races the bright fire of the sun!
If only I could stop my flight, 1140
folding my wings on my back,
above my bedroom in my native country,
and stand in the dances
†where I stood when a girl at a noble wedding
and, leaving my mother's side,
danced in revelling rounds with my friends,
striving to outdo them in grace
as we competed in the rich luxuriance of our hair,
and I shadowed my cheeks, 1150
flinging around them
my gorgeous veil, my clustering curls.†

Enter THOAS.

THOAS. Where is the Greek woman, the warden of the temple? Has she already begun the sacrifice of the strangers?
Are their bodies glimmering in the flames of the holy
shrine?

Enter IPHIGENIA *carrying the image of Artemis.**

CHORUS. Here she is. She can tell you everything clearly, my lord.

THOAS (*with a start*). Why have you lifted the goddess's image from its pedestal which it is sin to touch. Why are you carrying it in your arms, daughter of Agamemnon?

IPHIGENIA. My lord, stay where you are in the portico.*

THOAS. Something unprecedented must have happened in the 1160 temple, Iphigenia. What is it?

IPHIGENIA. I avert the evil omen.* I say this for the sake of Purity.

THOAS. An extraordinary start to your explanation. Speak plainy.

IPHIGENIA. The victims which you have captured for me are not pure.

THOAS. What was it that made you realize this? Or is it mere conjecture?

IPHIGENIA. The image of the goddess turned backwards from its place.

THOAS. By itself—or did an earth tremor turn it round?

IPHIGENIA. By itself. And it closed its eyes.

THOAS. What was the cause? Was it the strangers' pollution?

IPHIGENIA. Yes, that was the only cause. For the two of them have done terrible things.

THOAS. Can it be that they killed someone on the shores of our 1170 barbarian land?

IPHIGENIA. They came here polluted by kindred blood which they had shed.

THOAS. Whose blood? I am eager to know.

IPHIGENIA. They killed their mother.* Both of them held the sword.

THOAS. By Apollo, no one would have dared to do this even among barbarians.

IPHIGENIA. They have been chased out of the whole of Greece.

THOAS. Is it because of this that you are taking the statue outside?

IPHIGENIA. Yes, out under the holy air to free it from the stain of bloodshed.

THOAS. How did you realize that the two strangers were polluted?

IPHIGENIA. I questioned them when the image of the goddess turned backwards.

THOAS. A wise child of Greece to see so sharply.   1180

IPHIGENIA. Even so, they dangled an attractive bait to catch my heart.

THOAS. What, by telling you some pleasant news from Argos to put a spell on you?

IPHIGENIA. Yes, that my only brother Orestes enjoys good fortune.

THOAS. Their motive of course being to make you so happy at the news that you would spare them?

IPHIGENIA. They also told me that my father is alive and well.

THOAS. And you naturally took the goddess's part.

IPHIGENIA. Yes, because I hate the whole of Greece, the land that destroyed me.

THOAS. What should we do about the strangers then? Tell me.

IPHIGENIA. We must show reverence to the hallowed custom.

THOAS. Is not the holy water ready then, and your sword?   1190

IPHIGENIA. I want to wash them first with sacred water of purification.

THOAS. Water from the spring or from the salt sea's spray?

IPHIGENIA. The sea washes away all that is bad from men.*

THOAS. Of course. They would then die as a more holy sacrifice for the goddess.

IPHIGENIA. Yes, and what I am doing will have a happier outcome.

THOAS. Well, don't the waves break close to the temple here?

IPHIGENIA. We must be on our own, for I shall perform other rituals as well.

THOAS. Take them where you wish. It is not my custom to watch the holy mysteries.

IPHIGENIA. I must also purify this image of the goddess.

THOAS. Yes indeed, if the stain of matricide has touched it.   1200

IPHIGENIA. It has, for otherwise I would not have lifted it from its pedestal.

THOAS. Your piety and your forethought are right and proper.

IPHIGENIA. Let me have what you know I need.* THOAS. It is up to you to tell me this.

IPHIGENIA. You must tie up the strangers. THOAS. But where could they go if they escaped from you?

IPHIGENIA. You cannot trust a Greek. THOAS. Attendants, go
and bind them.

IPHIGENIA. And they must bring the strangers out here . . .
THOAS. This shall be done.

IPHIGENIA. . . . their heads hidden in their robes. THOAS. Yes,
to avoid polluting the fiery sun.

IPHIGENIA. And send some of your servants with me. THOAS.
These ones will accompany you.

IPHIGENIA. And send someone to tell the citizens . . . THOAS.
Of what emergency?

IPHIGENIA. . . . that they must all stay in their houses.
THOAS. In case they should meet the murderers?   1210

IPHIGENIA. Yes, for such encounters bring pollution. THOAS.
You, go and tell them . . .

IPHIGENIA. . . . that no one should come within sight of them.
THOAS. You show a thoughtful concern for our city.

IPHIGENIA. And for the friends who should concern me most.
THOAS. You mean me, I take it.

⟨IPHIGENIA. A natural conclusion.⟩* THOAS. And how natural it is that all our city should admire you.

IPHIGENIA. You must stay here before the goddess's shrine
and . . . THOAS. What must I do?

IPHIGENIA. . . . purify the temple with cleansing fire. THOAS.
Yes, so that it will be free from pollution when you return.

IPHIGENIA. And when the strangers come outside . . . THOAS.
What should I do?

IPHIGENIA. . . . hold your cloak in front of your eyes. THOAS.
Yes, so that I receive no pollution.

IPHIGENIA. And if I seem to be taking too much time . . .
THOAS. How long should I wait?

IPHIGENIA. . . . do not be surprised. THOAS. Perform the goddess's rituals properly, at your leisure.   1220

IPHIGENIA. I pray that this purification may happen as I
wish. THOAS. I join you in that prayer.

ORESTES and PYLADES are led out of the temple in bonds.

IPHIGENIA. But look, now I see the strangers coming out of
the temple, and the sacred robe and adornments of the
goddess's image, and new-born lambs, so that I may wash
away the pollution of bloodshed with their blood, and

flaming torches, and everything else that I prescribed for purifying the strangers and the goddess. And I bid the citizens to shun this pollution—all whose hands are consecrated to the goddess as wardens of her temple, all who come to offer sacrifice for marriage, and all who are heavy with child. Fly from hence! Stand afar off, so that this defilement may fall on no one.

O virgin queen, daughter of Zeus and Leto, if I wash you 1230 clean of these men's blood pollution and make my sacrifice where it is proper, you will dwell in a pure temple* and we shall be blessed. The rest I shall not say, yet I know all is plain to the gods, who know more than is spoken, and to you too, goddess.

THOAS *enters the temple.* IPHIGENIA, ORESTES, *and* PYLADES *go out.*

CHORUS (*sings*). Son of a glorious mother, Leto's son,*
whom she bore long ago
in the fertile valleys of Delos, god with the golden hair,
skilful master of the lyre,
who joys in the bow's sure aim! His mother,
leaving the famous birth-place, brought her son   1240
from the sea-beaten ridge of Mount Cynthus
to the summit of Parnassus,
mountain of torrential waters,
fellow-reveller with Dionysus.
Here the Python, its face like wine, its back glinting with
    many a hue,
lorded it in the grove, lush with the bay tree's shadowing
    greenery,
a gigantic monster born from the earth
guarding the earth's oracle.
Still, still a child,   1250
while you still frisked in your loving mother's arms,
you slew it, o Phoebus, you took possession of the sacred
    oracle
and now sit on the holy tripod, dispensing to mortals on
    your throne of truth
divine oracles from your shrine hard by Castalia's flowing
    waters,
your temple sited in the middle of the world.

But since he had dispossessed Themis child of Earth
of the sacred oracle,   1260
Earth herself engendered
night visions, dreams,
which told to the cities of mortals
all that would come to pass soon and thereafter,
told them in sleep
as they lay in the dark earth-beds.
And thus the earth goddess wrested away from Phoebus
his honour as a prophet as she jealously championed her
    daughter.
But lord Phoebus, rushing on swift foot to Olympus,   1270
clasped the high throne of Zeus in his infant arms
and begged him to banish the rage of the goddess of earth
    from his home at Delphi.
And Zeus laughed because his son had come to him at so
    tender an age
eager to receive the worship with all the gold it brought.
And he shook his locks as he promised to end the voices of
    the night
and he removed from mortals dream-revelations of truth
and restored to Loxias his tribute of honour   1280
and to mortals their confidence in his oracle's chants
at his throne thronged round with all its visitors.

Enter MESSENGER.

MESSENGER. O temple guards and ministers of the altar,
where is Thoas, the king of this land? Open up the closely-
bolted gates and call the country's ruler out of the temple.

CHORUS. What is it, if I may presume to speak uninvited?

MESSENGER. The two young men have got clean away thanks
to the schemes of Agamemnon's daughter. They have 1290
stowed the sacred image in the hold of a Greek ship and are
making their escape from this land.

CHORUS. What you have said is incredible. But the king of our
country, whom you wish to see, has rushed off from the
temple.*

MESSENGER. Where to? He must be told what is happening.

CHORUS. We don't know. But go and follow him and tell him
what you have to report wherever you find him.

MESSENGER. See the duplicity of the female sex! You too have played your part in this business.

CHORUS. You are mad. What have we to do with the strangers? 1300 Off with you to the palace gates as fast as you can go!

MESSENGER. Not until somebody can tell me whether the ruler of the land is inside or not. Ho there, open the bolted doors—I'm talking to you inside—and tell our master that I am here at the gates with my heavy cargo of bad news!

THOAS enters.

THOAS. Who is causing this uproar at the temple of the goddess, pounding at the gates and making the interior resound?

MESSENGER. These women were lying to steer me away from the temple. They said that you had gone away. So you were 1310 inside after all.

THOAS. What were they hoping to gain by this?

MESSENGER. I shall tell you about them later. Listen to the urgent information. Iphigenia, the maiden who served the altar here, has gone from this land with the strangers and taken the holy image of the goddess. The purification ceremony was a trick.

THOAS. What are you saying? How did she manage it?

MESSENGER. She is saving Orestes. You will find it amazing.

THOAS. Orestes? The son of Tyndareus' daughter, do you mean?

MESSENGER. Yes, the man the goddess had dedicated to her 1320 altar.

THOAS. A wonder! What stronger name can I find for it?

MESSENGER. Don't go searching for a different word, but listen to me. Take a clear-eyed view of the situation and as you listen, think up some method of pursuit by which we can hunt the strangers down.

THOAS. Speak, for you talk good sense. It is no short voyage on which they sail as they flee, and so they will not escape my ship.

MESSENGER. When we came to the sea-shore where the ship of Orestes stood at its hidden mooring, the daughter of Agamemnon motioned to us—the men you sent with her to hold the strangers' bonds—bidding us to stand far away as 1330

though she wished to offer the mysterious rites of purification
which she had come to perform, while she walked on her
own behind us holding the strangers' bonds in her hands.
And this struck me as suspicious, though it did not worry
your servants, master. After a time, in order that we should
think that she was doing something significant, she raised a
loud cry and started singing outlandish laments like a witch,
pretending that she was washing away the blood pollution.

But when we had been sitting there a long time, we
began to be afraid in case the strangers broke loose, killed 1340
her and took flight. However, fearing to see rites that we
should not see, we went on sitting there in silence. Finally,
though, we all said the same thing, that we should go to
where they were even though we weren't meant to. Then
we saw the Greek ship with the blades of its sweep of oars
all ready like wings and fifty sailors holding those oars on
the oar-pins,* and the young men standing free of their
bonds by the ship's stern. Some of the Greeks were steady-
ing the bows with poles, others were fastening the anchor to 1350
the catheads,* while others hurriedly carried ladders in their
hands and let them down for the foreign girl, dropping them
into the sea from the stern.

And when we saw her cunning trickery, we no longer felt
respect for her as a priestess, we seized hold of her and of the
mooring-cables, and tried to drag the steering-oars of the
fair-sterned ship out through the stern-holes.* Words hurtled
to and fro: 'What right have you to sail off stealing the
image of the goddess and smuggling the priestess from this
land? Who are you? Who is your father?' And he said: 'I am 1360
Orestes, this woman's brother—to be plain with you—, the
son of Agamemnon, and here I have my sister whom I lost
from home and am taking away with me.' However, we still
hung on to the foreign girl and tried to force her to come
with us to you. That was how I got these terrible bruises on
my cheeks. For they were not carrying swords—neither
were we—, their fists came crashing against us, and with
darting legs the two young men joined in kicking us in the 1370
ribs and stomach so that pain and exhaustion came on us
together. Scarred by these dreadful marks, we fled to the
cliffs behind the beach, some of us with bloody wounds on

our heads, others with them on our faces. We took our stand
on the heights and fought more cautiously, pelting them
with stones. But the archers standing on the stern held us
off with arrows and made us keep our distance.

Meanwhile—for the sea's surge was driving the ship 1380
towards the land, yet the maiden was afraid to wet her feet
in the surf—Orestes hoisted her up on his left shoulder,
waded into the sea, leaped onto the ladder and set his sister
down inside the well-benched ship together with the image
of the daughter of Zeus which fell from the sky. Then from
the middle of the ship a voice cried out: 'O sailing men of
Greece, take hold of your oars and churn the breakers white.
We have achieved what we came to achieve on this voyage
to the inhospitable strait between the Clashing Rocks!' They
roared out a cry of joy and struck the briny waters. And 1390
while the ship was inside the harbour, it made straight for
its mouth, but while it was passing through that, it got into
difficulties as it crashed into the furious surges of the open
sea, for a terrible wind arose and suddenly forced the ship
astern. They rowed with steadfast effort as they struggled
against the breakers, but the waves' backward surge drove
the ship to land again. Agamemnon's daughter stood up and
prayed: 'O daughter of Leto, bring me your priestess safely
to Greece from this barbarian land and forgive my theft. You 1400
love your brother, goddess. Believe that I also love my kin.'
In response to the girl's prayers the sailors chanted the victory hymn and, with shoulders stripped bare of their clothes,
they moved their oars in time to the bosun's shouts. But the
ship kept moving closer, closer to the rocks.*

And some of us rushed wading into the sea, while others
fastened lassoes of twisted rope to trees or rocks. And I immediately set out here to find you and report to you what has 1410
been happening there. Go then and take bonds and nooses
with you. For if the wind that swells the sea dies down, the
strangers have no hope of safety. Revered Poseidon, ruler of
the sea and Troy's protector, enemy to the family of Pelops,
will now, as I think, give you and the citizens the son of
Agamemnon to catch as your prey*—his sister too who has
forgotten the sacrifice at Aulis and stands convicted of
treachery to the goddess.

CHORUS. O miserable Iphigenia, you will fall into the tyrant's 1420
   hands with your brother and be killed again.
THOAS. All you citizens of this barbarian land, go, harness
   your horses and gallop along the shore. Wait for the Greek
   ship to be stranded and with the goddess's favour hurry to
   hunt the impious men. Others of you, drag down the speedy
   ships into the sea so that we can capture them by water or
   by land on horseback, and fling them over the rugged crags
   or impale their bodies on stakes.* You women, you knew 1430
   about the plot, and later, when I have the leisure, I shall
   punish you. But now I have urgent business in hand. This
   is no time to pause.

                    ATHENA *appears above the temple.*

ATHENA. Where, where are you going in pursuit of the
   strangers, King Thoas? I am Athena. Hear my words. Stop
   your pursuit. Hold back your army's flood. It was fated by
   the oracle of Loxias that Orestes should come here as he fled
   the Furies' anger, to take his sister to Argos, to bring the 1440
   sacred image to my land, and find relief from the sufferings
   that afflict him now.
      This is what I have to say to you. As for Orestes, whom
   you now expect to capture on the salt sea's surge and then
   kill—already Poseidon is smoothing the ocean's back to stillness for his ship to cross. This the god does as a favour to
   me.
      And you, Orestes, learn my commands—for you can hear
   my divine voice though you are not here. Go on your way
   with the image and your sister. And when you come to
   Athens, that god-built city,* there is a place on the furthest 1450
   verge of Attica, opposite the ridge of hills above Carystus—
   a holy place. My people call it Halae. There build a temple
   and set up the image, naming it after the Taurian land and
   the troubles which you endured as you wandered over
   Greece driven by the Furies' stings. So for all future time,
   men shall sing to Artemis as Artemis Tauropolos. And estab-
   lish the following custom. When the people sacrifice at her
   feast, in compensation for the sacrifice she missed in you, let
   the priest apply the sword to a man's neck and draw blood, 1460
   for purity's sake and to pay the goddess honour.

And you, Iphigenia, must be the warden of this goddess's temple around the holy meadows of Brauron.* Here you shall be buried when you die and they will make offerings to you of the fine-textured clothes which women who die in childbirth leave in their houses.

I give orders that these Greek women should be sent away from this land as a reward for their true hearts.

Long ago I saved you, Orestes, when I pronounced upon the equal votes on the hill of Ares. And this will be the estab- 1470 lished principle—that when the votes are equal the defendant is acquitted.* Now carry your sister away from the land, son of Agamemnon. And you, Thoas, do not be angry.

THOAS. Athena, queen, it is a perverse man who hears the words of the gods and disobeys them. I am not angry with Orestes if he has gone off with the image of the goddess, nor with his sister either. Why should I be? Is it good to fight against the power of the gods? Let them go to your country 1480 with the goddess's image and set it up with good fortune. I shall send these women too to happy Greece as your command instructs. I shall stop the spearmen I am sending against the foreigners*—the oared ships too, goddess, since this is your wish.

ATHENA. It is well. Necessity is too strong for the gods, too strong for you. Come, breezes, waft Agamemnon's son to Athens. And I shall travel with you to keep the holy image of my sister safe.

CHORUS (*sings*). Go in your good fortune, 1490
happy to be counted among the number of the saved.
Pallas Athena, goddess revered
among mortals and immortals alike,
we shall do as you tell us.
For passing all joy, passing all hope
are the words which my ears have heard.

ATHENA, THOAS, and the MESSENGER *go out.*

O most reverent Victory,
I pray you to protect my life
and never cease to crown me.*

The CHORUS *goes out.*

BACCHAE

Characters

DIONYSUS also known as Bacchus, the divine son of Zeus and
Semele
TEIRESIAS, the blind prophet of Apollo
CADMUS, formerly king of Thebes, father of Agave and grand-
father of Pentheus
PENTHEUS, king of Thebes
SERVANT of Pentheus
MESSENGER from the mountain
MESSENGER, attendant of Pentheus
AGAVE, daughter of Cadmus and mother of Pentheus
CHORUS of Lydian women, devotees of Dionysus (Bacchus)

Glossary

bacchae: female followers of Bacchus, another name for
Dionysus
bacchanals: the revels of the followers of Bacchus (Dionysus)
bacchant: a devotee of Bacchus (Dionysus)
Bacchic: adjective of Bacchus (Dionysus)
Bromius: a title for Dionysus, meaning 'roaring'
Euoi: a Dionysiac cry of joy
Io: a cry of celebration
maenad: inspired, possessed, frantic women, the female followers of Dionysus
thyrsus (plural *thyrsi*): a fennel rod or wand with ivy leaves
attached to its tip

The action is set before the façade of the royal palace at Thebes.
On the stage is a vine-clad tomb from which smoke rises. DIONYSUS
*enters.**

DIONYSUS. I am the son of Zeus, Dionysus. Semele, the daughter of Cadmus, bore me once in a birth precipitated by the
lightning flame.* I have transformed my appearance from
god to man and come to this Theban land, and here I am at

the streams of Dirce and the waters of Ismenus.* I can see
near the palace this memorial of my lightning-struck mother
and the ruins of her house smouldering with the still living
flame of the fire of Zeus, an undying symbol of Hera's outrageous violence against my mother. And I praise Cadmus
who has forbidden men to tread on this ground,* my   10
mother's precinct, which I have hidden with a covering of
the vine's grape-clustered greenery.

I have left the gold-rich lands of the Lydians and
Phrygians and travelled to the sun-scorched uplands of the
Persians, to walled Bactra,* to the Medes' wintry terrain, to
wealthy Arabia, and the whole tract of Asia which lies by
the briny sea with its fair-towered cities full of Greeks and
barbarians mixed together. I came to this city before all   20
others in Greece when I had set Asia dancing and established my mysteries there, so that I should be a god manifest to mortals.

Thebes here is the first city of the land of Greeks that I
have roused to Bacchic cries, fastening a fawnskin around
their bodies and placing a thyrsus, my ivy-clad weapon, in
their hands.* For my mother's sisters—the last who should
have done so—denied that I, Dionysus, was the son of Zeus,
but said that Semele had been seduced by some mortal and
used Zeus as a cover for her sexual transgression. This, they
claim, was Cadmus' clever idea,* and they gloatingly spread   30
the story that her lies about her marriage were the reason
that Zeus killed her. So that is why I have driven those same
women from their homes in a mad frenzy, and they live on
the mountain in a state of violent delusion. I have forced
them to wear the trappings of my rites. And all the females
among the Thebans, all the women, I have sent maddened
from their houses. Mixing with the daughters of Cadmus
they sit together beneath the green firs on the roofless
rocks.* For this city must learn to the full—even if it does
not wish to—that it is still uninitiated in my bacchanals*   40
and I must speak on my mother Semele's behalf by appearing to mortals as a god whom Zeus begot.

So then, Cadmus has given the kingship and its honour
to Pentheus, his daughter's son, who fights against the
deity* in my person, pushes me from my libations and makes

mention of me nowhere in his prayers. To pay him back for
that, I shall show to him and all the Thebans that I am a
god. After I have set things to rights here I shall move on to
another land and reveal my godhead there. But if the   50
Thebans' city tries in its rage to take the bacchae from the
mountain, I shall lead my army of maenads and join battle.
It is for this reason that I have changed to this mortal form
and transformed my appearance to human shape.

[*To the off-stage* CHORUS] But you who have left Mount
Tmolus,* Lydia's defence, my company, you women whom
I have brought from the barbarians to consort with me as
we travel together, lift the drums which come from their
home in a Phrygian city, the invention of mother Rhea* and
myself. Here to this royal palace of Pentheus!* And sound   60
them so that the city of Cadmus may come and see.
Meanwhile I shall go to the glens of Cithaeron* where my
bacchae are and I shall join in their dances.

DIONYSUS goes out.

The CHORUS OF DIONYSUS' FOLLOWERS enter.

CHORUS OF DIONYSUS' FOLLOWERS (*singing and dancing to
the accompaniment of drums and pipes*).
Fom the land of Asia,
leaving behind sacred Tmolus
I speed in Bromius'* delightful labour,
in my weariness that is no weariness,
crying in joy to the Bacchic god.
Who is on the street, on the street?
Who is indoors? Let him come outside,*
and let all hush their voices to reverence,   70
for I shall always celebrate Dionysus
by singing the customary songs.

O happy the man
who, blest with knowledge of the mysteries of the gods,
lives a pure life
and initiates his soul in the Bacchic company
as he celebrates the gods in the mountains
in holy rituals of purity,
observes the mysteries
of the great mother Cybele,*

and, swinging the thyrsus high,   80
and garlanded with ivy,
does service to Dionysus.
On, bacchae, on, bacchae,
bringing home the god Bromius,
son of a god, Dionysus,
from the Phrygian mountains to the streets of Greece
wide for the dance, Bromius.

While his mother carried him once in her womb,
the lightning of Zeus took its winged flight
and in the forced labour of childbirth   90
she bore him prematurely,
leaving her life
with the blast of the lightning bolt.
At once Zeus, son of Cronos,
received him in his thigh, the secret recesses of birth,
and covering him up there,
closed it together with golden pins
to keep him hidden from Hera.
And he gave him birth when the Fates brought comple-
    tion,
the bull-horned god,*   100
and he garlanded him
with garlands of snakes—the reason why
the maenads wreathe their locks with their beast-born
    prey.*

O Thebes, nurse of Semele,
garland yourself with ivy,
be abundant, abundant with green
berry-rich bryony*
and consecrate yourself in Bacchus' worship
with branches of oak or fir,   110
decking your dress of dappled fawnskins
with white-haired curls
of braided wool.* Be reverent as you handle
the violent fennel rods. At once all the land will dance
whenever Bromius leads the companies
to the mountain, to the mountain where waits
the horde of women

stung to frenzy from their looms and shuttles*
by Dionysus.

O secret chamber of the Couretes   120
and all-sacred haunts of Crete
where Zeus was born,
where the Corybants invented for me in the cave
this triple-crested circle
of stretched hide.
And in the intense rites
they mingled its noise with the sweetly-calling breath
of Phrygian pipes and placed it in the hand
of mother Rhea to beat time for the bacchae's shouts of
    joy.
And the maddened satyrs   130
borrowed it from the mother goddess
and added it to the dances
of the biennial festivals
in which Dionysus rejoices.*

He* is welcome in the mountains when he falls
to the ground from the running companies,
dressed in the holy fawnskin,
in the hunt for the blood of the killed goat,
for the joy of eating raw flesh,*
as he hurries to the mountains of Phrygia, Lydia—   140
Bromius, leading the way.
Euoi!*
The soil flows with milk, it flows with wine, it flows
with the nectar of bees.
The Bacchic god, holding on high
the blazing flame of the pine torch
like the smoke of Syrian frankincense,
lets it stream from his wand
as he spurs on the stragglers
while they run and dance,
and rouses them with his joyous cries,
flinging his delicate locks into the air.   150
And amid the Bacchic shouts of joy he roars forth these
    words:
'On, bacchae, oh,

on, bacchae,
glittering pride of Tmolus, its river awash with gold,*
celebrate Dionysus in your song
to the beat of the loud-roaring drums!
With joyful shouts glorify the god of joyful shouting
in Phrygian cries and calls,
when the tuneful sacred pipe peals forth its sacred merri-   160
    ment,
in harmony with your wild journeying
to the mountain, to the mountain!'
Happily then, like a foal beside its grazing mother,
the bacchant skips with quick feet as she runs.

Enter the blind prophet TEIRESIAS *dressed like a maenad in a
fawnskin with a garland and a thyrsus.**

TEIRESIAS. Who is at the gate? Call Cadmus out of the palace,   170
Agenor's son who left the city of Sidon* and built these towering walls of Thebes. Will someone go and tell him that
Teiresias is looking for him. He himself knows what I have
come about and what I agreed with him, an old man in con-
sultation with one still older—we are to make thyrsi and to
wear fawnskins and to garland our heads with shoots of ivy.*

CADMUS *comes out of the palace, dressed like Teiresias.*

CADMUS. O my dearest friend, I have come out of the house
because I recognized your voice, the wise voice of a wise
man,* when I heard it from inside. I have come all prepared   180
with this, the god's gear. For he, my daughter's son
[Dionysus, who has appeared as a god to mortals], must be
magnified by us as far as we are able. Where must we go
from here to set our feet for the dance and shake our grey
heads? You must explain this to me, Teiresias, as one old
man to another, for you are wise, and I shall never grow
tired of striking the ground with my thyrsus all day and all
night. How delightful it is to have forgotten that we are old!*
TEIRESIAS. I see that you feel in the same state as I do. For I   190
am young too and shall join in the dance.*
CADMUS. Shall we go to the mountain in a carriage?
TEIRESIAS. If we do that, the god will not have the same honour.

CADMUS. Shall I take you there, one old man leading another
like a schoolboy?
TEIRESIAS. The god will lead us there without effort.
CADMUS. Are we the only men in the city who will dance to
Bacchus?
TEIRESIAS. Yes, for we alone show good sense. All the others
are fools.
CADMUS. We are delaying here too long. Take hold of my hand.
TEIRESIAS. There, take my hand in yours and make them a
pair.
[CADMUS. I am a mortal. I do not look down on the gods.
TEIRESIAS. In the eyes of the gods we mortals have no   200
wisdom.* The traditions which we have received from our
fathers, as old as time—no argument shall throw them
down, whatever wisdom is invented by high intelligence.]
CADMUS. Will anyone say that I have no respect for old age as
I go off to dance, my hair garlanded with ivy?
TEIRESIAS. No, for the god has made no distinction between
the young and the older—all should dance. He wishes to
take honour from everyone alike. In his desire to be magnified he discounts no one.
CADMUS. Since you, Teiresias, cannot see this light of day, I   210
shall become an interpreter for you in words. Here comes
Pentheus, Echion's son, to whom I gave the rule of the land.
He is coming towards the house in haste. How excited he is!*
What fresh news will he bring us, I wonder?

Enter PENTHEUS *with guards.*

PENTHEUS. I happened to be away from this land when I
heard of this disturbing misfortune which has fallen on the
city. Our women have left their homes in fabricated rites of
Bacchus. They sit in the shady mountains, honouring the
parvenu god Dionysus, whoever he is, with their dances,   220
they set up full mixing bowls in the middle of their companies, and they slink off one by one to lonely spots to serve
the lust of males, their pretence being that they are maenads
sacrificing, while in reality they put Aphrodite before
Bacchus.* All those I have caught, my servants guard with
their hands tied in the public jail. All who are not there, I
shall hunt down* from the mountain[, Ino and Agave, who

bore me to Echion, and the mother of Actaeon, Autonoe I 230
mean].* I shall fasten them in iron snares and put a quick
stop to these pernicious Bacchic rites.

And they say that some foreigner, some wizard sorcerer,
has come here from the land of Lydia, his fragrant hair
falling in golden locks, his complexion wine-coloured. He
has the charms of Aphrodite in his eyes* and keeps company
day and night with young girls, dangling before them his
Bacchic mysteries. If I catch him within the boundaries of
this land, I shall stop him making his thyrsus ring and toss- 240
ing back his hair—by cutting his head from his body.*

That is the man who says that Dionysus is a god, it's that
man who claims that Dionysus was once sewn up in Zeus'
thigh. In fact he was destroyed by the fire of the thunderbolt
with his mother because she lied about a marriage with
Zeus. This is terrible. Does it not deserve the noose—to commit such arrogant impiety, whoever the stranger may be?

(*He notices* CADMUS *and* TEIRESIAS) But here is another marvel. I see the wonder-watcher Teiresias in a dappled fawnskin and my mother's father—what a laugh!*—worshipping 250
Bacchus with a fennel rod. I am shocked, father, to see you
old men divorced from good sense. Won't you shake off your
ivy? Won't you set your hand free from the thyrsus, father
of my mother?

It was you, Teiresias, who persuaded him to do this. You
want to introduce this extra god to men as a novelty and so
watch your birds and reap the rewards from burnt offerings.* If your grey-haired old age did not protect you, you
would be sitting in chains in the middle of the bacchae for
importing these wicked rites. For when the liquid gleam of 260
the grape-cluster shines for women at the feast, I say that
there is no longer anything healthy in their rites.

CHORUS. What impiety! Stranger, do you not respect the gods
and Cadmus who sowed the earth-born crop of men?* You
are Echion's son. Will you dishonour your family?

TEIRESIAS. When a wise man starts arguing from a just basis,
it is no great task for him to speak well. But while you have
a ready flow of words as if you spoke sensibly, there is no
sound thought in what you say. The capable speaker whose 270
influence is based on self-assurance is a bad citizen: he lacks

good sense. This new god whom you make fun of—I could
not tell you how great he will be throughout Greece. For,
young man, there are two fundamental elements among
mankind. The goddess Demeter—she is Earth,* call her
whichever of those names you will—she nurtures men with
dry food. And the god who came next, the son of Semele,
invented, to balance Demeter's gift, the liquid drink of the
grape and introduced it to men, the drink which puts an end   280
to sorrow for wretched mortals when they are filled with the
juice of the vine, and gives sleep to bring forgetfulness of
their daily round of cares.* There is no other cure for our
toils. He, a god himself, is poured in libations to gods and
thus it is through him that men have their blessings.

Do you mock him because he was sown up in the thigh
of Zeus? I shall explain to you what a fine thing this is.
When Zeus snatched him from the fire of the thunderbolt
and took his new child up to Olympus, Hera wanted to   290
throw it out of heaven. Zeus took the sort of counter-mea-
sure you would expect from a god. He broke off a portion of
the air of heaven which surrounds the earth and gave this
to Hera as a hostage, getting Dionysus out of the way of her
jealous rage. And after a time mortals came to say that he
was sewn in the thigh of Zeus, changing the name because,
god though he is, he was once a hostage to a goddess, and
thus making a new story.*

This god is a prophet. For mad Bacchic possession brings
considerable prophetic skill. When the god comes upon the   300
body in his might, he makes those he maddens tell the
future. And he has taken a share in the war-god's sphere.
For when an army stands armed in its ranks, terror can
make it scatter before it touches a spear. This too is a madness from Dionysus. One day you will see him by the rocks
at Delphi leaping with his pine torches over the upland
between the two peaks,* shaking and brandishing his
Bacchic staff, great throughout Greece.

But, Pentheus, listen to me. Do not be so over-sure that   310
power rules in human affairs, and do not persuade yourself
that you are right if you think something but your thought
is sick. No, receive the god into your land, pour libations to
Bacchus, worship him and garland your head. It is not for

Dionysus to force women to be chaste, but chastity [in all circumstances and at all times] depends on their nature. You must look at all the facts. The chaste woman will not be corrupted even amid the Bacchic rites. Do you see? You rejoice when the people stand at the gates and the city magnifies 320 the name of Pentheus. He too, I think, delights in being honoured.

And so I and Cadmus, whom you mock, will crown ourselves with ivy and dance. A grey-haired duo we may be— but still we must dance. And I shall not be persuaded by your words and fight with the gods. For you are mad, most cruelly mad. You cannot cure your sickness either with drugs or without them.

CHORUS. Old man, you bring no disgrace on Phoebus in what you have said and you show wisdom in honouring Bromius, a great god.

CADMUS. My boy, Teiresias has given you good advice. Dwell 330 with us, not beyond the boundary of the laws. For now you are up in the air and your thinking is folly. Even if, as you say, this Dionysus is not a god, he should still be called one by you. And you should tell a lie for credit's sake and claim that he is Semele's son. Thus it will appear that she has given birth to a god and honour will accrue to all our family.* You have seen the lamentable fate of Actaeon, torn to pieces by the flesh-eating dogs which he had reared because he had boasted in the mountain glades that he was better at 340 hunting than Artemis.* Do not suffer the same fate. Come over here, let me crown your head with ivy. Pay honour to the god with us.

PENTHEUS. Keep your hands off me! Off with you to your Bacchic rites! Do not wipe your foolishness off on me! But I shall punish this fellow who has taught you your folly. Go someone as quickly as possible, and when you come to the seat of this man where he observes his birds, prise it up with levers and turn it upside down. Pile everything all together in a confused mass and throw his wool ribbands* to the 350 winds and storms. By doing that I shall hurt him most. And let others comb the city and track down the foreigner who looks like a girl and is bringing this new infection on our women and corrupting their beds. If you catch him, bring

him here in chains so that he can meet his punishment of
death by stoning* and find his Bacchic rites in Thebes turning to ashes.

TEIRESIAS. You stubborn man, you do not know what you
  are saying. Before this you were out of your mind. Now you
  are altogether mad. Let us go, Cadmus, and let us beg the   360
  god, on behalf of this man, savage though he is, and of our
  city, not to do anything drastic. Come with me with your ivy
  staff, and try to support my body as I shall yours. For it
  would be a shameful thing if two old men fell down. Still, let
  come what will come. Men must be slaves to the Bacchic
  god, the son of Zeus. Be careful that Pentheus does not bring
  sorrow* on your house, Cadmus. I base what I say not on
  my prophetic skill, simply on the facts. For the words of a
  fool are folly.

TEIRESIAS and CADMUS *go out together.* PENTHEUS *goes into the palace.*

CHORUS (*sings*). Purity,* queen of the gods,
    Purity, flying over the earth   370
    on your golden wing,
    do you hear these words of Pentheus?
    Do you hear his impure blasphemy
    against Bromius, the son of Semele,
    the god who is first of the blessed ones
    at the fair-garlanded festivities?
    He is the god whose sphere it is
    to bring men together in the dances,
    to laugh to the pipe's music,   380
    and put an end to cares,
    whenever the gleam of the grape's cluster
    glints at the gods' feast,
    and the mixing bowl casts sleep over males*
    amid the ivy-wreathed merriment.

    The words of unbridled mouths,
    the thoughts of lawless folly
    end in tears,
    while the life of calm and sanity   390
    sails a voyage tossed by no storm
    and holds families together.
    For though the heavenly gods dwell

far off in the upper air,
they still watch what men do.
Mere cleverness is not wisdom.*
To think thoughts more than mortal
leads to a short life. In view of this
what man would pursue greatness
and fail to win what lies at hand?
This is the way the mad behave,   400
men whom I judge fools.

May I come to Cyprus,
Aphrodite's island
where the Loves which enchant men's hearts
dwell in Paphos
which the streams of the barbarian river
with its hundred mouths
fertilize without rain,
and to the region of Pieria in all its beauty
where the Muses dwell,   410
the sacred slope of Olympus.
Lead me there, Bromius, Bromius,
god of the loud Bacchic worship.
There are the Graces, there is Desire, there
it is lawful for the bacchae to hold their rites.*

The god, the son of Zeus,
rejoices in festivities,
and he loves Peace, bringer of prosperity,
the goddess who rears children.*   420
He gives to rich and humble
an equal share in the pleasure of wine
which banishes sorrow.
But he hates the man to whom it means nothing
to live a blessed life to the end
by day and happy night
†and to keep one's heart and mind in wisdom
away from haughty men.†
Whatever ordinary people have thought it right   430
to live by, that I would accept.

Re-enter PENTHEUS. *Enter a* SERVANT *with guards bringing on*
DIONYSUS.

SERVANT. Pentheus, we have come here after hunting down
the quarry which you sent us for. We have fulfilled our mission. But we found this wild beast tame. He didn't sneak off
in flight but gave us his hands quite willingly. With no pal-
lor, no change in his wine-coloured complexion, he laugh-
ingly told us to tie him up and lead him away, and he waited   440
there, making my task easy. And I felt ashamed and said,
'Stranger, it is not that I want to arrest you. I do it on the
orders of Pentheus who sent me.'*

Now as for the bacchae you locked up, the ones you
arrested and bound in the fetters of the public prison, they
have been set loose and have gone off to the mountain
glades where they skip about calling upon Bromius as a god.
The bonds broke loose from their feet of their own accord
and the bolts unfastened the doors without mortal hands.
This man has come here to Thebes fraught full with wonders. But it is up to you to decide what comes next.   450

PENTHEUS. Let go of his hands. Now that he is in the net, he
is not so nimble that he will escape me.

Well, physically you are not unhandsome, stranger, to a
woman's taste at any rate—and that is why you have come
to Thebes. You have long flowing locks, which prove you no
wrestler. They fall right by your cheek, laden with desire.*
And you keep your skin deliberately white since you hunt
Aphrodite with your beauty by avoiding the sun's rays and
skulking in the shadows. First tell me of what race you are.

DIONYSUS. There is no need for me to hesitate over my   460
answer. It is easily given. I suppose you know of flowery
Tmolus by report.

PENTHEUS. I know of it.* It encircles the city of Sardis.

DIONYSUS. I am from there, and Lydia is my fatherland.

PENTHEUS. From what source do you bring these rites to
Greece?

DIONYSUS. Dionysus himself initiated me, the son of Zeus.

PENTHEUS. Is there a Zeus there who begets new gods?

DIONYSUS. No, it is the same Zeus as the one who married
Semele here.

PENTHEUS. And was it in a dream or face to face that he laid
compulsion on you?

DIONYSUS. It was face to face, and he gave me his rituals.   470

PENTHEUS. What form do these rituals take for you?

DIONYSUS. That must not be told to those uninitiated in Bacchic worship. They must not know.

PENTHEUS. What benefit do the rituals bring to the sacrificers?

DIONYSUS. It is not right for you to hear, but it is worth knowing.

PENTHEUS. You faked that answer skilfully to make me want to hear.

DIONYSUS. The rituals of the god hate a man who practises impiety.

PENTHEUS. The god, just what was he like? Tell me, for you say you saw him clearly.

DIONYSUS. He appeared in the form he chose. I did not arrange this.

PENTHEUS. Here again you have sidetracked me with fine but empty words.

DIONYSUS. An ignorant man will think another's wise words 480 folly.

PENTHEUS. Was it Thebes that you came to first with your imported god?

DIONYSUS. Every one of the barbarians dances in these rituals.

PENTHEUS. Yes, for they are much more foolish than Greeks.

DIONYSUS. In this respect they are far cleverer. But their customs are different.

PENTHEUS. Do you perform your sacred rituals at night or by day?

DIONYSUS. Mainly by night. The night has solemnity.

PENTHEUS. This is your insidious method of corrupting women.

DIONYSUS. You can find immorality by daylight too.

PENTHEUS. You must pay the penalty for your wicked sophistries.

DIONYSUS. And you must pay for your ignorance and your 490 impiety towards the god.

PENTHEUS. How bold the bacchant* is—and not unexercised in speaking!

DIONYSUS. Tell me what I must suffer. What fearful thing will you do to me?

PENTHEUS. First I shall cut off your love-locks.

DIONYSUS. My hair is sacred. I grow it for the god.

PENTHEUS. Now give me this thyrsus from your hands.

DIONYSUS. Take it from me yourself. I carry it for Dionysus.

PENTHEUS. We shall guard your body inside in prison.

DIONYSUS. The god will free me whenever I wish.*

PENTHEUS. When you stand among the bacchae and call him.

DIONYSUS. He is here close by even now and sees what I suf- 500
fer.

PENTHEUS. And where is he? He is not manifest to my eyes.

DIONYSUS. He is where I am. In your impiety you cannot see
him.

PENTHEUS. Lay hold on him. He is showing contempt for me
and for Thebes.

DIONYSUS. I tell you not to tie me up—sensible words to the
senseless.

PENTHEUS. Tie him up, I say—my authority counts here, not
yours.

DIONYSUS. You do not know what your life is, or what you
are doing, or who you are.

PENTHEUS. I am Pentheus, the son of Agave and of my father
Echion.*

DIONYSUS. You have a name fit to sorrow for.*

PENTHEUS. Off with you. Shut him in the stables nearby so
that he can see the black darkness. Do your dancing there. 510
As for these women, the partners in crime you have brought
here with you, either we shall sell them off or I shall put a
stop to these pounding thuds of their drums and keep them
as slaves at the loom.*

DIONYSUS. I am willing to go. For what I should not suffer, I
shall not. But be sure that Dionysus will exact punishment
for this violence—the god you say does not exist. For in
wronging me, you put him in chains.

                    DIONYSUS is taken out. Exit PENTHEUS.

CHORUS (*sings*). Daughter of Achelous,*
blessed maiden, queen Dirce,   520
once you took in your streams
Zeus' new-born child
when Zeus his father snatched him from the undying fire
and hid him in his thigh, with this shout:
'Come, Dithyrambus,* come
to this male womb.

I reveal you to Thebes, o Bacchic god,
so that she may call you by that name.'
But you, o blessed Dirce, 530
drive me away
as I hold my garlanded companies on your bank.
Why do you reject me? Why do you shun me?
One day—by the joy
of Dionysus' vine clusters—
one day you will care about Bromius.

[What fury, what fury he shows!]
He reveals his earth-born ancestry,
Pentheus,
the old dragon's brood, 540
whom earth-begotten Echion begat*
to be a wild-faced monster, not a human being,
taking on the gods like a murderous giant.
He will soon tie me,
the slave of Bromius, in his knots,
and he already holds inside his house
my fellow-reveller
hidden in a dark prison.
Do you see this, o son of Zeus 550
Dionysus, your prophets
in a struggle with oppression?
Come down from Olympus, lord,
brandishing your thyrsus faced with gold,
and check the violence of a murderous man.
Where then on Nysa, nurse of wild beasts,
or on the Corycian peaks,* o Dionysus,
do you lead your companies
with your thyrsus?
And perhaps amid the tree-rich coverts of Olympus 560
where Orpheus once with the music of his strings
brought together the trees,
brought together the wild beasts.*
O blessed Pieria,
the god of ecstatic cries reveres you, and he will come
to set you dancing amid the bacchic revelry,
and will lead the whirling maenads,

crossing the swift-flowing Axios   570
and the river Lydias,* the father who gives wealth
and its blessings to mortals,
and who I have heard
enriches with his fairest waters
a land of fine horses.*

DIONYSUS (*chants off-stage*). Io, bacchae,
   hear my voice, hear,
   io, io bacchae.

CHORUS (*chants*). What calls, what calls are these of the god
     of cries
   which summon me? Where have they come from?

DIONYSUS (*chants*). Io, io, I cry again,   580
   I, the son of Semele, the son of Zeus.

CHORUS (*chants*). Io, io, master, master,
   come then to our company,
   o Bromius, Bromius.

DIONYSUS (*chants*). Shake the floor of the earth, sovereign
   spirit of earthquake.

CHORUS (*chants*). Ah, ah!
   Soon the palace of Pentheus will be shaken apart
   and collapse.*
   Dionysus is everywhere in the palace.
   Worship him!—Oh, we do worship him!   590
   —You saw how those stone lintels
   ran apart? It is Bromius, lord of thunder,
   who shouts his triumph inside the house.

DIONYSUS (*chants*). Kindle your thunderbolt's flashing fire,
   burn the house of Pentheus to nothing, to nothing.

The fire on Semele's tomb flares up.

CHORUS (*chants*). Ah, ah,
   can you not see the fire, do you not perceive
   around this holy tomb of Semele
   the flame which Zeus' thunder-flung bolt
   left here long ago?
   Throw, throw your trembling bodies   600
   to the ground, maenads.
   For our lord will come upon this palace
   turning it upside down—the son of Zeus.

DIONYSUS *enters from the palace.*

DIONYSUS (*chants*). Barbarian women, have you fallen to the
  ground
so stunned by fear? It seems that you saw the Bacchic god
shaking asunder the house of Pentheus. But lift up
your bodies, take courage, and put away this trembling from
  your flesh.
CHORUS (*chants*). O light of our day, our leader in the
  ecstatic rituals,
how joyful I am to see you, all alone in my isolation.
DIONYSUS (*chants*). Did you fall into despair when I was   610
  being taken inside—
thinking that I was about to fall into the snares of
  Pentheus' dark dungeon?
CHORUS (*chants*). How could I fail to? Who will protect me if
  you meet disaster?
But how were you freed from your encounter with a man
  of sin?
DIONYSUS (*chants*). I won my safety by myself, easily,
  effortlessly.
CHORUS (*chants*). Didn't he fasten your hands with knots of
  rope?
DIONYSUS (*chants*). That was just the way I made a fool of
  him—though he thought he was tying me up,
he did not touch or grasp me but fed on empty hopes.
He found a bull* by the stables where he had taken me
  and shut me in,
and he tried to rope this up with nooses around its knees
  and fetlocks
as he panted out his rage, dripping sweat from his body,   620
biting his lips. I was nearby
sitting quietly watching him. And during this time
Bacchus came and levered up the house and kindled
the fire on my mother's tomb. When he saw this, thinking
  the palace was in flames,
he rushed this way and that, telling his servants
to bring water. And every slave was engaged on the task,
  but toiled in vain.
Then thinking I had escaped, he abandoned his efforts,

snatched a dark sword, and darted inside the palace.
And then Bromius—as it seems to me: I give my own
    impression—
created a phantom in the courtyard. In his rage Pentheus   630
    rushed upon this
and tried to stab bright vapour, thinking he was killing
    me.
On top of that the Bacchic god piled these further indigni-
    ties on him.
He smashed his palace to the ground. All lies shattered.
He has seen a most bitter end to my imprisonment.
    Dropping his sword,
he has collapsed in exhaustion. A mere man, he had the
    hardihood
to join battle with a god. I have come quietly
out of the palace to you with no thought for Pentheus.
But I think—indeed there is the sound of tramping feet
    inside the palace—
that in an instant he will come out in front here.
    Whatever will he find to say after all this?
No matter, for I shall make light of him even if he comes   640
    snorting rage.
A wise man should always keep a balanced and easy
    temper.*

Enter PENTHEUS.

PENTHEUS. I have suffered terrible things. The stranger who
just now was bound fast with rope has escaped me. (*with a
start*) But look! Here is the man. What is going on? How can
I be seeing you in front of my house? How did you get out?

DIONYSUS. Stand still.* Put a stop to your anger and calm
down.

PENTHEUS. How have you managed to escape your bonds and
come out here?

DIONYSUS. Did I not say—or did you not hear—that someone
would free me?

PENTHEUS. Who? You are for ever mentioning new, unex-   650
pected things.

DIONYSUS. The one who grows the rich-clustered vine for
men.*

PENTHEUS. . . . .
DIONYSUS. You insult Dionysus over what is his glory.
PENTHEUS. I order that every gate in the circle of walls should be locked.
DIONYSUS. What is the point of that? Cannot gods go over walls?
PENTHEUS. You are clever, clever—except where you should be clever.
DIONYSUS. Where I should be clever, there above all I am so.

A MESSENGER *enters.*

But first listen to this man who has come from the mountain to tell you something, and hear what he has to say. We shall remain here, we shall not run away.
MESSENGER. Pentheus, ruler of this Theban land, I have come 660 here from Mount Cithaeron where the dazzling falls of white snow never melt.
PENTHEUS. And what weighty message do you bring?
MESSENGER. I have seen the holy bacchae whose white limbs flashed away spear-swift in their madness. And I have come here wishing to tell you and the city, my lord, that they do strange things, things that go beyond wonder. I want to hear whether I can tell you what has happened there with complete freedom of speech—or should I check my tongue? For I fear your speed of thought, my king, your sharp tem- 670 per and your all too kingly spirit.
PENTHEUS. Speak—you are in no danger of being punished by me, whatever you say. [After all, it is not right to show anger against just men.]* But the more strange the things you say about the bacchae, the more severe the penalty I shall exact from this man who has corrupted the women with his wiles.
MESSENGER. The pasturing herds of cattle were just climbing onto the upland country at the time when the sun sends forth its beams to heat the world. I saw three companies of 680 female dancers. Autonoe was in charge of one, your mother Agave of the second, and Ino of the third. And all of them were sleeping, their bodies relaxed, some of them leaning their backs on fir-tree needles, others amid oak leaves, their heads flung down at random on the ground—chastely, and

not, as you say, made drunk by the wine-bowl and the
music of the pipe, and slinking off on their own to hunt
Aphrodite in the wood. But when your mother heard the
lowings of the horned cattle, she stood up in the middle of
the bacchae and cried her Bacchic cry to make them stir   690
themselves from sleep. The women, casting deep slumber
from their eyes, leapt upright, a marvel of good order to look
upon,* young women and old and maidens still unwed. And
first they let their hair down onto their shoulders, and all
those whose fawnskins' binding knots had worked loose tied
them up and girdled the dappled hides with snakes which
licked their cheeks. Some of them held a roe deer or wild
wolf-cubs in their arms and all the recent mothers, whose
breasts were still swollen for the offspring they had abandoned, gave to these their white milk. They put on garlands   700
of ivy, of oak, and of flower-clustered bryony. And one of
them took her thyrsus and struck it against a rock, from
which the dewy wetness of water leapt forth. Another
plunged her fennel rod into the earth's surface, and for her
the god spurted up a spring of wine. Then all who felt a longing for the white drink scraped at the ground with their fin-
gertips and took jets of milk in their hands. And from their   710
ivy-clad thyrsi dripped sweet streams of honey.* So, if you
had been there and seen these things, you would have
approached this god, whom you now hold cheap, with
prayers.

　　We herdsmen and shepherds came together to outdo each
other in our accounts [as we described their strange and
wondrous actions]. And someone who had tramped the
town and was a glib speaker* said to all of us, 'You men who
live on the sacred upland plateaus, do you want us to hunt
Agave, Pentheus' mother, from her Bacchic rites and do our   720
king a favour?' We thought his words made good sense, and
we lay in ambush hiding ourselves in the leafy thickets. At
the appointed time the women began to rouse their thyrsi
for the Bacchic rites, calling in unison on Bromius, the son
of Zeus, god of ecstatic cries. And all the mountain and the
animals joined them in their Bacchic worship—there was
nothing that did not move with the running. Agave happened to be leaping near me and I jumped out, eager to

snatch hold of her,* emptying the thicket where we were   730
hiding. She shouted out, 'O my running hounds, we are the
quarry of these men's hunt. But follow me, follow me, with
your thyrsi in your hands as weapons.' So we ran away and
escaped being torn to pieces by the bacchae, while they
turned against the young cows which were grazing upon the
grass. They held no iron weapons in their hands.* You
would have seen one of them wrenching in two a full-
uddered young heifer which bellowed, while others were
rending, tearing mature ones apart. You would have seen   740
ribs or a cloven hoof flung up and down. These hung under
the fir trees dripping, all fouled with blood. Bulls which till
then had been arrogant, their anger mounting into their
horns, stumbled to the ground dragged down by the countless hands of girls. Their hides were torn apart quicker than
you could have closed your royal eyes.

Like birds rising high, they went at a run across the low-
land plains which produce fine crops for the Thebans by the   750
streams of Asopus. They swooped down like an enemy on
Hysiae and Erythrae which stand in the hill-country of
Cithaeron in its lower regions, and ransacked everything
from top to bottom. They seized children from the houses
and all of these that they placed on their shoulders were held
there by no bonds, yet did not fall [to the black ground.
Neither did bronze or iron].* They carried fire on the locks of
their hair, and it did not burn them. Thus plundered by the
bacchae, the villagers resorted to arms in a passion of rage.
Thereupon we saw a terrible sight, my lord. The villagers'   760
pointed spears, whether tipped with bronze or iron, drew no
blood, while the bacchae shot their thyrsi from their hands
and kept wounding them and making them turn and run
away. Women did these things to men. A god certainly
helped them.

Then they went back to where they had started from, to
the very springs which the god had sent up for them, they
washed off the blood, and the snakes licked the drops from
their cheeks making their skin gleam.

And so, my master, receive this god, whoever he is, in
this city. For he is great in other respects, and especially in   770
this particular thing that they say of him—that, as I hear,

he has given to mortals the vine that puts an end to sorrow.
If wine no longer existed, then there would be no Aphrodite
or any other sweet delight still left for mortals.

CHORUS. I am frightened to speak out freely what I have to say
to the king, but nevertheless it shall be said. Dionysus is inferior to none of the gods.

PENTHEUS. Already this violent blasphemy of the bacchae
blazes up close to us like fire. It reflects great discredit on the
Greeks. But it is imperative not to hestitate. Off with you, go   780
to the Electran gate.* Order all the heavy infantry and those
that ride swift-footed horses to assemble—and all who bran-
dish light shields and pluck the bowstring with their
hands—since we shall march against the bacchae.* For it is
certainly beyond endurance if we are to suffer what we now
suffer at the hands of women.

DIONYSUS. You hear my words, Pentheus, but they make no
impression on you. However, even though I suffer this bad
treatment at your hands, I still tell you that you should not
take up arms against a god. No, you should do nothing.   790
Bromius will not tolerate your dislodging the bacchae from
the mountains of joy.

PENTHEUS. Do not tell me what to think. You have escaped
from jail. Do you want to stay free? Or shall I renew your
punishment?

DIONYSUS. I would pay him sacrifices rather than kick against
the goad in rage—a mere mortal taking on a god.

PENTHEUS. I *shall* pay him sacrifices—in women's blood, as
they deserve. I shall shed it in rich measure in Cithaeron's
glens.

DIONYSUS. You will all be routed. And this brings disgrace—
for bacchae to turn your shields of beaten bronze with their
thyrsi.

PENTHEUS. I am locked together with this stranger and can   800
find no escape from the hold.* He will be silent neither when
he suffers nor when he acts.

DIONYSUS. Sir, it is still possible to set this matter right.*

PENTHEUS. By doing what? By being a slave to my slave
women?

DIONYSUS. I will bring those women here without the use of
weapons.

PENTHEUS. Alas! This is some trick which he is now devising against me.

DIONYSUS. How can it be a trick if I am willing to save you by my skills?

PENTHEUS. You have all planned this together so that you can worship Bacchus in perpetuity.

DIONYSUS. Certainly I planned this—you can be confident of that—together with the god.

PENTHEUS. Bring me out weapons here, and you, stop talking!

DIONYSUS. Ah!*   810
Do you want to see them sitting together on the mountain?

PENTHEUS. Very much so, and I would give an infinite weight of gold for that.

DIONYSUS. How is it that you have conceived so great a passion for this?

PENTHEUS. I should be sorry to see them drunk.

DIONYSUS. But would you nevertheless be glad to see what is bitter to you?

PENTHEUS. You can be sure of that—I want to sit in silence beneath the firs.

DIONYSUS. But they will hunt you out even if you go secretly.

PENTHEUS. No, I shall go openly. This advice of yours is good.

DIONYSUS. Should we lead you then, and will you undertake the journey?

PENTHEUS. Lead me as quickly as you can. I shall hold any   820
delay against you.

DIONYSUS. Then put fine linen clothes around your body.*

PENTHEUS. Why that? Am I to stop being a man and join the female sex?

DIONYSUS. Yes, so that they don't kill you if you are seen there as a man.

PENTHEUS. Another piece of good advice. How clever a fellow you have been all along!

DIONYSUS. Dionysus gave me full instruction in this.

PENTHEUS. How could your advice to me be successfully realized?

DIONYSUS. I shall come inside your palace and dress you.

PENTHEUS. In what clothes? Do you mean a woman's dress? But I feel shame at this.

DIONYSUS. Are you no longer eager to be a spectator* of the maenads?

PENTHEUS. What do you say you will fling around my body? 830
DIONYSUS. First I shall make your hair hang long on your head.*
PENTHEUS. What is the next feature of my costume?
DIONYSUS. Robes that fall to your feet. And on your head will
be a headband.
PENTHEUS. And will you put anything else on me in addition
to those things?
DIONYSUS. Yes, a thyrsus for your hand, and a dappled skin
of a fawn.
PENTHEUS. I shan't be able to put on a woman's clothes.
DIONYSUS. But you will cause bloodshed if you join battle with
the bacchae.
PENTHEUS. Rightly said. First I must go to reconnoitre.
DIONYSUS. Yes, it is certainly wiser than to hunt for trouble
by inflicting it.
PENTHEUS. And how shall I avoid being seen by Cadmus'
people as I go through the city?   840
DIONYSUS. We shall go through empty streets. I shall lead the
way.
PENTHEUS. Anything is better than that the bacchae should
laugh at me.
DIONYSUS. Let us go into the house . . .
PENTHEUS. . . . I shall decide whatever seems best.*
DIONYSUS. You may. Whatever you decide, for my part I am
ready and at hand.
PENTHEUS. I think I shall go in. Either I shall march with arms
or I shall follow your advice.*   *Exit* PENTHEUS.

DIONYSUS. Women, this man is walking into the casting net.
He will come to the bacchae—and there he will pay the
penalty by his death. Dionysus, it is your work now. I call
upon you, for you are not far away. Let us take vengeance 850
on him. First of all, drive him out of his mind, sending dizzy
madness upon him, since if he is sane, he will certainly not
be willing to put on women's clothes, while if he drives off
the track of sanity, he will put them on. I want him to win
laughter from the Thebans as he is led through the city in a
woman's form—after those earlier threats of his with which
he inspired such terror! But I shall go to dress Pentheus in
the clothes which he shall take to the Underworld when he

goes there slaughtered at his mother's hands. He shall recognize Dionysus the son of Zeus and see that he is by turns a 860
most terrifying and a most gentle god to mortals.

Exit DIONYSUS.

CHORUS (*sings*). Shall I ever in night-long dance
set my white feet
in the Bacchic revel
and fling my head back to the dewy air
like a fawn at play
in the meadow's green joyfulness
when she escapes the fearsome hunt,
leaping clear of the ring of watchers
over the close-woven nets.   870
And the huntsman shouts
to urge his dogs to speed,
while she, swift as a storm
in her effortful racing,
bounds over the water-meadow,
joying in places void of men and the green life
that springs under the shadowy hair of the forest.

What is wisdom?* Or what god-given prize
is nobler in men's eyes
than to hold one's hand in mastery
over the head of one's enemies?   880
What is noble is precious—that ever holds true.

The power of the gods moves slowly
but surely none the less.
It corrects those men
who worship senselessness
and in their mad folly
do not magnify the gods
who cover with elaborate devices
the unhastening foot of time
as they hunt down the man without religion.   890
For in thought and behaviour
one should never go beyond traditional ways.
It costs little
to regard these things as having power:
whatever it is that comes from god

and what has always been the tradition established
by nature and long time.

What is wisdom? Or what god-given prize
is nobler in men's eyes
than to hold one's hand in mastery
over the head of one's enemies?   900
What is noble is precious—that ever holds true.

Happy the man who has escaped
from a storm at sea and found harbour.
Happy the man who has overcome hardships.
In various ways one man surpasses another
in wealth and power.
And there remain countless hopes
for countless people. Some of these
find fulfilment for mortals in wealth,
while others vanish.   910
The man whose life is blessed from day to day—
him I count happy.

Enter DIONYSUS.

DIONYSUS. You who are eager to see what you should not,
   eager to seek what should not be sought, Pentheus I say,
   come out in front of the house. Let me see you dressed in
   female get-up as a maenad, a bacchant,* so that you can spy
   on your mother and her company. You look like one of
   Cadmus' daughters.

*PENTHEUS enters dressed as a maenad in a wig and a long linen
   dress, and holding a thyrsus.*

PENTHEUS. How strange! I think I see two suns and a double
   Thebes, our seven-gated city. And I think that you lead the   920
   way before me as a bull and that horns have grown on your
   head. Were you perhaps a beast all the time? You have certainly been changed into a bull.*
DIONYSUS. It is the god who walks together with you. He was
   hostile before but now he is at peace with us. Now you see
   what you should see.
PENTHEUS. How do I look then? Don't I carry myself like Ino
   or Agave, my mother?

DIONYSUS. As I look at you, those are the very women I think
I see. But this lock of your hair has slipped from its place. It
isn't as I tucked it beneath your headband.

PENTHEUS. As I shook it backwards and forwards acting my 930
Bacchic role inside the palace, I must have dislodged it from
its place.

DIONYSUS. But I, whose concern it is to be your servant,
shall put it back where it should be. But hold your head
upright.*

PENTHEUS. There! You must set me straight. I have put myself
in your hands.

DIONYSUS. And your girdle is loose and the pleats of your
dress do not hang evenly to below your ankle.

PENTHEUS. Yes, I think so too—by my right foot at any rate.
But on this side the dress is straight at the tendon.*

DIONYSUS. You will certainly regard me as the first of your
friends when you see that the bacchae are chaste, contrary 940
to what you say.

PENTHEUS. Will I be more like a bacchant if I hold the thyrsus in my right hand or in this one?*

DIONYSUS. You should lift it up in your right hand, in time
with your right foot. I am delighted by your altered mind.

PENTHEUS. Would I have the strength to carry the folds of
Cithaeron, bacchae and all, on my shoulders?*

DIONYSUS. You could if you wanted to. The way you thought
before was unhealthy. Now you think as you should.

PENTHEUS. Should we take along crowbars, or should I put 950
my shoulder or arm beneath the mountain's crests and tear
it up with my bare hands?

DIONYSUS. You really mustn't destroy the shrines of the
Nymphs and the haunts of Pan where he plays his pipes.*

PENTHEUS. Good advice. Women are not to be conquered by
brute force. I shall hide myself beneath the firs.

DIONYSUS. You will be hidden as you should be hidden when
you come in secret to spy on the maenads.

PENTHEUS. Think of it! I feel that they are in the thickets,
caught like mating birds in the delicious nets of love.

DIONYSUS. Aren't you on a mission to guard against this very
thing? Perhaps you will catch them, if you are not caught 960
first.

PENTHEUS. Escort me through the middle of the land of Thebes.
For I am the lone man of them all who dares this deed.*

DIONYSUS. You alone bear the burden for this city, you alone.
That is why the destined contests lie in store for you. Follow
me. I am your guide and shall bring you safely to that place.
But another will take you back from there . . . PENTHEUS.
Yes, my mother.

DIONYSUS. . . . for all to see. PENTHEUS. That is why I am going.

DIONYSUS. You will not return on foot . . . PENTHEUS. You
want to pamper me.

DIONYSUS. In your mother's arms . . . PENTHEUS. You are
determined to spoil me.

DIONYSUS. Yes, spoil you in my fashion. PENTHEUS. I lay hold   970
on what I deserve.

DIONYSUS. You are an amazing man, truly amazing, and you
go to amazing sufferings. Through these you will find a
glory that towers to heaven.* Stretch out your hands,
Agave, and Agave's sisters too, you daughters of Cadmus.
I am leading this young man to a great contest and the
winner will be Bromius and myself. Everything else the
event will show.

                                  DIONYSUS leads PENTHEUS out.

CHORUS (*sings*). On, swift hounds of Frenzy,* on to the
      mountain
where the daughters of Cadmus join in worship.
Sting them to madness
against the man who comes dressed up in a woman's   980
      costume
to spy upon the maenads in his frenzy.
First of all his mother will spot him
as he peers from some precipitous rock or pinnacle,
and will shout out to the maenads,
'Who is this who has come to the mountain, come to the
      mountain, o bacchae,
tracking the mountain-running women of Cadmus' race?
What creature gave him birth?
For he was not born from women's blood
but from a lioness, he,   990
or from the race of Libyan Gorgons.'*

Let Justice come plain for all to see, let it come
sword in hand, stabbing
right through the throat
the ungodly, unlawful, unrighteous one
from Echion's earth-born breed.

The man who sets forth with injustice in his mind
and madness in his heart, crazily daring in his lawless rage
†against the Bacchic rites and your mother's worship†,
his aim to master the invincible by force—   1000
†death is an ungainsayable teacher
of moderate opinions
in what concerns the gods.
To act as a mortal should brings a life free from grief.
I do not begrudge the wise their wisdom—but I happily
    pursue
the other things which are great and plain to see,
the things that lead life towards what is beautiful,†*
to show holy reverence through the day and into the night,
and casting aside all that transgresses the laws of justice
to honour the gods.*   1010

Let Justice come plain for all to see, let it come
sword in hand, stabbing
right through the throat
the ungodly, unlawful, unrighteous one
from Echion's earth-born breed.

Appear to our sight as a bull
or a many-headed snake
or a fire-blazing lion to look upon.
Come, o Bacchus, as a wild beast,   1020
with smiling face throw your deadly noose
around this hunter of the bacchae
when he has fallen beneath the maenads' drove.

Enter MESSENGER, *an attendant of Pentheus.*

MESSENGER. O house [of the old man from Sidon, who sowed
    the earth-born crop of the serpent snake in the ground],*
    once you were happy in the sight of all of Greece, but how
    I lament for you now. I am a mere slave, but even so [good
    slaves sympathize with their masters' misfortunes].

CHORUS. What is it? Do you bring us any news fom the bacchae?
MESSENGER. Pentheus, son of Echion, is dead.   1030
CHORUS (*sings*). O lord Bromius, you stand revealed as a
  great god.
MESSENGER. What do you mean? What is this you say? Do
  you rejoice over the catastrophe of one who was my master,
  woman?
CHORUS (*sings*). I am a foreigner and I cry 'Euoi' in my barbarian song. For I cower no more in fear of prison.
MESSENGER. Do you think the men of Thebes so spineless
  ⟨that they will not punish you⟩?*
CHORUS (*sings*). It is Dionysus, not Thebes but Dionysus,
  who has power over me.
MESSENGER. I understand your attitude, except that it is not
  proper, women, to exult over horrific deeds.*   1040
CHORUS (*sings*). Speak, tell me. By what fate did the lawless
  man die as he pursued his lawless schemes?
MESSENGER. When we left the settlements of the Theban
  land and moved on from the streams of Asopus, we began
  to strike into the hill-country of Cithaeron, Pentheus and
  I—for I was following my master—and the stranger who
  led us on our way to see the sight. Well, first we sat in a
  grassy valley, keeping silent every movement of foot and
  tongue so that we could see without being seen. There was 1050
  a ravine, shut in by cliffs, refreshed by waters and thick-
  shaded with pines where the maenads sat, their hands
  occupied in delightful tasks. Some of them were restoring
  what had been a thyrsus by wreathing it again with locks
  of ivy, while others were singing Bacchic songs to each
  other in antiphony, like fillies released from the patterned
  yoke.*
    But the wretched Pentheus did not spot the crowd of
  women and said this: 'Stranger, where we are standing, my
  eyes cannot reach the maenads in their diseased frenzy. But 1060
  if I climbed up a towering fir tree on the banks of the ravine,
  I could see their foul antics properly.' What followed next
  was that I saw the stranger do astonishing things. Laying
  hold of the topmost, heaven-piercing branch of a fir,* he
  pulled it down, down, down to the black ground. And it was

bent like a bow or a rounded wheel when its curving out-
line is traced by a string fixed to a peg.* Thus the stranger
pulled the mountain tree with his hands and bent it to the
ground. This was no mortal action that he performed. And
seating Pentheus on the fir branches, he began to let the tree 1070
go upright smoothly, moving hand over hand and taking
care not to unseat him, and it towered sheer to the sheer
heaven, with my master sitting on its back. But rather than
seeing the maenads, he was seen by them. For he was just
becoming visible as he sat on high—the stranger could no
longer be seen—and a voice from the sky—it was Dionysus
as I guess—shouted out: 'You young women, I bring the
man who makes fun of you and of me and of my rites. But 1080
take vengeance on him.' And as the voice said these things,
a blaze of awful fire flashed between heaven and earth. The
sky fell silent, the wooded glade held its leaves in stillness,
and you could not have heard any wild beast's cry.* The
bacchae, their ears failing to take in the sound clearly, stood
upright and darted their eyes about them. But he gave them
his command a second time, and when the daughters of
Cadmus plainly understood the Bacchic god's order, they
shot forward with all the speed of a wood pigeon, [their feet 1090
moving fast and intensely, the mother Agave and her sisters]
and all the bacchae with them, and they leapt through the
ravine with its swollen torrent and over the broken cliffs,
frantic with the god's breath upon them.

And when they saw my master sitting on the fir tree, they
first climbed onto a rock which towered opposite and tried
to pelt him with a powerful volley of stones; and they shot
fir-branches at him like javelins, while others hurled their
thyrsi through the air at Pentheus. It was a grisly shooting 1100
exercise, but they did not reach their target.* For the pitiable
man sat high, beyond the reach of their fanaticism. But he
was trapped—there was no escape. In the end they used
their oak branches as levers on the roots of the fir and tried
to tear it up with their crowbars not of iron. But when they
failed to bring this labour to fulfilment, Agave spoke: 'Come,
stand round in a circle and take hold of the trunk, maenads,
so that we can capture this climbing beast and stop him
reporting* the secret dances of the god.'

They set their innumerable hands on the fir and tore it up 1110
from the ground. Perched on high, he hurtled from his high
seat down to the ground and as he fell, he poured out innumerable cries of sorrow, Pentheus the sorrowful. For he was
learning that he was close to disaster. His mother, as priestess, was the first to begin the slaughter and she fell upon
him. But he flung the band from his head* so that the
wretched Agave could recognize him and not kill him, and
he touched her cheek,* saying: 'It's me, mother, your son
Pentheus, whom you bore in the house of Echion. O mother,
pity me and do not kill me for what I have done wrong.* I 1120
am your son.' But Agave, frothing foam and whirling her
twisted eyes, was far from sanity. The Bacchic god held her
possessed, and she paid no heed to Pentheus. She seized his
left arm in her hands, set her foot on the wretched man's
ribs, and tore out his shoulder—not through her own
strength: it was the god who made her handiwork easy. And
Ino wrenched his flesh apart as she performed the same
action on the other side, and Autonoe and the whole crowd 1130
of bacchae went at it. Everyone shouted out together—
Pentheus groaning as long as he went on breathing, the
women yelling their cries of triumph at the sacrifice. One of
them carried an arm, another a foot still in its shoe, his ribs
were laid bare as they tore him apart, and with their bloody
hands they all played ball with Pentheus' flesh.

The body lies in scattered fragments, one bit beneath the
jagged rocks, another in the wood's thick foliage. To find it
all is no easy task. As for his wretched head—which, as it
happened, his mother took up in her hands—, she has fixed 1140
it on the top of her thyrsus and is carrying it across
Cithaeron for all to see as if it were the head of a mountain-
lion. She has left her sisters behind amid the dancing maenads. And she comes here into our walled city exulting in
her ill-fated hunt, calling upon the Bacchic god, her fellow
hunter, her partner in the chase, the splendid victor whose
victory-prize for her is tears.

Well, I shall take myself out of the way of this tragedy
before Agave comes to the house. Moderation and piety 1150
towards the gods—these are the noblest ends, and I think
that mortals who practise them possess the truest wisdom.*

The MESSENGER *goes out.*

CHORUS (*singing*). Let us dance in praise of the Bacchic god,
 in his praise let us shout aloud
 the doom of Pentheus, the serpent's offspring,
 who put on female attire
 and took up †the sure fennel-rod, the weapon of Death,†*
 as his splendid thyrsus,
 having a bull to lead him to disaster.
 You bacchae, daughters of Cadmus,   1160
 you have sung a famous victory-song
 but it ends in groans, in tears.
 This is a noble conquest—†to plunge a dripping hand
 in the blood of one's child.†
(*speaking*) But look, I see Agave, Pentheus' mother, rushing to
 the palace, her eyes rolling. Welcome her to the revel of the
 god of ecstatic cries.

> *Enter* AGAVE *carrying the head of Pentheus.** (AGAVE *and the*
> CHORUS *sing their lines up to* 1199.)

AGAVE. Asian bacchae . . . CHORUS. Why do you address
 me, lady?
AGAVE. We bring from the mountain to the palace
 this new-cut tendril,*   1170
 our blessed prey.
CHORUS. I see it and shall receive you into our revel band.
AGAVE. I caught the young cub
 without nets or snares,
 as you can see.
CHORUS. From where in the wilderness?
AGAVE. Cithaeron . . . CHORUS. Cithaeron?
AGAVE. slaughtered him.
CHORUS. Who was it that struck him? AGAVE. That privi-
 lege was mine first.
 I am called Agave the blessed in the companies.
CHORUS. Who else struck him? AGAVE. It was Cadmus . . .   1180
CHORUS. Cadmus? AGAVE. . . . . whose children
 laid their hands on this wild beast—but after me, after me!
 Yes, it was a happy hunt.
 So join in the feast. CHORUS. Why should I join you, poor
 creature?*

AGAVE. The calf is young, his cheek just growing downy
   beneath his crest of soft hair.
CHORUS. Yes, by the hair it looks like a beast of the wild.
AGAVE. Bacchus the clever huntsman
   cleverly set his maenads   1190
   upon this beast.
CHORUS. Yes, our lord is a hunter.
AGAVE. Do you give praise? CHORUS. I do.
AGAVE. And soon the people of Cadmus . . .
CHORUS. And indeed your son Pentheus . . .
AGAVE. will praise his mother
   for catching this quarry of the lion's brood.
CHORUS. A strange quarry. AGAVE. And strangely caught.
CHORUS. Are you exultant? AGAVE. I rejoice,
   for I have done great, great and manifest things
   in this hunt.

CHORUS. Then, wretched woman, show the citizens the prey 1200
   you have carried here, your prize of victory.
AGAVE. O you who dwell in this fair-towered city of the land
   of Thebes, come to see this wild beast, the prey which we
   daughters of Cadmus have caught in our hunt, not with the
   Thessalians' thonged javelins* or with nets, but with our
   white arms and hands. After that, why should one throw
   the javelin and get hold of the armourer's handiwork?
   There's no need. It was with our hands and nothing else
   that we caught this beast and tore its limbs all in pieces.   1210
      Where is my father, the old man? Let him come near.
   And where is Pentheus, my son? Let him take ladders with
   solid steps and raise them against the house so that he can
   nail to its entablature the lion's head* which I have brought
   here from the hunt.

Enter CADMUS *with attendants carrying the remains of Pentheus
on a bier.*

CADMUS. Follow me, carrying the lamentable weight of
   Pentheus, follow me, my attendants, in front of the house. I
   sought for his body with endless effort and bring it here. I
   found it torn to pieces in the glens of Cithaeron and picked up 1220
   nothing in the same spot. [It lay in the wood which made it

hard to find.] For I heard from someone of the dreadful deeds
of my daughters when I had already arrived in the city. I had
come inside its walls with the old man Teiresias on my return
from the bacchae. I turned back again to the mountain and
started to recover this boy, whom the maenads killed. And I
saw Autonoe, who bore Actaeon* to Aristaeus long ago, and
Ino together with her, both poor women still stung with
frenzy amid the woods. But someone told me that the third,
Agave, was rushing here in a Bacchic trance, and what I 1230
heard proves to be true, for I see her—a tragic sight.

AGAVE. Father, you can boast the greatest boast—that you of
all mortals have fathered the best daughters by far. I am
talking of all of them, but especially myself. I abandoned the
shuttles by the looms and have risen to greater things—to
hunting wild beasts with my bare hands.* I have won this
prize for excellence and carry it, as you see, in my arms so
that it can be hung up on your house. Take it in your hands, 1240
father, and in your exultation at my hunting, call your
friends to a feast. For you are blessed, truly blessed, since we
have performed such exploits.

CADMUS. [O sorrow that knows no measure, from which the
eyes flinch, o deed of murder, the exploit of your unhappy
hands!] A fine sacrificial offering to the gods have you struck
down, and now you invite this city of Thebes and myself to
a feast. I cry alas for your woes, then for mine. For the god 1250
lord Bromius has destroyed us justly but all too well—and
he is of our family.

AGAVE. How curmudgeonly old men are, how their eyes
scowl. If only my boy could prove a lucky hunter, like his
mother in her ways, whenever he goes after the wild beasts
with the young men of Thebes. But he is only good for fighting against the gods. You must warn him about this, father.
Would someone call him here to my sight so that he can see
me, Agave the blessed.

CADMUS. Alas, alas. If you all realize what you have done, you
will suffer terrible grief. But if you stay for ever in this state 1260
you are in now, you may not be fortunate but you will
escape misfortune in your illusion.

AGAVE. What is wrong with what has happened, what cause
of grief is there?*

CADMUS (*pointing*). First turn your eyes to the sky here.

AGAVE (*looking at the sky*). There. Why did you suggest that I should look at this?

CADMUS. Is it still the same, or do you think that it is changing?

AGAVE. It seems brighter than before and more translucent.

CADMUS. And is this fluttering sensation still present in your head?

AGAVE. I don't understand what you mean. But somehow I am coming back to myself. Something has changed in my mind. 1270

CADMUS. Will you listen and answer clearly?

AGAVE. Yes, since I have forgotten what we said before, father.

CADMUS. What house did you go to when you married?

AGAVE. You gave me to Echion, the Sown Man as they call him.

CADMUS. So who was the son you bore to your husband in his house?

AGAVE. Pentheus, the fruit of his father's and my love.

CADMUS. Well then, whose face are you holding in your arms?*

AGAVE. A lion's—or so the huntswomen assured me.

CADMUS. Look properly then. It is only a moment's effort.

AGAVE (*with a gasp*). What is this I see? What is this that I am carrying in my hands? 1280

CADMUS. Look at it closely and you will reach a clearer understanding.

AGAVE. I see a sight that brings me infinite pain and misery.

CADMUS. It doesn't seem to you to be like a lion, does it?

AGAVE. No, but—o misery—I am holding the head of Pentheus.

CADMUS. I mourned him before you recognized him.

AGAVE. Who killed him? How did he come into my hands?

CADMUS. O agonizing truth, how untimely your discovery!

AGAVE. Tell me—for my heart leaps with fear of what is to come.

CADMUS. You killed him together with your sisters.

AGAVE. Where did he die? Was it at home, or in what place? 1290

CADMUS. It was just where the dogs once tore Actaeon to shreds.

AGAVE. Why did this unhappy man go to Cithaeron?

CADMUS. He went there to insult the god and your bacchae.

AGAVE. And how did we rush off there?

CADMUS. You were mad, and the whole city had been driven into a bacchic frenzy.

AGAVE. It is Dionysus who has destroyed us—now I realize this.

CADMUS. His divinity had been outraged. You did not believe that he was a god.

AGAVE. And where is my son's beloved body, father?

CADMUS. I tracked it down with difficulty and bring it here.

AGAVE. Is every limb laid decently by limb?* 1300

   .   .   .   .

AGAVE. What part of my madness fell upon Pentheus?

CADMUS. He proved himself like you in showing the god no reverence. And therefore Dionysus joined you all together in one ruin, you and this son of yours, and so he has destroyed the house and me, for I, who fathered no male children myself, now see this young shoot of your womb, you poor woman, so foully, so shamefully slaughtered.

It was through you, my child, that the house recovered its sight, it was you who held my halls together, you, my daughter's son. You struck terror into the city. And no one, when 1310 he looked on you, wanted to insult old Cadmus, for you would give due punishment.* But now I shall be a dishonoured exile from this house,* I Cadmus the Great, who sowed the Thebans' race and reaped that most noble of harvests. O dearest of men—for though you no longer exist, you will still be numbered among the dearest to me, my child—no longer will you touch this chin of mine and embrace me, calling me your mother's father, and saying, 'Who does you wrong, who dishonours you, old man? Who troubles your heart and 1320 brings you distress? Tell me so that I can punish the man who wrongs you, my father.' But now I am wretched and you are miserable and your mother is pitiable, your family miserable. If there is any man who scorns the deities, let him look on this man's death and believe in the gods!

CHORUS. I grieve for you, Cadmus. But your son has met a punishment which he deserved, however painful it is for you.

AGAVE. O father, you see how much my fortunes have changed . . .*

DIONYSUS appears above the house.

DIONYSUS. You will be transformed into a snake, and your 1330
wife Harmonia, the daughter of Ares* whom you, a mortal,
took in marriage, will change her form to that of a savage
serpent. And, as the oracle of Zeus says, you will drive an
ox-drawn cart with your wife at the head of barbarians and
you will destroy many cities with your numberless army.
But when they ransack the oracle of Loxias,* they will meet
with a miserable return home. But, as for you and
Harmonia, Ares will save you and settle you yet living in the
land of the blessed. I Dionysus tell you this, the son of no 1340
mortal father but of Zeus. If you had known how to be wise
when you were unwilling,* you would now have the son of
Zeus as your ally and be happy.
CADMUS. Dionysus, we beseech you, we have wronged you.*
DIONYSUS. You have understood me too late. You did not
know me when you should have.
CADMUS. We realize that. But you have come down on us
with too heavy a punishment.
DIONYSUS. Yes, for I, a god, was treated with outrage by
you.
CADMUS. It is not fitting that gods should be like mortals in
their rage.
DIONYSUS. My father Zeus long ago assented to these things.
AGAVE. Alas, it is settled, old man—a miserable exile.   1350
DIONYSUS. Then why do you delay to perform what necessity
decrees?   *DIONYSUS disappears.*

CADMUS. O my daughter, we have all come to disaster—how
terrible the disaster!—you, wretched Agave, and your sisters, and my wretched self. I shall arrive among foreigners,
an ancient alien, and besides there is the oracle which tells
me that I must lead an army of mixed barbarians to Greece.
And I shall take Harmonia, my wife, the daughter of Ares,
when she has assumed her wild snake's form, to the altars
and graves of the Greeks as I lead my spearmen, a snake 1360
myself. I, Cadmus, poor wretch, shall not sail the downward-plunging river Acheron and find peace.*
AGAVE. My father, I shall lose you and go into exile.
CADMUS. Why do you fling your arms round me, my wretched

child, as a young swan shelters the old one, hoary and helpless?

AGAVE. I must. Where can I turn to in my exile from my
fatherland?

CADMUS. I do not know, my child. Your father is little help.

The rest of the play is chanted.

AGAVE. Farewell, our palace, farewell, city of my fathers,
  I leave you for misery,
  a fugitive from my bridal chamber.   1370

CADMUS. Go then, child, . . . Aristaeus' son . . .

AGAVE. I grieve for you, father. CADMUS. And I grieve for
    you, my child,
  and I shed tears for your sisters.

AGAVE. Yes, for terribly has Lord Dionysus
  visited this brutality
  upon your house.

CADMUS. Yes, for he suffered terrible things from us,
  since his name found no honour in Thebes.

AGAVE. Farewell, my father. CADMUS. Farewell, wretched
    daughter.
  But to find fair fortune would be a hard journey indeed.   1380

AGAVE. Take me, friends, where I can find my sisters,
  my miserable fellows in exile.
  May I go
  where accursed Cithaeron cannot see me
  nor can I see Cithaeron with these eyes,
  where no dedicated thyrsus can bring me memories.
  All that must be the concern of other bacchae.

          CADMUS and AGAVE go out in different directions.

CHORUS. The divine will manifests itself in many forms,
  and the gods bring many things to pass against our expec-
    tation.
  What we thought would happen remains unfulfilled,   1390
  while the god has found a way to accomplish the unex-
    pected.
  And that is what has happened here.*

                  The CHORUS goes out.

IPHIGENIA AT AULIS

Characters

AGAMEMNON, King of Argos and commander of the Greek army
OLD MAN, the slave of Agamemnon and his wife Clytemnestra
MENELAUS, king of Sparta and brother of Agamemnon
CLYTEMNESTRA, wife of Agamemnon
IPHIGENIA, daughter of Agamemnon and Clytemnestra
ACHILLES, a Greek hero, leader of the Myrmidons
MESSENGER from the retinue of Clytemnestra
MESSENGER from the Greek army

CHORUS of women of Chalcis in Euboea

The action is set before Agamemnon's tent at Aulis. [Enter
AGAMEMNON *holding wooden writing tablets, and the* OLD MAN.*
Both characters chant their lines until 48.

AGAMEMNON. Old man, come here*
  in front of the tent.
OLD MAN. I am coming. What new plan do you have in
    mind,
  King Agamemnon? AGAMEMNON. Hurry! OLD MAN. I'm
    hurrying.
  My old age is very wakeful
  and my eyes remain keen-sighted.
AGAMEMNON. Whatever can this star be that passes
  with blazing light, darting still in mid-heaven
  near the Pleiades on their seven paths?*
  There is not a sound from the birds
  or the sea. The winds are hushed   10
  and silence holds the strait of Euripus.*
OLD MAN. Why are you darting about outside your tent,*
  King Agamemnon?
  Still there is silence over Aulis here,
  and the guards on the walls do not stir.
  Let us go inside. AGAMEMNON. I envy you, old man,
  I envy any man who has passed through life

free from danger, in obscurity, with no glory.
Those in high renown, I envy less.*
OLD MAN. And yet it is they who have success in life.   20
AGAMEMNON. But that success is an unsteady thing,
    and while high rank has its sweetness,
    it brings pain to the man who achieves it.
    Now the will of the gods swerves against him
    and overturns his life, now it is men
    whose manifold, perverse counsels
    shatter him.
OLD MAN. I do not admire this in a man who leads us.
    It was not so that you could find success everywhere,
    Agamemnon, that Atreus begat you. You must meet with   30
    both joy and sorrow, for you are only mortal.
    Even if you do not like it,
    what the gods will, will be. But you fail to understand this.
        No,
    you have lit a lamp* and are writing on this tablet
    which you still hold in your hands,
    and you constantly erase what you have written,
    seal the pine tablets* up and break them open again,
    and fling them on the ground
    shedding a big rich tear* down your cheeks,
    and in your helplessness   40
    you lack no symptom of madness.
    What troubles you? What new sorrow oppresses you, my
        king?
    Come, talk it over with me.
    You will be speaking to a good and trustworthy fellow.
    For Tyndareus sent me, a loyal man, to your wife,
    as part of her bridal dowry long ago.*
AGAMEMNON. Leda,* the child of Thestios, had three daugh-
    ters, Phoebe and Clytemnestra, my wife, and Helen. To woo 50
    Helen there came the young men who were most blest by for-
    tune among the Greeks. Terrible threats and jealousy arose
    between them at the prospect of failing to win the maiden,
    and her father Tyndareus was in a quandary over this.
    Should he give her or not? How could he best achieve a for-
    tunate outcome? And the idea came to him that the suitors
    should join in an oath, should clasp each other's right hand,

burn sacrifices and pour libations, and swear to this—that   60
whichever of them should have the daughter of Tyndareus
as his wife, they should all join to help him if anyone took
her from her home and ran off with her, ousting her husband
from his marriage; and they should go on an expedition and
by force of arms overthrow Greek or barbarian city alike. And
when they had pledged themselves—it was a neat scheme
with which the crafty invention of old Tyndareus caught
them—he allowed his daughter to choose whichever of the
suitors the sweet winds of love* should waft her to. And she
chose—O that he had never taken her!—Menelaus. And to   70
Sparta there came from the Trojans this man who had
judged the goddesses*—as men tell the tale—dazzling in the
finery of his robes, aglitter with gold, with all the luxury of
the east.* He fell in love with Helen and she with him, and,
finding Menelaus away from home, he snatched her off and
went to his ox stalls on Mount Ida. So Menelaus rushed the
length and breadth of Greece in a frenzy, reminding everybody of the old oath they had sworn to Tyndareus—that they
must help the husband if he was wronged.

After that the Greeks darted forth to fight. They took their   80
armour and came, with a force of ships and shields too, and
many horses and chariots, to Aulis here, built by its narrow
strait. And then they chose me to be general, out of respect
for Menelaus since I am his brother. If only someone else had
won this honour and not me! When the expedition had been
gathered together and was all assembled, we sat at Aulis
idle, unable to sail. And Calchas the seer* announced the
divine will to us in our helplessness. I had to sacrifice my
daughter Iphigenia, the flesh of my flesh, to Artemis who   90
dwells in this place.* And we could sail to Troy and sack the
city if I performed this sacrifice, but if I did not sacrifice her,
it was not to be. When I heard this, I ordered Talthybius* to
make a loud announcement that all the army should dis-
perse—for I could never bring myself to kill my daughter. At
that, my brother brought all kinds of argument to bear and
persuaded me to go through with a terrible deed. So I wrote
on folding tablets which I dispatched to my wife, telling her
to send my daughter here so that she can marry Achilles. I   100
wrote with pride of the man's high worth and said that he

was not willing to sail with the Achaeans unless a bride from
my family went to Phthia.* For I had this means of persuasion to use on my wife—to weave my lies about marriage
for the girl. We are the only ones of the Achaeans who know
the situation, Calchas, Odysseus, Menelaus, and myself.

My decision then was dishonourable, and now I am
repairing that dishonour by writing a countermand on this
tablet which you have seen me tying and untying in the   110
dark, old man. But come now, take this letter and off with
you to Argos.* But I shall read to you all that is written and
lies concealed in these folded tablets. For you are faithful to
my wife and my home.

The characters sing until 301.

OLD MAN. Speak and make it plain, so that what my tongue
    says
may be in harmony with what you have written.
AGAMEMNON (*reading his letter*).
    I send you this tablet, o daughter of Leda,
    in addition to the former one,
    to tell you not to send your child
    to sheltered Aulis,*
    the bay enfolded by the wing of Euboea's promontory.   120
    We shall feast our daughter's wedding
    and sing her wedding song at another time.
OLD MAN. And what of Achilles? If he is robbed of this
    marriage,
    will he not feel great indignation and resentment
    against you and your wife? This is a real danger.
    Explain what you are writing.
AGAMEMNON. Achilles has lent his name, nothing more
    substantial.
    He does not know about the marriage or what we are up
    to—
    or that I am bespoken
    to give my daughter to him   130
    to embrace as a bride
    in the marriage bed.
OLD MAN. You have acted with terrible boldness, King
    Agamemnon,

in promising your daughter as wife to the son of the
    goddess,
when you meant to bring her here to be slaughtered for
    the Greeks.
AGAMEMNON. O misery! I was out of my mind.
    Alas! I am falling into mad ruin.
    Be off with you, move fast,
    go with a young man's speed.   OLD MAN. As fast as I   140
    can, my king.
AGAMEMNON. Do not sit by woodland springs,
    or fall beneath the spell of sleep.
OLD MAN   *indignantly*). Quiet! Say no more.
AGAMEMNON. As you pass any place where roads diverge,
    always keep your eyes open in case you fail to spot
    a carriage passing you with its rolling wheels,
    bringing my daughter here
    to the ships of the Greeks.
OLD MAN. I shall.   AGAMEMNON. †If she has left her
    chamber door
    and you meet her with her escort,   150
    turn round the horses' bridles,†
    and hurry her back to the Cyclops' palace.*
OLD MAN. But if I say this, how shall I win belief
    with your daughter and your wife?
AGAMEMNON. Keep safe the seal which you carry
    on these tablets. Go! The glimmering dawn
    and the fiery four-horsed chariot of the Sun
    now bring a gleam of whiteness to the sky here.*
    Shoulder your share of my troubles. No mortal   160
    is prosperous or happy till the end.
    No one on earth has yet been free from sorrow.
                    AGAMEMNON *and the* OLD MAN *go out.*]

    The CHORUS *of women from Chalcis in Euboea enter.**

CHORUS (*sings*). I came along the sandy shore
    of Aulis on the sea,
    where I put into port across the waters
    of Euripus' narrow strait,
    leaving my city of Chalcis,
    nurse of the sea-neighbouring waters

of famous Arethusa.*   170
My purpose was to view the army of the Achaeans
and the sea-faring oars
of the Achaean demi-gods whom, as our husbands say,
red-haired Menelaus*
and nobly-born Agamemnon
are leading with a fleet of a thousand ships
to Troy
in quest of Helen,
whom Paris the oxherd took   180
from Eurotas,* reedy river,
the gift of Aphrodite
when the Cyprian goddess* joined in strife
by the dewy waters of a spring—*
strife with Hera and Pallas over their beauty.

I came in haste through the sacred grove of Artemis,
scene of so many sacrifices,
my cheeks turning red
with the fresh bashfulness of a young woman,
eager to see the strong guard of the shield-bearing Greeks,
their armed encampment   190
and their numberless horses.
And I saw the two Ajaxes sitting together,
the son of Oileus and the son of Telamon,
the glory of Salamis,*
and Protesilaus* and Palamedes,
whom the son of Poseidon begot,
as they sat taking delight
in the ever-shifting patterns of the draughts board,*
and Diomedes enjoying
the pleasures of discus-throwing,   200
and beside him Meriones,
Ares' son, a wonder to men,
and the son of Laertes from his mountainous island,*
and together with him Nireus,
handsomest of all the Achaeans.

And I saw, his feet as fleet as the wind,
light-running Achilles
whom Thetis gave birth to

and Chiron trained to perfection,*
saw him racing in his armour   210
over beach, over shingle,
swift of foot
as he raced hard against a four-horsed chariot,
rounding the course for victory's sake.
And the charioteer was shouting,
Eumelus, Pheres' grandson—
I saw his horses, so beautiful,
their bits gold-chased,
as he struck them with his goad—   220
the middle ones who carried the yoke
dappled with flecks of white on their manes,
the trace-horses outside them
sweeping close round the turnings of the race-track,*
bays with spotted fetlocks. The son of Peleus
went bounding along by these in his armour,
beside the chariot's rail
and its wheels.   230

[And I went on to count up their ships,
to see something wondrous,*
so that I could glut my woman's eyes
with a sight that brought me pleasure honey-sweet.
Holding the right wing
of the fleet
was the warlike force of Myrmidons from Phthia
with fifty fierce ships.
High on their sterns the Nereid goddesses* stood
in golden images,   240
emblems on the ships of Achilles' armament.

Nearby were the ships of the Argives,
equal in number to these,
their commanders Mecisteus' son
whom his grandfather Talaus brought up,*
and Sthenelus, son of Capaneus.
Next there lay at anchor the son of Theseus*
who had led sixty ships from Attica,
his emblem the goddess Pallas Athena
placed in a winged chariot   250

drawn by horses with uncloven hoofs,
a blazon signalling good fortune to sea-faring men.

And I saw the Boeotians' sea armament—
fifty ships
decorated with emblems.
For them it was Cadmus
grappling with a golden dragon
on their ships' curving stern.
The earth-born Leitus*
led the fleet.   260
And from the land of Phocis* ⟨there were ships⟩
and there too was the son of Oileus leading vessels of
    Locris
equal to these in number.
He had come from the famous city of Thronium.

And from Cyclops-built Mycenae
the son of Atreus* led
the mustered crews of a hundred ships.
With him was his brother to share the command,
as kin supporting kin,
so that Greece could take revenge   270
on the woman who fled from her home
for marriage to a barbarian.
From Pylos I saw the ships
of Gerenian* Nestor,
their blazon a picture of the river Alpheus, their neigh-
    bour,
footed like a bull.*

From the Aenians was a muster of twelve ships
which King Gouneus commanded.
Then, near these
were the lords of Elis   280
with men whom the whole army called Epeians.
Eurytus was their leader.
He led the warlike force of the Taphians
with their white oars,
though Meges, child of Phyleus, was their king.
He had left the Echinades islands,
inhospitable to sea-faring men.*

And Ajax, nursling of Salamis,
†united his right wing
to the force of those on his left   290
—he was moored nearby them—† linking them with his
    ships
which were stationed at the end of the line,
his twelve supremely manoeuvrable vessels.*
As I had heard of it, so did I observe
this sea-faring host.
If anyone sets his barbarian boats
against this,
he shall not return home—
such an armada
have I seen here,   300
and I heard some things at home
about the summoned host, which I keep in my mind.*]

MENELAUS enters, holding the writing tablets, with the OLD MAN,
    who is trying to snatch them back from him.

OLD MAN. Menelaus*, this is an outrage. You must not do this.
MENELAUS. Stand back! You are all too faithful to your master.
OLD MAN. What you reproach me with brings me honour!
MENELAUS. You'll be sorry if you do what you ought not to do.
OLD MAN. You shouldn't have broken open the writing tablets
    which I was carrying.
MENELAUS. And you shouldn't have been carrying what will
    bring disaster on all the Greeks.
OLD MAN. Quarrel about this with someone else.* Let me have
    the letter.
MENELAUS. I won't let go. OLD MAN. Neither will I.   310
MENELAUS. Then I'll soon give you a bloody head with my staff.
OLD MAN. Well, it is a noble thing to die for one's master.
MENELAUS. Let go. For a slave, you are talking far too much.

MENELAUS still has the letter. AGAMEMNON *enters.*

OLD MAN. My master, we are being wronged. This man has
    used force on me, Agamemnon, and snatched your letter
    from my hand. He flatly refuses to deal justly with us.
AGAMEMNON. What's going on?* What is this noisy quarrel
    outside my tent?

MENELAUS. My words have a better right to be spoken than his.
AGAMEMNON. Why have you got into a quarrel with this man, Menelaus? Why are you pulling him about so violently?

The OLD MAN *goes out.*

MENELAUS. Look me in the face so that I can get started on the story without any evasions.   320
AGAMEMNON. Do you think that Agamemnon, son of Atreus, is going to tremble and not look you in the eye?*
MENELAUS. Do you see this tablet, which carries a disastrous message?
AGAMEMNON. I see it. First of all hand it over.
MENELAUS. Not before I show what is written there to all the Greeks.
AGAMEMNON. Have you really opened the seal? Do you know what you have no right to know?
MENELAUS. Yes, I opened it, and you'll be sorry that I did—I have brought your underhand mischief to the light.
AGAMEMNON. Just where did you catch him? By the gods, what an impudent spirit you have!
MENELAUS. I caught him as I waited to see whether your child would come to the army from Argos.
AGAMEMNON. Why must you keep watch on my affairs? Doesn't this brand you an impudent scoundrel?
MENELAUS. Because the wish to do so provoked me to it. I am   330
not your slave.
AGAMEMNON. Is not this outrageous? Will you not let me manage my own affairs?
MENELAUS. No, for your thoughts are crooked, shifting with every moment.*
AGAMEMNON. What a fine gloss you have put on your base deed!* A clever tongue is a hateful thing.
MENELAUS. Yes, but a mind devoid of steadfastness makes a man unjust and untrustworthy to his friends. I want to put you to the question. You must not turn from the truth in a passion, and I for my part shall not press things too far.
    You know, when you were eager to be the commander of the Greeks against Troy—to all appearances reluctant, yet willing enough in your heart—you know how humble you were, clasping every hand, keeping open house for any   340

citizen who wanted to visit you and allowing everyone, high
or low, to talk to you even if they did not expect it. In behaving like this, you sought to buy popularity against all com-
ers. And then, when you had your power, you sang a
different tune.You were no longer as friendly as before to
your one-time friends. It was hard to get access to you since
you stayed behind barred doors and were rarely to be seen.*
Do you remember? A good man should not change his ways
when he achieves greatness. Rather, it is then most of all
that he should prove steadfast to his friends, at the time
when his success enables him to help them most. This is the
first point for which I criticize you, the first where I have
found you at fault.

Then again, when you and the united army of the Greeks   350
came to Aulis, you proved a man of straw. You were panic-
stricken by the fortune the gods sent us when no favourable
wind would blow us Troywards. The Greeks spread the word
that you should disband the ships—no pointless suffering at
Aulis for them. How helpless you looked, how confused at
the thought that, though you ruled a thousand ships, you
would not fill the plain of Troy with your spearmen. So you
called for me. 'What am I to do?' you said. 'What solution
can I find? or where?'—so that you didn't lose your command and forfeit glorious honour. And then when Calchas
amid the holy offerings bade you sacrifice your daughter to
Artemis and said that if you did, the Greeks could sail, your
heart rejoiced. You gladly promised to sacrifice your child.   360
And you willingly wrote to your wife—nobody forced you,
don't say that they did—telling her to send your child here
on the pretext of marriage with Achilles.* And now you
have been caught sending a different message, since you are
no longer willing to be the killer of your daughter. Have you
shifted yet again? Most certainly you have. This is the same
sky above us as heard your former words.

Countless men have shared your experience. They have
problems and toil away at them, but then come out of it
badly, some through the citizens' foolish misjudgement, but
some deservedly since it lies in them that they cannot keep
their city safe. Unhappy Greece,* it is for her above all that   370
I myself lament, for she wishes to do something good, yet

will let the barbarians escape—those nobodies who laugh at
her—because of you and your daughter. I hope I shall never
make anyone ruler of a country or commander of an army
because of his manliness. A city's general must have intelligence. Every man is up to that position if he possesses understanding.

CHORUS. It is a terrible thing when brothers join in conflict
and fling violent criticism at each other.

AGAMEMNON. I wish to say in my turn where I find fault with
you, but I shall be brief and avoid assuming too scornful and
superior an expression. No, I shall speak more moderately
since it is my brother that I am talking to. After all, a good   380
man is accustomed to show respect to others. Tell me, why
are you snorting with rage, your face flushed in anger? Who
is wronging you? What do you want? Do you desire to win
a good wife? I could not provide you with one. You certainly
proved a bad master of the one you did have. Then am I, a
man with no grievance, to pay the penalty for your misfortunes? It is not my advancement to high office that needles
you. No, you want to hold a beautiful woman in your arms,
casting discretion and honour to the winds. The desires of a
base man are evil. But if I made the wrong decision before
and have now thought better of it, am I out of my mind?
No, it is rather you who are mad. You lost a bad wife and
want to take her back, though the god gave you good for-   390
tune when she went. The suitors were misguided when in
their eagerness to win the bride, they swore Tyndareus'
oath. It was hope, a goddess as I think, who made it happen
rather than you and your strength. Take them and go on
your expedition. In their hearts' folly they are ready. The
gods are not devoid of wisdom. No, they are able to recognize oaths which were sworn without validity because they
were made under compulsion. I will not kill my child. And
your fortunes will not prosper, in defiance of what is just, by
your vengeance on a worthless bedfellow, while nights and
days waste me away in tears, the perpetrator of a lawless
and unjust deed against the daughter of my flesh.

  That is what I have to say to you. It is brief, clear, and   400
easy enough. If you do not wish to be sensible, I shall put
my own affairs in good order.

CHORUS. What you have just spoken is different from what you said before.* But it is good to hear you talk of sparing your child.*

[MENELAUS. Alas! I can see then in my misery that I have no friends.

AGAMEMNON. Ah, but you have, if you do not seek your friends' ruin.

MENELAUS. How can you show that you were born from the same father as myself?

AGAMEMNON. I want to share with you in wisdom, not in folly.

MENELAUS. Friends should join in their friends' distress.

AGAMEMNON. Ask for my help by treating me well, not by causing me sorrow.

MENELAUS. Do you not think it right to share in the efforts of Greece?*   410

AGAMEMNON. Some god has brought this sickness on Greece and on you.

MENELAUS. Take pride in your sceptre then, and betray your brother. But I shall go to other friends and other plans.

Enter MESSENGER.

MESSENGER. O king of all the Greeks,* Agamemnon, I have come bringing you your child whom you named Iphigenia in your palace. Her mother is accompanying her, your Clytemnestra in person, as well as your son Orestes, so that you can take pleasure in seeing him after your long absence from home. But since they have travelled far, they are cool-   420
ing and refreshing their feet by a fair-flowing spring, women and fillies alike.* We turned the horses loose in the mead-ows' grass so that they could feed themselves. As for myself, I have come here before them to prepare you. For the army has discovered—after all, news spreads quickly—that your daughter has arrived. The whole host is running to see the sight. They want to look at your child. Yes, those of blessed estate are regarded by all as famous, the observed of all observers. The soldiers are saying: 'Does this mean a mar-   430
riage? Or what is going on? Is it because he misses her that the king has sent for his young daughter?' And you might have heard this too: 'They are consecrating the young girl to Artemis,* the ruler of Aulis, in preparation for her wed-

ding. Who is the bridegroom?' Come then, bring the baskets,* start the sacrificial rite and garland your heads. And
you, King Menelaus, rehearse the wedding song! Let the
pipe sound forth in the tents! Let the earth thud with
the noise of stamping feet. For this day has dawned with the
promise of happiness for the maiden.]

AGAMEMNON. Good. But go inside the tent. As fortune takes   440
its course, the rest will turn out well.

Exit MESSENGER.

AGAMEMNON. Alas! What can I say in my misery? Where can
I begin? Under what yoke of necessity have I fallen? A god
has outwitted me and proved far cleverer than all my clever
plans. Men of low birth have some advantages. They can
weep without restraint and speak freely. But for the man of
noble birth there is no relief from unhappiness.* We have
solemnity to rule our lives and are slaves to the common   450
people. I am ashamed to pour forth tears, but then I am
ashamed, poor wretch that I am, to hold them in, now that
I have plumbed these terrible depths of disaster.

 Well then, what shall I say to my wife?* How shall I
receive her? What expression shall I assume when I meet
her? I had troubles enough already but by coming here
when I did not ask her to, she has dealt me the final blow.
Yet it was perfectly reasonable that she could accompany
her own dear daughter to give her in marriage—and at that
marriage she will find that I am a criminal. As for the
wretched virgin—why do I call her virgin? Hades, it seems,   460
will soon marry her*—Oh how I pity her! I think I hear her
supplicating me: 'O father, will you kill me? May you make
such a marriage, may anyone you love!' Orestes will be
there nearby. He cannot talk yet but he will scream out inar-
ticulate, though only too comprehensible cries. Alas, it was
Priam's son, Paris, who brought me to this when he made
his marriage with Helen—and destroyed me!

CHORUS. I feel pity too—as far as a foreign woman may grieve
for the sorrows of kings.   470

MENELAUS. My brother, take your hand in mine.

AGAMEMNON. Here is my hand. For yours is the victory, mine
the misery.

MENELAUS. I swear by Pelops,* whom they call the father of
my father and yours, and by Atreus who begat us, that I
shall open my heart to you, speaking frankly, with no ulte-
rior motive but simply saying what I think. When I saw
tears falling from your eyes, I pitied you, I myself shed tears
for you in my turn,* and I withdraw the words I spoke
before. I am not your enemy. No, I am putting myself in   480
your position. And I advise you not to kill your child and not
to prefer my interests to yours. For it is not right that you
should sorrow while all goes well for me and that your child
should die while my family looks on the light of day.

What do I want then? Could I not make another marriage, an excellent one, if you will say that it is marriage I
desire? Am I to win Helen* by losing a brother—the last person I should lose—, exchanging good for evil? I was mad
and headstrong until I examined your situation closely and
saw what it means to kill one's child. And besides that, pity   490
for the wretched girl swept over me as I thought about our
kinship, for the girl who is about to be sacrificed for the sake
of my marriage. What has your daughter to do with Helen?
Disband the expedition! Let it go from Aulis! Wet your eyes
with tears no longer, brother. No longer make me weep with
you. Whatever concern you may have in the oracles about
your daughter, let them be no concern of mine. My interest
in this business I make over to you.

But you will say that I am a different man from the one   500
who spoke so violently. That is perfectly natural. I have
changed out of love for my brother, the son of the same parents. To act in the best way as occasion arises—that is how
an honourable man behaves.

CHORUS. You have spoken noble words, worthy of Tantalus,*
the son of Zeus. You bring no shame on your ancestors.

AGAMEMNON. I thank you, Menelaus, because against my
expectation you have suggested an honourable course of
action in a manner which reflects your worth. Strife between
brothers* arises through love of a woman or ambition to take
over the house. I detest the type of brothers' bond which   510
leads to bitterness for both of them. However, we have come
to a point where necessity dictates our fortunes. We must
carry out the bloody murder of my daughter.

MENELAUS. What is this?* Who will force you to kill your own child?

AGAMEMNON. The whole assembled host of the Achaeans.

MENELAUS. Not if you send Iphigenia back to Argos.

AGAMEMNON. I could do that secretly, but there is something that we cannot keep secret.

MENELAUS. What is that? You must not fear the people too much.

AGAMEMNON. Calchas will tell the prophecy to the Argive army.

MENELAUS. Not if he dies first.* This presents no problems.

AGAMEMNON. The whole breed of seers is an abomination— 520 always on the make.

MENELAUS. †Yes, hateful and useless—while alive.†*

AGAMEMNON. But are you not afraid of something else that comes to my mind?

MENELAUS. How can I understand what you're talking about if you won't tell me?

AGAMEMNON. The vile son of Sisyphus* knows all of this.

MENELAUS. Odysseus cannot do you or me any injury.

AGAMEMNON. He is always sly and sides with the mob.

MENELAUS. It is ambition, a terrible evil, that possesses him.

AGAMEMNON. Don't you think that he will stand in the midst of the Argives and speak out the oracles which Calchas revealed, saying how I promised to make the sacrifice to 530 Artemis and then lied about it? Will he not then carry the whole army with him and tell the Argives to kill you and me and next slaughter the girl? And if I escape to Argos, they will come there, destroy the city and raze it to the ground, Cyclopean walls and all. Such thoughts torment me. Wretched Agamemnon, to what helplessness have the gods reduced you now today?

Please take care of one thing for me, Menelaus, when you go among the army—see that Clytemnestra does not learn 540 of this before I take my daughter and hand her down to Hades, so that I may endure my torment with the fewest tears. And you, keep silent, you foreign women.

AGAMEMNON and MENELAUS go out.

CHORUS (*sings*). Happy are they*
who share in the joys of marriage

with a temperate spirit
when Aphrodite proves moderate—
enjoying a calm free from the stings
of mad desire, for when desire is there,
golden-haired Eros bends his bow
with two arrows of his delights,
one bringing a fortunate fate,   550
the other leading life into confusion.
That one I banish,
o most beautiful Cypris,*
from our bedrooms,
Rather may my pleasures be moderate,
my desires pure,
and may I have my part in Aphrodite
but abjure her when she comes in full force.*

Mortals have different natures,
different habits. But what is truly noble
is always clear.   560
Education and upbringing
make a great contribution to virtue.
And a sense of shame is itself wisdom
†and has the surpassing grace
of discerning the path of duty
through reason.† Then reputation brings
ageless glory to human life.
It is a great thing to hunt after virtue,
for women in a chaste love at home;
among men in their turn   570
†self-discipline in its countless forms†
raises their city to greatness.

You came, o Paris, to the place where you were reared
an oxherd among white heifers
on Mount Ida
playing your barbarian tunes
and, as you breathed on the reeds,
imitating the Phrygian pipe of Olympus,*
your full-uddered cows were feeding
while the judgement of the goddesses awaited you—   580
the judgement which sent you to Greece.

You stood before the throne of Helen
with its inlay of ivory,
and as you gazed at each other
you gave her your gift of love and with love
you were yourself transported.
And for that you are bringing strife, yes, strife—
Greece with her spears and ships,
upon Troy's citadel.

CLYTEMNESTRA, *holding the baby Orestes, and* IPHIGENIA *enter on a carriage. They are accompanied by attendants.*

[CHORUS (*chants*). Ah! Ah! Great is the happiness   590
of the great.* See Iphigenia,
the daughter of the king, my princess,
and Clytemnestra, Tyndareus' daughter.
From what high ancestry were they born!
To what imposing destinies have they come!
In the eyes of less fortunate mortals
the powerful and the wealthy are gods.

Let us stand close, young women from Calchis,
let us support the queen as she leaves her chariot
in case she stumbles as she steps to the ground,   600
let us give gentle hands in soft courtesy
so that the famous child of Agamemnon
may not be frightened the moment she arrives,
and let us not trouble or alarm
these foreigners from Argos—
we are foreigners too.

CLYTEMNESTRA. I take this as a favourable omen, your kind-
ness and your auspicious words. I have some hopes of happiness for the marriage to which I have come as escort to 610
the bride. (*To her attendants*) Come, unload from the carriage the wedding gifts I am bringing for the girl and take
them carefully inside. And you, my child, leave the horse-
drawn carriage and place your weak, delicate, and dainty
feet* on the ground. And you young women, take her on
your arms and help her down from the carriage. Will someone give a supporting hand to me as well so that I can
leave my seat in this vehicle with decorum? And you girls,

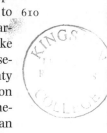

stand at the front of the yoked horses. For a horse looks 620
frightened when no one soothes it. And take this child,
Orestes, Agamemnon's son.* He's still a baby. Are you
sleeping, my child, lulled by the motion of the carriage?
Wake up for the marriage of your sister, and be happy. For
you, nobly-born yourself, will become the kinsman of an
excellent man, the god-like offspring of Nereus' daughter.*
Sit here beside my feet, my child. You, Iphigenia, stand
next to your mother and give these foreign women a picture of my happiness.*

AGAMEMNON *enters.*

Here is your dear father. Speak to him. King Agamem- 630
non, my most revered lord, we have come in obedience to
your commands.]*

IPHIGENIA. Mother, I shall outrun you—do not be angry—
and clasp my father heart to heart. O father, I want to run
to you before the others and clasp my father heart to heart.
It has been so long. I want to look at you. (*To Clytemnestra*)
Don't be angry.*

CLYTEMNESTRA. So you should, my child. Of all the children
I bore to your father, you have always been the one who
loved him best.

IPHIGENIA. My father,* what joy it is to see you after so long 640
a time!

AGAMEMNON. Joy for your father too! You speak for both of
us there.

IPHIGENIA. Greetings. You have done well to bring me here,
father.

AGAMEMNON. Can I say that, my child, or can I not? I do not
know.

IPHIGENIA (*with a start*). But how troubled you look in spite
of your happiness at seeing me.

AGAMEMNON. A king and a commander has many cares.

IPHIGENIA. Give yourself to me now. Put these anxious
thoughts aside.

AGAMEMNON. I am altogether yours. I am thinking of nothing else.

IPHIGENIA. Smooth out this frown then and look on me with
love.

AGAMEMNON. Look! I have all the joy I can have in seeing you, my child.

IPHIGENIA. And even then do tears pour from your eyes?   650

AGAMEMNON. A long separation is in store for us.

IPHIGENIA. I do not know what you mean, dearest of fathers, I do not know. Where do they say that the Phrygians* dwell, father?

AGAMEMNON. In a place . . . ah! if only Priam's son Paris had never dwelt there!

IPHIGENIA. You are voyaging to a distant land, my father, and leaving me.

AGAMEMNON. O my daughter, you will come to the same place as your father.* The more sensibly you speak, the more you make me pity you.

IPHIGENIA. I shall talk nonsense then if that will make you happy.*

AGAMEMNON (*aside*). Alas, I do not have the strength to keep silent. (*to Iphigenia*) You're a good girl.

IPHIGENIA. Stay at home, father, for your children.

AGAMEMNON. That is my wish, but my sorrow is that I cannot wish it.

IPHIGENIA. A curse on wars and Menelaus' wrongs!

AGAMEMNON. What has already brought me ruin will ruin others too.

IPHIGENIA. What a long time you have been away on the   660 gulf of Aulis!

AGAMEMNON. Even now something prevents me from sending the expedition on its way.

IPHIGENIA. Alas! If only it was †proper for us both that I should sail with you!

AGAMEMNON. A voyage yet lies in store for you as well and on it you will forget† your father.*

IPHIGENIA. Shall I sail with my mother or travel alone?

AGAMEMNON. Alone, alone, away from your father and mother.

IPHIGENIA. Can it be that you want me to live in another   670 home, father?

AGAMEMNON. We must let this matter be. It is not right for girls to know such things.

IPHIGENIA. Put all to rights at Troy, my father, and hurry back to me from there.

AGAMEMNON. First I must make a certain sacrifice here.

IPHIGENIA. Well, you must have regard for what is holy with religious rites.

AGAMEMNON. You will discover about this. For you will stand near the holy water.*

IPHIGENIA. Then am I to lead the dances round the altar, father?

AGAMEMNON. I count you happier than myself because you do not understand at all. Go inside the tent—it is not pleasing that girls should be seen in public. But first kiss me and give me your hand, for you are going to dwell far away from 680 your father for all too long.

O these breasts and cheeks, o this blond hair,* what a sorrow has this city of the Phrygians and Helen proved for us! I'll say no more, for a sudden flood of tears overcomes me as I touch you. Go into the tent.   IPHIGENIA *goes inside.*

I beg you to forgive me, daughter of Leda, if I have shown too much sorrow at the prospect of giving my daughter to Achilles. To send away one's child in marriage is a happy event, but nevertheless it tears at the parents' hearts when a father hands over his children to other houses after all his 690 trouble in bringing them up.

CLYTEMNESTRA. I am not so devoid of understanding. You can be sure that I myself will suffer the same pain—so I cannot criticize you—when I lead out my daughter to the sound of the wedding song. But getting used to it will help to dry the tears. As to the name, I know who it is that you have betrothed our child to, but I want to discover about his family and where he was born.

AGAMEMNON. Asopus* was the father of a daughter, Aegina.

CLYTEMNESTRA. Which god or mortal married her?

AGAMEMNON. Zeus. And he begat Aeacus, the king of Oenone.

CLYTEMNESTRA. And who was the son of Aeacus, who inher- 700 ited his house?

AGAMEMNON. Peleus, and Peleus married Nereus' daughter.

CLYTEMNESTRA. Did a god give her to him or did he take her in defiance of the gods?

AGAMEMNON. Zeus, who had the authority to do so, betrothed her to him and gave her away.*

CLYTEMNESTRA. Where did he marry her? Was it beneath the heaving sea?

AGAMEMNON. It was where Chiron* lives on the holy foothills of Olympus.

CLYTEMNESTRA. Where they say that the centaur race dwells?

AGAMEMNON. It was there that the gods feasted Peleus' wedding.

CLYTEMNESTRA. Did Thetis or his father bring up Achilles?*

AGAMEMNON. Chiron did, so that he might not learn the ways of evil men.

CLYTEMNESTRA. Ah. Wise was the teacher, and wise the 710 father who entrusted his son to a wiser influence.

AGAMEMNON. Such is the man who will be your daughter's husband.

CLYTEMNESTRA. I can find no fault with him. Which Greek city does he live in?

AGAMEMNON. By the banks of the river Apidanos in the land of Phthia.

CLYTEMNESTRA. Will he take our daughter there?

AGAMEMNON. That will be the business of the master who has won her.*

CLYTEMNESTRA. May they meet with good fortune. On what day will he marry her?

AGAMEMNON. At the time of the full moon.*

CLYTEMNESTRA. Have you already made the sacrifice to the goddess for our daughter?

AGAMEMNON. I am on the point of doing so. That is the very event that occupies me now.

CLYTEMNESTRA. In that case will you postpone the marriage 720 feast till later?

AGAMEMNON. Yes, when I have made the sacrifice which I must make to the gods.

CLYTEMNESTRA. Where shall we hold the banquet for the women?

AGAMEMNON. Here by the Agives' fair-sterned ships.

CLYTEMNESTRA. Good, if it must be so. I pray for fair fortune even so.

AGAMEMNON. You know what you must do, lady? You must follow my instructions.

CLYTEMNESTRA. In what? I am accustomed to obey you in everything.

AGAMEMNON. I myself here, where the bridegroom is . . .

CLYTEMNESTRA. In the mother's absence, what will you do that should fall to me?

AGAMEMNON. I shall give away your daughter with the Achaeans to assist me.

CLYTEMNESTRA. And where must I be at the time?   730

AGAMEMNON. Go to Argos and take care of your daughters.

CLYTEMNESTRA. And leave my child? Who will hold the marriage torch on high?

AGAMEMNON. I shall supply the ceremonial torch for bride and groom.

CLYTEMNESTRA. This is not the custom, and such things must be treated seriously.

AGAMEMNON. It is not proper for you to be away from home amid the crowd of soldiers.

CLYTEMNESTRA. But it *is* proper for me as the mother to give away my daughter.

AGAMEMNON. Yes, and it is proper that the girls at home should not be on their own.

CLYTEMNESTRA. They are well and securely guarded in the maidens' quarters.

AGAMEMNON. Do what I say.

CLYTEMNESTRA. No, by the sovereign goddess of Argos.* [You go to arrange what needs to be done outside, while I look   740
after everything indoors* and see to what is needed for brides at their wedding.   CLYTEMNESTRA *goes out.*

AGAMEMNON. Alas! My preliminary strike was useless. I wanted to send my wife away from here far from my sight, but my hopes have been baffled. I make clever plans and devise schemes against those I love best—but am defeated everywhere. Still, despite that I shall go to consult with the soothsayer Calchas and make the best I can of what the goddess wishes, which will bring no happiness to me and torment to the Greeks. A wise man must keep a woman who is helpful and good in his house—or avoid marriage alto-   750
gether.   AGAMEMNON *goes out towards the army.*

CHORUS (*sings*). There will indeed come to Simois*
and its silvery swirling waters
the assembled army of the Greeks

aboard its ships and with its arms—
come to Ilium, the plain of Troy,
Phoebus' land,
where I hear that Cassandra, adorned with a garland
of green-leafed laurel,
tosses her golden locks
whenever the god breathes upon her   760
and compels her to prophecy.
The Trojans will stand
on the citadel of Troy and its circle of walls,
when Ares of the bronze shield comes near
over the sea,
as the Greeks row their fine-prowed ships
near to Simois' streams,
wishing to take back from Priam
Helen, sister
of the twin sky-dwelling Dioscuri,   770
back to the land of Greece,
won by the shields and spears of Achaean warriors.

The war-god will circle Pergamum, the Phrygians' city,
around its stone towers
with his spirit of slaughter,
will cut throats and †hack off heads,
will ransack Troy's city†
from top to bottom
and make girls and the wife of Priam
weep many tears.   780
And Helen, the daughter of Zeus,
will weep many tears
for deserting her husband.
May there never come to me or my children's children
such a prospect as the doom
that will befall the Lydian women decked in gold
and the wives of the Phrygians,
as they say these words to one another
at the loom: 790
'What man, †tightening his grasp on my luxuriant locks
   as I weep,†
will pluck me as a flower is plucked,

from my country as it dies?'
It is all because of you, daughter of the long-necked swan,
if the story is really true
that Leda met with a winged bird
when Zeus had altered his form—
or have poets in their inspired writings
introduced this fable to men—
an inept and empty fiction?   800

Enter ACHILLES.

ACHILLES. Where can I find here the commander of the
   Achaeans? Will one of his servants let him know that
   Achilles, the son of Peleus, is in front of his tent looking for
   him? The fact is that we do not wait near Euripus under the
   same circumstances.* For some of us who sit here on the
   shore are not yet married and have left our houses unprotected, while others have wives and children. So passionate
   a longing for this expedition has seized hold on Greece—the
   gods must be playing a part in this. And so it is right that I 810
   should make my own business clear. Anyone else can state
   his case if he wants to. I have left the land of Pharsalus and
   my father Peleus and, as I wait by the Euripus with its faint
   currents, I have to restrain my Myrmidons.* They are for
   ever harassing me, saying, 'Achilles, why are we waiting?
   How much time must we spend here counting the days until
   we sail for Troy? Act, if you are going to act! If not, lead the
   army home and don't wait here because the sons of Atreus
   are delaying.']

Enter CLYTEMNESTRA *from the tent.*

CLYTEMNESTRA. O son of the divine daughter of Nereus, I
   heard you talking from inside and have come out in front of 820
   the tent.
ACHILLES (*recoiling*). O lady Modesty,* what woman is this
   that I see? How beautiful she is!
CLYTEMNESTRA. It is not surprising that you do not know
   who I am since you have not met me before. I approve of
   your respectful modesty.
ACHILLES. But who are you? Why have you come to the army
   gathered here—a woman among men plated in armour?

CLYTEMNESTRA. I am the daughter of Leda, Clytemnestra is my name, and my husband is King Agamemnon.

ACHILLES. You do well to be brief in telling me the main facts. But it is not proper for me to join in conversation with a woman. 830

CLYTEMNESTRA. Stay! Why are you running away? Join your right hand with mine as a prelude to a happy marriage.

ACHILLES. What do you mean? I join my right hand with yours? I should feel shame before Agamemnon if I were to touch what I have no right to touch.

CLYTEMNESTRA. You have every right, for you are marrying my child, o son of the sea-goddess, the daughter of Nereus.

ACHILLES. What is this marriage you are talking about? I am at a loss for words, lady. Perhaps you are a bit crazy and that is why you are talking so strangely.

CLYTEMNESTRA. It is natural for everyone to feel modesty when meeting new friends, especially when they are speak- 840 ing about marriage.

ACHILLES. I never paid court to your daughter, lady, and no talk of marriage ever came to me from Atreus' sons.

CLYTEMNESTRA. What can this mean? You for your part must guess at my meaning. I am amazed at what you say.

ACHILLES. Well may you be amazed. We both have to rely on guesswork here. We were both misled equally by what we were told.

CLYTEMNESTRA. Can I really have been treated so outrageously? I am looking for a marriage which seems to be imaginary. I am deeply ashamed.

ACHILLES. Perhaps someone is making fools of both of us. But 850 don't give it another thought. Don't take it to heart.

CLYTEMNESTRA. Goodbye.* I cannot look at you face to face any more. I have proved to be a liar—and the victim of treatment which I do not deserve.

ACHILLES. I bid you goodbye as well. I am going to look for your husband inside this tent.

The OLD MAN *appears in the entrance to the tent, which he has half-opened.*

OLD MAN. Stranger,* descendant of Aeacus, wait. It's you I'm talking to, you, the son of a goddess, and you, the daughter of Leda.

ACHILLES. Who is this who has half-opened the entrance to the tent and is calling us? How terrified he sounds!

OLD MAN. I'm a slave—I'm not too proud to admit it. What has happened leaves me with no choice.

ACHILLES. Whose slave? Not mine. My slaves and Agamemnon's live apart.

OLD MAN. I am the slave of this lady in front of the tent. Her father Tyndareus gave me to her.   860

ACHILLES. I'll stay. Please tell me why you stopped me.

OLD MAN. Is it really just the two of you standing in front of the tent?

ACHILLES. You will be speaking only to the two of us—so come out of the king's tent.

The OLD MAN comes out onto the stage.

OLD MAN. O fortune, o my foresight, save those I wish to save!

ACHILLES. We shall have to wait to hear what he has to say. He is taking his time.

CLYTEMNESTRA. I guarantee you protection. Do not hold back if you want to say something to me.

OLD MAN. Then do you know who I am and how well-disposed I feel towards you and your children?

CLYTEMNESTRA. I know that you are an old slave of my house.

OLD MAN. And you know that King Agamemnon took me as part of your dowry?

CLYTEMNESTRA. You came to Argos with me and have been   870
mine all this time.

OLD MAN. That is so. And I am well-disposed towards you, less so to your husband.

CLYTEMNESTRA. Now at last reveal to us what you are holding back.

OLD MAN. The father who begat your daughter is about to kill her with his own hand.

CLYTEMNESTRA. What are you saying? I refuse to believe this, old man. You are out of your mind.

OLD MAN. With his sword he will stain the wretched girl's white neck with blood.

CLYTEMNESTRA. What outrageous cruelty to me! Has my husband gone mad?

OLD MAN. He is sane except where you and your child are concerned. There he has lost all sense.

CLYTEMNESTRA. But for what reason? What avenging demon drives him on?

OLD MAN. It is an oracle, so Calchas says, at any rate—so that the expedition can set sail.

CLYTEMNESTRA. Sail where? What cruelty to me! What cruelty to the girl whom her father is about to kill! 880

OLD MAN. To the house of Dardanus,* so that Menelaus can win back Helen.

CLYTEMNESTRA. Is it then destined that Helen can only return if Iphigenia is killed?

OLD MAN. You know it all. Her father is about to sacrifice your daughter to Artemis.

CLYTEMNESTRA. What was the reason for the false marriage by which he brought me from home?

OLD MAN. He wanted you to be happy to bring your child here to marry Achilles.*

CLYTEMNESTRA. O my daughter, you have come here to meet your death, you and your mother too.

OLD MAN. I pity you both equally in your sufferings. Agamemnon has nerved himself to do a terrible deed.

CLYTEMNESTRA. O misery! It is all over for me. I can no longer hold back my welling tears.

OLD MAN. If losing your children is a painful loss, let your tears flow.

CLYTEMNESTRA. But where do you say you learnt this from, old man? How did you find it out? 890

OLD MAN. I was going with a letter for you about the former message.

CLYTEMNESTRA. Did the letter tell me not to bring the girl here to her death, or confirm the previous instructions?

OLD MAN. No, you were not to do so. For your husband was in his right mind then.

CLYTEMNESTRA. So, if you were carrying the letter, how was it that you did not hand it over to me?

OLD MAN. Menelaus snatched it from me. He is to blame for all these evils.

CLYTEMNESTRA. O child of Nereus' daughter, Peleus' son, do you hear this?

ACHILLES. Yes, I hear that you are wretched, and I do not view the way I have been treated as a trivial matter.

CLYTEMNESTRA. They are going to kill my child, and it was by the promise of a marriage to you that they tricked me.

ACHILLES. I too find your husband at fault and I do not take it as lightly as you may think.

CLYTEMNESTRA. I shall feel no shame in falling at your 900 knees,* though I am a mortal while you are the son of a goddess. For why should I be proud? She is my child. She comes first. I must fight for her.* Come to my aid, o son of a goddess, in my misery, help the girl who was called your wife— falsely, but even so. It was for you that I garlanded her and led her here to marry you. But as it is I have brought her to be slaughtered. It will be levelled as a reproach against you if you fail to protect her. For although you were not joined with her in marriage, you were still called the beloved husband of the unhappy girl. By your chin, by your right hand, by your mother—I call on you because your name, which 910 ought to be defending me, has destroyed me—I have no altar to take refuge at except your knees, and there is no friend nearby. You hear of the cruelty of Agamemnon who will stop at nothing. As you see, I have arrived here, a woman in a camp full of unruly sailors who are bold when it comes to evil deeds, though helpful when they wish to be. If you have the courage to hold your hand over me in protection, we are saved. If not, we are lost.

CHORUS. There is a strange power in motherhood. It has its own magic. This is an instinct all humans share—to fight for their children.

[ACHILLES. My proud spirit swells within me and urges me on. But I have learnt to be moderate in my grief over misfortune 920 as well as in my joy over prosperity with her billowing sails. For moderate men have reasoned how to show good judgement as they go through life. So while there are times when it is pleasant not to be too sensible, there are also occasions when it is useful to exercise that good judgement. As for me, brought up as I was in the house of Chiron, the most pious of men, I have learnt straightforward ways. And I shall obey the sons of Atreus when they lead well, but when they lead badly I shall not obey them. Here and in Troy I shall show 930

myself to be a free spirit and, as far as I am able, I shall fight
the good fight.

As for you, so cruelly treated by those closest to you, I
shall set this matter right with all the vigour a young man
can muster. That much pity I shall show you. And your
daughter, who was declared my bride, will never be slaughtered by her father. I shall not allow your husband to involve
me in his trickery. For it is my name that will kill your
daughter even if it does not wield the knife. Your husband
is to blame. My body will no longer be untainted if the girl   940
dies because of me and her marriage to me, the victim of terrible, unendurable suffering, of an outrage so unjust that it
defies imagination. I shall be proved the most cowardly of
the Greeks, a mere cipher—and Menelaus will be counted a
man!—no son of Peleus I, but of some avenging demon, if
your husband uses my name to murder her. By Nereus,
reared in the waves of the sea, the father of Thetis who gave
me birth, King Agamemnon shall not lay a hand, no, not a   950
finger on your daughter. He shall not touch her dress. Or
Sipylus, that barbarian stronghold from which our generals
draw their descent,* will prove a mighty power and Phthia
find no fame the whole world over. If Calchas begins the sacrifice with the barley* and the purifying water, he will regret
it. What kind of man is a seer? A man who tells a few truths
and many lies—and that is when things are going well for
him. When things go badly, he is finished.

I do not say this because of the marriage. Countless girls
seek to be my bride. But Agamemnon has insulted me bru-   960
tally. He ought to have asked me himself for the use of my
name to trap his child. It was mainly by the thought of me
that Clytemnestra was persuaded to betroth her daughter to
me in marriage.* I would have given my name for the
Greeks if that was what was causing the voyage to Troy to
founder. I would not have refused to promote the common
interest of my comrades in arms.* But as it is I am of no
account, the commanders do not trouble themselves
whether they treat me well or badly. As for this sword of   970
mine, before I go to Troy I shall defile it †with murder, stains
of blood,† and it shall soon know if anyone is going to take
your daughter from me.

Be calm. I have appeared to you like an all-powerful god,
though I am not one. Even so, that is what I shall become.
CHORUS. What you have said, son of Peleus, is worthy both of
you and of the sea-goddess, that reverent divinity.
CLYTEMNESTRA. Ah! What words can I find to praise you that
do not go too far and yet do not forfeit your good will by
falling too short. When good men are praised, there is a kind
of resentment in what they feel towards those who praise 980
them if they praise them excessively. I am ashamed of forcing my sad story on you, for my sorrows are my private sickness and you are uninfected by them. But it is nobly done
when the good man comes to the help of the unfortunate
even though he is remote from them.

Show us pity for we have suffered piteously. First of all, I
thought that I would have you as my son-in-law and fed on
empty hopes. Then the death of my daughter may perhaps
prove a bad omen for your marriage when it comes, and
that is something you must guard against. But what you 990
said at the beginning and what you said at the end—both
were spoken well: if you wish it, my daughter shall be saved.
Do you want her to clasp your knees as a suppliant? That is
not how a maiden should behave, but if you desire it, she
will come out wearing a modest, open expression. However,
if I can win the same result from you if she is not here, let
her remain in the tent. Her pride has its own dignity. But
nevertheless we must plead with every resource we can
muster.
ACHILLES. Do not bring out the girl before me here. And let
us not expose ourselves to ignorant criticism, lady. Soldiers, 1000
all together like this and free from personal worries, love
malicious, back-biting gossip. In any case, whether the two
of you supplicate me or not, it will come to the same thing.
Before me lies a single mighty endeavour—to deliver you
from disaster. Listen to me and rest assured of this one thing:
I shall not lie to you. If my words are lies and empty mock-
ery, may I perish. But as I hope for life, I shall save the girl.
CLYTEMNESTRA. May you always be happy, you friend of the
unfortunate.
ACHILLES. Listen to me then—so that this matter may turn
out well.

CLYTEMNESTRA. What do you mean? I must listen to you. 1010
ACHILLES. Let us persuade her father to think better of the
    matter.
CLYTEMNESTRA. He is something of a coward and is too fear-
    ful of the army.
ACHILLES. But reason surely can outwrestle fear.
CLYTEMNESTRA. My hopes are cold. But tell me what I must do.
ACHILLES. First of all, beseech him not to kill his child. And if
    he goes against you, you must come to me. †For if you per-
    suaded him to grant your desire,† there would be no need
    for me to interfere, since that secures her safety. I should
    become a better friend to a friend and the army would not 1020
    find fault with me, if I managed the affair by reason rather
    than by force.* †If things reach a successful conclusion, they
    will please your friends and you, even if I give you no help.†
CLYTEMNESTRA. How sensibly you have spoken. I must do
    what you think best. But still, if I do not gain what I desire,
    where shall I see you again? Where must I come, poor
    woman, to find your hand to champion me in my misery?
ACHILLES. I shall protect you where you need a protector. We
    must not let anyone see you going through the host of the 1030
    Greeks in frantic agitation. And do not disgrace your father's
    house. For Tyndareus* does not deserve to be ill spoken of.
    He is great among the Greeks.
CLYTEMNESTRA. So be it. I must perform your bidding. If the
    gods are wise, you will find good fortune as a just man. But
    if they are not, what point is there in all our efforts?
        ACHILLES *and* CLYTEMNESTRA *go out, the latter into the tent.*]

CHORUS (*sings*). What joyous sounds did the god of the mar-
        riage song ring out
    to the strains of the Lybian lotus pipe*
    and the lyre that loves the dance
    and the pipes of reed,
    when the fair-tressed Muses of Pieria   1040
    who stamp their golden sandals on the ground
    at the feasts of the gods
    came along the ridge of Mount Pelion*
    to the wedding of Peleus,
    celebrating in their melodious songs

Thetis and the grandson of Aeacus
on the centaurs' mountains throughout Pelion's woods?
And the descendant of Dardanus,
the beloved plaything of Zeus' bed,   1050
was drawing off wine
mixed in the depths of golden bowls,
Ganymede the Phrygian.*
And along the bright white sands
the fifty daughters of Nereus
celebrated the wedding as they twirled
in the circles of the dance.*

And with their staffs of silver fir,* with their garlands
of fresh foliage, the revelling company
of human horses, the centaurs, came   1060
to the feast of the gods and the wine-bowl of Bacchus
and loudly they cried: 'O daughter of Nereus,
the son you bear
will be a great light to Thessaly—
so Chiron, instructed in the art of Phoebus,*
has declared.
He will come at the head of his Myrmidons
with their spears and shields
to burn the famous land of Priam to ashes,   1070
his body clad in his suit of golden armour,
the work of Hephaestus' forge,
which he will receive as a gift
from his divine mother,
from Thetis who bore him.'*
Then it was that the gods poured blessings
on the wedding of the first of the Nereids,*
the daughter of a noble father,
and her marriage with Peleus.

But as for you,* the Argives will crown your head,   1080
the beautiful tresses of your hair,
like a dappled heifer,
a pure heifer brought down
from the mountain caves of rock,
bloodying your throat with gore.
You were not brought up

where the shepherd blows his pipe or where the herdsman
  whistles,
but by your mother's side, to be dressed as a bride one
  day
for a wedding with a son of Inachus.*
Where is the face of Shame, where is the face of Goodness   1090
  now?
Do they have any power?—
when what is impious holds sway
and men turn their back on Goodness
and ignore her.
Anarchy holds dominion over laws
and mortals cannot make common cause in the struggle
to avoid the anger of the gods.

[CLYTEMNESTRA *enters.*

CLYTEMNESTRA. I have come from the tent as I watch for my
  husband who went out some time ago and is not yet back.
  My wretched daughter is in tears, sounding despair in many   1100
  different tones, for she has heard about the death which her
  father is planning for her. But look. Agamemnon is
  approaching just when I was talking about him. The
  moment he arrives, he will stand convicted of planning an
  unholy act against his own child.

AGAMEMNON *enters.*

AGAMEMNON. Daughter of Leda, it is opportune that I have
  found you outside the tent. I want to say some things to you
  which it is not proper for a bride to hear, without the girl
  being there.
CLYTEMNESTRA. What is it? Why does this strike you as an
  opportune moment?
AGAMEMNON (*resignedly*). Fetch the girl out of the tent to join   1110
  her father. The holy water is ready, as is the barley to cast
  on the cleansing fire, and the heifers which must fall before
  a marriage, snorting black blood from their nostrils, in sacrifice to the goddess Artemis.
CLYTEMNESTRA. You make a good show with your words,
  but how I should call your actions good, I do not know.
  Come outside, daughter—for you are aware of all that your

father intends to do—take your brother Orestes in the folds
of your dress and bring him here, my child.

<small>IPHIGENIA</small> enters, holding Orestes.

Look, here she is in obedience to your commands. As for the 1120
rest, I myself shall say it for my daughter and for myself.

AGAMEMNON. My child, why are you weeping? Why aren't
you still smiling at me, but staring down at the ground and
holding your dress in front of your eyes?*

CLYTEMNESTRA. Alas! Which of my woes should I start my
speech with? Every one of them could be brought in any-
where, at the beginning, at the end, and in the middle.

AGAMEMNON. What is it? You are all* looking at me with the
same confusion and distress in your eyes.

CLYTEMNESTRA. Reply to what I ask you like an honourable
man, husband.

AGAMEMNON. There is no need for that command. I am will- 1130
ing to listen to your questions.

CLYTEMNESTRA. Your child and mine—are you about to kill
her?

AGAMEMNON (*with a start*). Ah! You have spoken out of turn
and you suspect what you have no right to.

CLYTEMNESTRA. Be quiet. First answer again what I asked
just now.

AGAMEMNON. If you ask a reasonable question, I shall give
you a reasonable answer.

CLYTEMNESTRA. But that is the question I am asking you, and
that and nothing else is what you must answer.

AGAMEMNON. O mistress fate, my fortune, and my evil genius!

CLYTEMNESTRA. My evil genius too, and hers, a single one for
us three doomed creatures.

AGAMEMNON. How have you been wronged?

CLYTEMNESTRA. You ask that—of me? This mind of yours is
no mind at all.*

AGAMEMNON (*aside*). All is over for me. My secrets are betrayed. 1140

CLYTEMNESTRA. I know everything. I have discovered what you
are about to do to me. Your very silence says that you agree—
your every groan. Spare yourself the labour of speaking.

AGAMEMNON. Look, my lips are shut. (*aside*) Why should I tell
lies and so add shamelessness to my tally of woes?

CLYTEMNESTRA. Listen then. I shall reveal my meaning plainly and speak in hinting riddles no longer. First of all— and this will be my first reproach against you—you married me against my will. Indeed, you won me with violence by killing Tantalus,* my former husband. †And you wafted my 1150 baby to your share of captives,†* tearing him from my breast with brute force. The two sons of Zeus, my brothers,* came on their flashing white steeds to make war on you. But my father, old Tyndareus, saved you when you became his suppliant, and despite everything else you took me to be your wife. In that marriage I was reconciled to you and your house, and you will bear witness how irreproachable I was as a wife, proving chaste in my sexual conduct as well as building up your estate, so that you rejoiced to enter the 1160 house and were happy when you went away.* It is a rare catch for a man to win such a wife, while there is no lack of bad ones.

After three daughters, I bore you this son. And you are cruelly robbing me of one of the girls. If someone asks you why you will kill her, tell me, what will you say? Or must I speak for you? So that Menelaus can take back Helen. It would be a fine thing to pay for a bad woman with the life of a child! We are buying what we hate the most with what 1170 we love the best.

Another point—if you go off to fight, leaving me in the house and staying at Troy in a long separation from me, what do you imagine will be my feelings back at home every time I see each chair she used to sit in standing empty, the maidens' chambers empty?—while I sit alone with nothing to do but weep, for ever singing my lament for her: 'The father who begat you has destroyed you, my child. He killed you himself, no one else. His alone was the hand.'—†the father who has left such a motive for hatred in the house.†* It needs only a slight pretext and I and the girls you have 1180 left behind will receive you as it is fitting you should be received. By the gods then, do not force me to become a traitor to you, and you must not prove a traitor to me.

So then, you will kill your daughter. What prayers will you utter? What blessing will you beg should fall on you as you slaughter your child? A grim journey back—after your

shameful departure from home? But do you expect me to
pray for some good for you? We would surely believe that
the gods are fools if we call down blessings on murderers. On 1190
your return from Argos, will you hold your children in your
arms? But you have no right to do so. And which of the children will even meet you with a look if you are to kill the one
you embrace? Did you pause to consider this, or are you
only interested in parading your sceptre and giving your
army orders? These would have been the right words to say
to the Greeks: 'Achaeans, do you wish to sail to the
Phrygians' land? Cast lots to see whose child must die.' This
would have been fair—not that you should pick out your
daughter as a sacrificial victim to give to the Greeks. Fair too 1200
for Menelaus to kill Hermione* for her mother. After all, the
quarrel was his. But as things are, I, who have been loyal to
your bed, shall be robbed of my child, and the woman who
sinned will get back her girl under her roof in Sparta and
find happiness.

Answer me if anything I have said was not well said. But
if I did speak well, then do not kill your child and mine. This
will show that you are a man of judgement.

CHORUS. Listen to her. To join in saving a child is a noble 1210
thing, Agamemnon. No one will gainsay that.

IPHIGENIA. If I had the voice of Orpheus,* father, with the
power to persuade by my song so that I could make rocks
follow me and charm all those I wished to with my elo-
quence, I would have used it. But as it is I shall offer the only
skill that I possess, my tears. They are my only resource. I
press my body, which this lady bore to you, close to your
knees as though it were a suppliant's branch.* Do not kill
me before my time. It is sweet to see the light of day. Do not
force me to look on the underworld. I was the first to call
you father,* you were the first to call me child. I was the first 1220
to climb up on your knees and give you loving kisses and
take them in return. And this is what you used to say: 'Shall
I see you happy, my child, in your husband's house, leading
a palmy life worthy of your royal father.' This was my reply
as I reached up to clasp the chin which I take hold of now:
'And what about you? Shall I receive you in my house with
a loving welcome, father, when you are old, and so repay

the tender care with which you brought me up?' I can 1230
remember these words but you have forgotten them and
want to kill me. Do not do it, I beg you, by Pelops and by
Atreus your father and by my mother here who suffered
long ago the agony of bringing me to birth and endures this
second agony now. What do I have to do with the marriage
of Helen and Paris? Why must I die because he came to
Sparta? Look at me, turn your eyes this way, and kiss me so
that as I die I may have this at least as a remembrance of 1240
you, if my words cannot persuade you.

Brother, you are only a tiny champion for your friends,
but weep with me none the less and beg your father that
your sister should not die. Even in infants there is an inborn
sense of life's cruelties. Look, he can say nothing but still he
pleads with you, father. Show me mercy. Pity me and do not
kill me. Yes, by your chin, we supplicate you, we your two
darlings, this one here but a nestling, the other already
fledged.

The success of my whole case rests on this single point.
This light of day is very sweet for men to look upon and 1250
what is below the ground is nothing. The person who prays
to die is mad. To live basely is better than to die nobly.*

CHORUS. Cruel-hearted Helen, because of you and your marriage a great struggle has come to the sons of Atreus and
their children.*

AGAMEMNON. I understand what calls for pity and what does
not, and I love my children. I would be mad if I did not love
them. It is a terrible thing for me to bring myself to do this
deed, lady, and terrible also not to do it. But whether I want
to or not, I have to. Both of you can see what a vast army
is here with its armada, how many Greeks, masters of 1260
bronze arms. They can never sail against the towers of
Ilium, never overturn the famous foundations of Troy, if I do
not sacrifice you, as the seer Calchas says. In the army of the
Greeks there rages some mad desire* to sail with all speed to
the land of the barbarians and put an end to the rape of
Greek wives. They will kill my girls in Argos, and the three
of you, and me as well, if I frustrate the oracle of the goddess. It is not Menelaus who has made me his slave, my
child, no, I am not guided by his wishes. It is Greece* for 1270

which I must sacrifice you whether I want to or no. There's
the necessity that masters me. Greece must be free, as far as
that lies in your power, my child, and in mine, and as
Greeks, her men must not be robbed of their wives through
force.*   AGAMEMNON *goes out.*

CLYTEMNESTRA (*chants*).
   O my child, o you foreign women,
   O my own misery over your death,
   your father is running away. He has surrendered you to
      Hades.
IPHIGENIA (*chants*).
   I cry for myself, my mother. For the selfsame song against
      our fortune
   has fallen to us both,   1280
   and the light of the sky and this brilliant sun
   are mine no longer.

(*sings*)
   Ah! Ah!
   Snow-beaten valley of the Phrygians
   and Ida's mountains, where Priam once
   cast out his tender baby,
   taking it far away from its mother
   and dooming it to death,
   Paris,* who was called the child of Ida,
   the child of Ida in the Phrygians' city,   1290
   if only you had never given a home
   to Alexandros, the ox-herd reared among the oxen,
   a home by the sparkling waters
   where the springs of the Nymphs lie
   and the meadow,
   lush with its green shoots,
   and roses and hyacinths
   for goddesses to pick. There once
   Pallas came and Cypris, the schemer,   1300
   and Hera and Hermes, Zeus' messenger—
   Cypris, vain* of the love which she inspires,
   Pallas, proud of her martial prowess,
   and Hera, of the royal bed of Zeus—
   they came to judgement,

to a hateful contest in beauty
which meant death for me,
a death which brings glory to the maidens of Greece,   1310
and Artemis has won her sacrifice
as a prelude to the voyage to Ilium.
But my father has gone,
o mother, o mother,
he has betrayed me, deserted me, his wretched daughter.
O my misery, bitter,
bitter was the sight of Helen, name of ill omen,
and I am being killed, murdered,
impiously slaughtered by an impious father.

If only Aulis had not received
the sterns* of bronze-beaked ships   1320
into this anchorage,
the fleet that was taking the army to Troy!
If only the breath of Zeus on Euripus
had not held back the voyage, of Zeus who whirls the winds
to suit all kinds of mortals,
some to be cheered by full sails,
while for others there is sorrow, and for others the clamp
    of necessity.
Here they are sailing out, here furling their sails,
here they simply wait.
We humans are mere creatures of a day, and full of   1330
    suffering,
yes, full of suffering is our life. It is a hard undertaking
for men to find out their fate.
Ah!
I cry out against the daughter of Tyndareus
who brings great torments, great woes upon the Greeks.

CHORUS. I pity you. You have met with calamity. O that you
    never had!
IPHIGENIA. My mother,* you who gave me birth, I see a
    troop of soldiers approaching.
CLYTEMNESTRA. And the son of the goddess, Achilles, child,
    the man for whom you came here.
IPHIGENIA. Open up the tent please, servants, so that I can 1340
    hide myself.

CLYTEMNESTRA. Why are you running away, my child?

IPHIGENIA. I am ashamed to look upon Achilles here.

CLYTEMNESTRA. Why?

IPHIGENIA. The sad business of my marriage makes me feel ashamed.

CLYTEMNESTRA. This is no time for false delicacy, considering what has happened. I tell you, you must stay. Pride is no use to us if we are to find help.

ACHILLES enters with attendants carrying his armour.

ACHILLES. Daughter of Leda, you unfortunate woman . . .

CLYTEMNESTRA. There you speak the truth.

ACHILLES. The Greeks are shouting terrible things . . .

CLYTEMNESTRA. What are they shouting? Tell me.

ACHILLES. . . . about your child . . . CLYTEMNESTRA. What you say bodes ill.

ACHILLES. . . . that she must be slaughtered. CLYTEMNESTRA. And no one is speaking against this?

ACHILLES. I myself met with some noisy shouting.

CLYTEMNESTRA. What were they shouting?

ACHILLES. That I should be stoned to death. CLYTEMNESTRA. Not because you tried to save my child?   1350

ACHILLES. Yes, for just that. CLYTEMNESTRA. Who would have dared to lay a hand on you?

ACHILLES. All the Greeks.* CLYTEMNESTRA. But wasn't the Myrmidon army there to protect you?

ACHILLES. They were the bitterest in opposing me. CLYTEMNESTRA. It is all over with us then, my child.

ACHILLES. Why, they taunted me, calling me the slave of my hoped-for marriage. CLYTEMNESTRA. And what did you answer?

ACHILLES. I forbade them to kill my future wife . . . CLYTEMNESTRA. Yes, and you were right to.

ACHILLES. . . . the wife her father promised me. CLYTEMNES-TRA. . . . and sent for from Argos.

ACHILLES. But I was overwhelmed by the uproar. CLYTEMNES-TRA. Yes, the mob is a terrible, destructive force.

ACHILLES. But I shall protect you nevertheless. CLYTEMNES-TRA. And fight all alone against a multitude?

ACHILLES. Do you see these men who carry my arms?

CLYTEMNESTRA. Blessings on you for your sense of honour.

ACHILLES. Well, I shall have my reward.* CLYTEMNESTRA.
Will my child not be slaughtered now?   1360
ACHILLES. No, at least not with my consent. CLYTEMNESTRA.
Will someone come to lay hold of the girl?
ACHILLES. Many will come, and Odysseus will lead her away.
CLYTEMNESTRA. What, the son of Sisyphus?*
ACHILLES. The very same. CLYTEMNESTRA. On his own ini-
tiative—or instructed by the army?
ACHILLES. Chosen, and willing too. CLYTEMNESTRA. They
are choosing a vile man to commit a vile murder.
ACHILLES. But I shall hold him off. CLYTEMNESTRA. Will he
drag her away by force if she is unwilling to go?
ACHILLES. Certainly, and by her golden hair. CLYTEMNES-
TRA. What must I do then?
ACHILLES. Hold your daughter tightly. CLYTEMNESTRA. If
that is all I have to do to save her, she will not be slaughtered.
ACHILLES. But it will certainly come to that.
IPHIGENIA. Mother,* you must listen to my words. For I see
that you are angry with your husband for no reason. It is
not easy for us to go through with the impossible. It is right 1370
to thank the stranger* for his generous heart. But you
should think of this too. His reputation among the army
must not be destroyed. We should be no better off and he
would be ruined. Hear what has settled in my mind, mother,
as I thought about this. I have made the decision to die. I
want to do this gloriously, to reject all meanness of spirit.
Only consider these things with me, mother, and you will
see how nobly I am speaking. Greece in all its greatness*
now looks to me and no one else, on me depends the voyage of the ships across the sea and the overthrow of the
Phrygians; and if the barbarians try to seize our women 1380
from happy Greece in the future, it lies with me to stop them
by ensuring that they pay for the ruin of Helen whom Paris
snatched away. Through my death I shall secure all this and
my fame as the liberator of Greece will be for ever blessed.

And indeed it is right that I should not be too much in
love with life. You bore me for the common good of the
Greeks, not for yourself alone. Will countless warriors, with
their shields their bulwark, will numberless oarsmen dare to
strike against the enemy and die for their fatherland when

Greece is wronged, and shall my life, my single life, prevent 1390
all this? †How could we argue that this is right?†

And let me come to the next point. This man must not
battle with all of the Greeks for a woman's sake, and die. It
is better that one man should see the light of day than any
number of women. If Artemis has decided to take my body,
am I, a mere mortal, to oppose the goddess? No, it is impossible. I give my body to Greece. Sacrifice me and sack Troy.
This shall be my lasting monument, this shall be my children, my marriage and my glory. It is right that the Greeks 1400
should rule barbarians, mother, and not barbarians Greeks.
For they are slaves and we are free.

CHORUS. The part you play, maiden, is a noble one. But fate
and the goddess—that is where the sickness lies.*

ACHILLES. Child of Agamemnon, a god meant to make me
happy—if I could only win you as a wife. I envy Greece
because she is blessed in you and you because you are
blessed in Greece. Your words were noble and worthy of
your fatherland. You have given up your struggle with the
gods, for they are too strong for you, and you have pondered
on what is good and what is inevitable. Now that I have
seen your character, I long still more to marry you. You 1410
have a noble heart. And consider this. It is my own wish to
serve you and to take you to my house, and it will bring me
grief—let Thetis be my witness—if I do not join battle with
the Greeks and save you. Think. Death is a fearful thing.

IPHIGENIA. It is enough that Helen's beauty should stir up
deadly strife for men. Do not kill anyone or be killed because
of me, but allow me to save Greece if I can.   1420

ACHILLES. You heroic spirit, I have nothing more to say to
this, since this is what you have decided and your thoughts
are noble. Why should one fail to speak the truth? But even
so, perhaps you may change your mind about this. Hear
then—for I shall tell you—what I plan to do. I shall go to
the altar and place my arms nearby. I shall not allow you to
be killed. No, I shall prevent it. You will take up my promise
soon enough when you see the sword close to your neck. I
shall not let you die because of a foolish impulse.* I shall go 1430
with these weapons of mine to the temple of the goddess and
wait for your arrival there.   *ACHILLES goes out.*

IPHIGENIA. Mother, why are you silent? Why these tear-filled eyes?*

CLYTEMNESTRA. In my misery I have good cause for a sorrowing heart.

IPHIGENIA. Stop. Do not make a coward of me.* Obey me in what I ask you.

CLYTEMNESTRA. Tell me what it is—you shall have no cause to complain of *me*, at any rate.

IPHIGENIA. Then do not cut off a lock of your hair,* or clothe your body in black robes.

CLYTEMNESTRA. Why do you say this my child—when I have lost you?

IPHIGENIA. But you have not. I have been saved and through me you shall win glory.*   1440

CLYTEMNESTRA. What do you mean? Must I not grieve for your death?

IPHIGENIA. No, no. For no tomb will be raised to me.

CLYTEMNESTRA. What? Is not burial customary for the dead?

IPHIGENIA. The altar of the divine daughter of Zeus will be my memorial.*

CLYTEMNESTRA. Well then, my child, I shall obey you. This is good advice.

IPHIGENIA. It comes from a happy woman, the benefactor of Greece.

CLYTEMNESTRA. What message from you should I give your sisters?

IPHIGENIA. Do not dress them in black robes either.

CLYTEMNESTRA. Should I say some loving word to the girls from you?

IPHIGENIA. Bid them farewell. And bring up Orestes here to manhood, I beg you.   1450

CLYTEMNESTRA. Hug him close to you and look at him for the last time.

IPHIGENIA. Dearest Orestes, you did everything you could to help your dear sister.

CLYTEMNESTRA. Is there anything I can do in Argos which will please you?

IPHIGENIA. Do not hate your husband, since he is my father.

CLYTEMNESTRA. He must run a terrible race because of you.*

IPHIGENIA. It was against his will and for the sake of Greece
that he destroyed me.
CLYTEMNESTRA. But it was by a foul trick, unworthy of Atreus.*
IPHIGENIA. Who will come to take me away before they tear
at my hair?
CLYTEMNESTRA. I shall go with you . . .
IPHIGENIA. No, not you. You show bad judgement there.
CLYTEMNESTRA. Yes I shall, holding tight to your robes.   1460
IPHIGENIA. Mother, obey me. Remain here. That will be bet-
ter both for myself and you. Let one of my father's atten-
dants here lead me to Artemis' meadow where I am to be
slaughtered.
CLYTEMNESTRA. Are you lost to me, my child?
IPHIGENIA. Yes, and I shall never come again.
CLYTEMNESTRA. You will leave your mother?
IPHIGENIA. As you see—and not as a girl should leave her.
CLYTEMNESTRA. Stay! Do not forsake me.
IPHIGENIA. I forbid you to let fall a tear.* And you, young
women, sing a propitious song for my fate, a song in praise
of Zeus' daughter Artemis. Let the Greeks keep propitious
silence. Let someone begin the sacrifice with the baskets, let 1470
the fire blaze with purifying barley meal, and let my father
walk round the altar from left to right,* for I come to give
salvation and with it victory to the Greeks.

(*sings*) Lead me on—the destroyer
of Ilium's city and the Phrygians.
Give me, bring me garlands to bind my head—
here is a lock of my hair to wreathe the altar—
and streams of purifying water.
Dance your swirling dance for Artemis   1480
around the temple, around the altar,
for Artemis the queen, the blessed one.
For with my blood,
shed in sacrifice if it must be,
I shall wash away the oracle.
O mother, my lady mother, I shall not
give you my tears.
They are not fitting at a holy rite.   1490
Ah, young women, ah,

join with me in singing the praise of Artemis,
the goddess across the strait from Chalcis,
where because of me, Iphigenia,
the sailors of the wooden ships
in Aulis' mooring on the narrow straits
are impatient for the end.
O land of Argos which gave me birth,
and Mycenae, my home . . .
CHORUS (*sings*). Are you calling on the city of Perseus   1500
constructed by Cyclopian hands?*
IPHIGENIA (*sings*). You brought me up to be a light for Greece.*
It causes me no regret that I die.
CHORUS (*sings*). Your glory shall live for ever.
IPHIGENIA (*sings*). Ah! Ah!
Bright torch of the day,
and Zeus' sunlight,
a different life,
a different fate shall be mine.
Farewell, beloved light.*

        IPHIGENIA *is led off.* CLYTEMNESTRA *goes into the tent.*

[CHORUS (*sings*). Ah! Ah!   1510
See the destroyer
of Ilium's city and the Phrygians
going on her way—garlands will be cast upon her head
and streams of purifying water—
†to sprinkle the altar of the goddess divine*
and her own lovely neck
with a dew of gushing blood
at the moment of slaughter.
The generous streams of purifying water
which your father will pour await you.†
The army of the Achaeans awaits you,
eager to go to the city of Troy.   1520
But let us invoke the daughter of Zeus,
Artemis, sovereign goddess,
as if this were a happy fate.
O maiden, maiden, your favour won
by a human sacrifice,
send the Greek army

to the land of the Phrygians
and the treacherous city of Troy,
and grant that Agamemnon
may crown the spears of Greece
with glorious fame, and his own brows   1530
with a glory that never dies.

Enter MESSENGER.

MESSENGER. Daughter of Tyndareus, Clytemnestra, come out
of the tent, so that you can hear my words.

Enter CLYTEMNESTRA holding Orestes.

CLYTEMNESTRA. I heard your voice and have come here, out
of my mind in an agony of fear. Surely you have not come
with news of another disaster to add to what I suffer now?
MESSENGER. No, I want to tell you something strange and
wonderful about your child.
CLYTEMNESTRA. Do not delay then, but let me know at once.
MESSENGER. Well then, my dear mistress, I shall make every- 1540
thing clear to you. I shall begin at the beginning in case my
excitement makes me incoherent as I tell you the story.

Well, we came to the grove of Zeus' daughter Artemis and
her flowery meadows where the army of the Achaeans had
gathered. We were leading your child. Immediately all the
Greeks crowded together shoulder to shoulder. And when
King Agamemnon saw the girl coming into the grove to be
slain, he groaned loudly, turned his head away from her and
burst into tears, pulling his robe in front of his eyes.*   1550
But she stood near to her father and said: 'O my father,
here I am beside you. I gladly give my body for my fatherland and for the whole land of Greece. Lead me to the altar
of the goddess, you Achaeans, and sacrifice me, if this is
what the oracle demands. So far as it depends on me, may
you have success, may you win victory with your spears and
come back to your fatherland. Therefore let no Greek lay a
hand on me. I shall offer my neck with a brave heart in 1560
silence.'

This is what she said. And as they listened, everyone mar-
velled at the courage and heroism of the maiden. Then
Talthybius—whose office it was—*called for a reverent

silence from the army. And the seer Calchas, drew a sharp
sword from its scabbard, placed it in a golden basket, and
put a garland round the girl's head. Next the son of Peleus
took the basket and the holy water too, quickly circled the
altar of the goddess, and said: 'O daughter of Zeus, o slayer 1570
of wild beasts, spinning your bright radiance through the
darkness of the night,* accept this sacrifice which we, the
Achaean army and King Agamemnon too, present to you,
the undefiled blood from a virgin's beautiful neck, and grant
that our ships sail on safely and take Troy's citadel.' The
sons of Atreus and the whole army stood staring down at
the ground.

The priest took the knife, uttered his prayer and looked at
her throat to see where he should strike. As for myself, a 1580
great anguish began to lay hold on my heart and I stood
there, my head drooping.* But suddenly there was a wonder
to behold. Everyone would have heard the thud of the blow
clearly, but the girl had sunk into the ground, nobody
knows where.

The priest shouted and the whole army echoed back the
cry. We had seen an unhoped for portent from one of the
gods and could scarcely believe our eyes. For a deer lay pant-
ing and struggling on the ground, an impressive sight in its
vastness and its beauty, and it was that creature's blood that
spattered all the altar. At this, Calchas cried with unimag- 1590
inable joy: 'Lords of the united Achaean army, do you see
this victim which the goddess has placed on her altar, a
mountain-running deer? She has gladly received this rather
than the girl. She does not wish to defile her altar with noble
blood. She is pleased to accept this sacrifice and will give us
favourable winds as we sail to attack Troy. So let every sailor
take good heart and go to his ship. For on this day we must
leave the hollow bay of Aulis and cross the swelling Aegean 1600
sea.' When the whole victim had been burnt to ashes* in
Hephaestus' fire, he prayed a suitable prayer to win a good
voyage.

Agamemnon has sent me to tell you this and to let you
know what fate the gods have given your daughter. She has
won glory throughout Greece, glory that will never die. I
was there, and I am telling you this as one who saw it.

Clearly your daughter has flown away to join the gods. Put
an end to your grief and lay aside your anger against your
husband. What the gods purpose cannot be foreseen by mor-   1610
tals. They save those they love. For this day has seen your
daughter dying and coming back to life.

CHORUS. How I rejoice to hear the messenger's report. He says
that your daughter is alive and living among the gods.

CLYTEMNESTRA (*chants*).
O my child, which of the gods has stolen you?
By what name can I call you? How can I be sure
that this story has not been made up to console me
so that I can lay to rest
my cruel grief over you?

CHORUS (*chants*).
But look, King Agamemnon is coming.
He brings you confirmation of the story.   1620

Enter AGAMEMNON.

AGAMEMNON. My wife, we may be happy for our daughter's
sake. For I tell you truly, she lives among the gods. You must
take this little baby and go off home, since the army has its
voyage in prospect. And farewell. It will be a long time
before I return from Troy and greet you again. May all go
well with you.*

CHORUS (*chants*).
May you reach the Phrygian land in happiness
and meet with a happy return
carrying most splendid spoils from Troy.
All the characters leave the stage.]

RHESUS

Characters

HECTOR, *commander-in-chief of the Trojans*
AENEAS, *a Trojan chieftain*
DOLON, *a Trojan*
MESSENGER, *a shepherd*
RHESUS, *king of Thrace*
ODYSSEUS, *a Greek chieftain*
DIOMEDES, *a Greek chieftain*
ATHENA, *a goddess*
ALEXANDROS, *also known as Paris, a Trojan chieftain, Hector's
    brother*
The CHARIOTEER *of Rhesus*
The MUSE, *mother of Rhesus*

CHORUS *of Trojan sentinels*

*The scene is set in Hector's area of the Trojan camp on the plain
outside Troy.* HECTOR lies on the ground on a bed of leaves. His
attendants lie around him, DOLON among them.The CHORUS of
Trojan guards enters.*

CHORUS (*chants*). Come to where Hector is sleeping.*
    Which of the prince's squires or soldiers
    is awake?
    He must hear the strange news reported
    by the men who are set to guard the whole army
    for the fourth watch of the night.*
    Lean on your elbow and lift up your head,
    open your eyelids and reveal your frightening gaze,*
    up from your bed of leaves that strew the ground,
    Hector. It is time to listen.   10
HECTOR (*chants*).
    Who is this? Is it a friend's voice? What man is it?
    What is the watchword? Say it.*
    Who are these men who come in the darkness,
    close to where I sleep. You must answer.

CHORUS (*chants*). We are the army's guards. HECTOR
  (*chants*). Why are you unsettled by alarm?
[CHORUS (*chants*). Do not be afraid. HECTOR (*chants*). I am
    not afraid.
  Surely there has not been an ambush in the night?
    CHORUS (*chants*). No.
HECTOR (*chants*).
  Then why have you left your guard-posts to rouse the
    army]
  if you do not have some night-news?
  Are you not aware
  how close we are to the Greek army   20
  as we lie all night in full armour?
CHORUS (*sings*). Take up your arms, Hector, and come
  to where the allies lie.
  Rouse them from their sleep, make them take up their
    spears.
  Send for your friends to join your company.
  Bridle your horses.
  Who will go to Panthus' son
  or Europa's,* the leader of the men from Lycia?
  Where are the interpreters of the victims' entrails,*   30
  where are the captains of the slingers,
  and the Phrygians'* archers?
  Span the horn-tipped bows with their strings.
HECTOR (*chants*). Though hearing what you say makes me
    fearful,
  you tell me not to be afraid. Your message is unclear.
  Are you alarmed by the scourge of trembling fear
  from Cronos' son Pan,* and has that made you leave your
    guard posts
  and rouse the army? What are you telling me? What news
  can I say that you are bringing? For you have spoken
    many words
  but have communicated no plain message.   40
CHORUS (*sings*). The Argive* army has been burning fires,
  Hector, all the dark night.
  The moorings of their ships are bright with torches.*
  And their whole army has gone in the night
  to Agamemnon's tent,

in an uproar, eager for some new pronouncement. Never
   yet before
has that host from across the sea been so frightened.
I can merely guess at what the future holds,
and have come to bring the news   50
so that you will never be able to level any criticism against
   me.

HECTOR. You have come at an opportune moment, even if your
message tells of fear. For those men are planning to elude my
watchful eye and to take flight from this land by sailing
away in the night.* These nocturnal beacons hold my gaze.
O fortune, you have robbed me amid my success, robbed this
lion of his feast, before I could kill the whole of the Argives'
army with this spear in one fell swoop. If the bright beams
of the sun had not failed,* I would not have held back my   60
triumphant spear until I had fired their ships and gone
through their huts killing Achaeans* with this deadly hand.
And I was eager to continue the fighting by night and to
take the god's tide of good fortune at the flood. However, the
experts and the seers who know of things divine persuaded
me to wait for the light of day and then to drive every single
Argive from the dry land. But the enemy are not waiting
for my soothsayers' advice. At night runaways gather
strength.

   But we must pass the order through the army with all dis-   70
patch that they are to wake from sleep and grasp their arms
that lie to hand so that our enemies, even in the act of leaping on board their ships, may be spear-split on their backs
and sprinkle the boarding-ladders with their blood,* or be
captured and snared in bonds, and learn to toil at the
Phrygians' fertile soil.*

CHORUS. Hector, you are rushing impetuously onwards before
you are sure what is happening. We do not know for certain
if the men are running away.

HECTOR. If they aren't,* what reason can there be for the
Argives' army to light the fires?

CHORUS. I do not know. But my heart is full of misgivings.

HECTOR. If you are afraid about this, you can be sure that   80
there is nothing that will not frighten you.

CHORUS. Never before now have the enemy kindled so many fires.

HECTOR. Never yet have they suffered shame like this as they fell in their army's rout.

CHORUS. It was you who brought that about. Now you must look to the future too.

HECTOR. My message is simple: to arm against the enemy.

CHORUS. Look. Here comes Aeneas. He is rushing with great urgency. He has some new matter to tell his friends.

Enter AENEAS.*

AENEAS. Hector, why have the guards gone fearfully through the army in the night to where you are sleeping? What night-news do they bring? Why has the army been disturbed?

HECTOR. Aeneas, case your body in your armour.   90

AENEAS. What is it? Is the news that the enemy have ambushed us under cover of darkness? Surely not?

HECTOR. The men are running away and boarding their ships.

AENEAS. What certain proof of this can you give me?

HECTOR. They have been lighting torches all night long. And I think that they will not wait until tomorrow. No, they will burn out their torches and leave this land in flight for home on their well-benched ships.

AENEAS. And your reaction to this is to take up arms. With what intention?

HECTOR. As they flee and leap onto their ships, I shall attack   100
them fiercely and keep them back here by my spear's might.*
After all the harm our enemies have done us, it would be shameful, and not only shameful but cowardly too, if we let them escape without a fight when the god has delivered them into our hands.

AENEAS. I wish that you were as reliable in counsel as in action. But then no man is master of every art. Each has a different gift, and while yours is fighting, others make sensible plans.*
You hear that the Achaeans are burning fire-beacons and you are carried away by the news. So you intend to lead your   110
army over the ditches* in the dark. And yet if you cross the trenches' hollow depths and find the enemy not fleeing from our land but facing your attack, I am afraid that you may be

defeated and never come back again. Tell me, how will the army get over the stakes in a rout? Then again, how will the charioteers drive across the causeways without shattering their chariots' axle-boxes?* But if you are victorious, you still have to deal with the son of Peleus, who sits there in reserve. He will not let you set fire to the ships* or seize Achaean cap- 120 tives, as you are expecting. For he is a fiery man and a tower of strength and boldness.

No, let us allow the army to sleep by their shields and rest from the labours of deadly war. And it seems a good idea to me to send a volunteer to spy on the enemy. If we find that they are taking flight, let us go and fall upon the Argive army. But if this lighting of beacons is leading us into some trap,* we shall find out what the enemy are scheming from our spy and then take counsel. That is what I recommend, 130 my lord.

CHORUS (*sings*).
This is good advice—change your mind and follow it.
I do not like a general's commands to risk disaster.
Yes, a swiftly-pacing spy
should go near to the ships—what plan could be better?—
to see why it is that the enemy are burning watch-fires
in front of where their vessels are stationed.

HECTOR. I give in to you since you all agree on this. Go, calm our allies. Perhaps the army may have heard about our night-council and become restless. I shall send someone to 140 spy on the enemy, and if we learn of any trickery from our foe, you will hear all about it and will be present to decide what we should do. But if they are rushing off in flight, you can expect our trumpet to sound. Listen out for it, for there will be no delay from me. No, I shall go close to their ship-ways to attack the Argives' army this very night.

AENEAS. Send your spy as soon as you can. Now you are thinking soundly. You shall see me fighting steadfastly beside you when the time comes.

HECTOR. Which of the Trojans present while we speak is will-ing to go as a spy to the Argives' ships? Who will become 150 this country's benefactor? Who will volunteer? I cannot serve the city of my fathers and the allies in everything myself.

DOLON. I am willing to risk this danger for our land and to go to the Argives' ships as a spy. And when I have discovered all the Achaeans' plans, I shall come back here. I shall undertake this task as you have outlined it.

HECTOR. Your tricky name suits you admirably, Dolon,* and you love your city. Your father's house was glorious before, but now you have made it doubly so.

DOLON. Since I am ready to undertake this task, should I not win a fitting reward?* After all, every act which promises 160 profit is done with twice the pleasure.

HECTOR. Yes, your claim is just and I agree with you. Name your reward. Anything except my royal power.

DOLON. I do not desire* the royal power with which you protect our city.

HECTOR. At least marry one of Priam's daughters and become my brother-in-law.

DOLON. I do not wish to marry above my station.

HECTOR. There is gold available if that is the gift you ask for.

DOLON. I have gold at home. I am not short of the means of 170 living.

HECTOR. What then do you desire from Ilium's* hidden hoard?

DOLON. Promise me my gifts if you capture the Achaeans.

HECTOR. You shall have gifts—but do not ask for the commanders of the ships.*

DOLON. Kill them. I do not bid you to spare Menelaus.

HECTOR. Surely you do not ask me to give you the son of Oileus?*

DOLON. Well-bred hands make bad farmers.

HECTOR. Which Greek's life do you want to hold to ransom?

DOLON. I told you before—I have gold at home.

HECTOR. Well then, you shall choose from the spoils in person.

DOLON. Fasten them up for the gods on their temples.   180

HECTOR. Then what gift greater than these will you ask me for?

DOLON. Achilles' horses.* A man must work for a worthwhile reward when he stakes his life in fortune's game of dice.

HECTOR. Ah, I too covet those horses. You are my rival. Born immortal from immortal sires, they bear the war-crazed son of Peleus. Poseidon, the lord of the sea, broke them in himself and, as they say, gave them to Peleus. But I shall not

raise your hopes only to cheat you of them. I shall give you
Achilles' team—a fine present to take home.   190
DOLON. Thank you. I assure you that, if I were to get them, I
would win the most beautiful gift the Phrygians have to offer
as the reward for my courage. You must not begrudge me
them. There are countless other things which you, as ruler
of this land, will delight in.
CHORUS (*sings*).
Great is your enterprise, great the prize you aim to win.
If you succeed, you will be blest.
This is a glorious task.* Yet it is a great thing
to become the kinsman of royalty.
Let Justice see to what comes from the gods,
but as for what men can do,   200
it seems a full reward for you.*
DOLON. I shall go. I shall visit my home and while I am there
I shall clothe my body in an appropriate garb and set out
from there to the ships of the Argives.
CHORUS. Why, what different dress will you wear instead of
this?
DOLON. One that accords with the stealthy tread of my mission.
CHORUS. It is right that a clever man should teach us something clever. Tell us, what costume will you dress your body
in?
DOLON. I shall fasten a wolfskin round my back and place the
beast's gaping jaws over my head. I shall fit the fore-feet to   210
my hands and the hind-legs to my legs and mimic a wolf's
four-footed lope. The enemy will find it hard to penetrate this
disguise* as I come near to the trenches and the barriers that
protect the ships. But when I set foot on an empty stretch of
land, I shall walk on two feet. This is the trick I have devised.
CHORUS. May Hermes, the son of Maia, lord of cheats,* bring
you successfully there and back. You know what you must
do. All you need is good fortune.
DOLON. I shall return safely, be sure of that, and I shall kill
Odysseus and bring his head to you. When you hold this   220
sure proof, you will agree that Dolon reached the Argives'
ships. Or I may kill Tydeus' son.* I shall come back home
with blood-stained hands before light returns to the earth.
                                        Exit DOLON.

CHORUS (*sings*). God of Thymbra and Delos,
    ever present in your temple in Lycia,*
    Apollo, great son of Zeus, come with your bow,
    come this night,
    escort the man on his mission and prove his saviour,
    and take the part of Dardanus' people,*   230
    O all-powerful one
    who built the ancient walls of Troy.*

May the man come to where the ships are stationed,
    may he arrive safe as a spy
    on the Greek army and turn back
    to the Trojan altars of his father's home.
    May he one day mount the chariot drawn by the horses
        from Phthia,*
    after our lord has destroyed the Achaeans' war-might—
    the mares which the god of the sea   240
    gave to Peleus, the son of Aeacus.

For he alone has had the courage to go to spy
    on the ship's stations, for the sake of his home and his
        native land.
    I admire his spirit. Certainly
    there are never enough brave men
    whenever it is sunless on the sea and the city
    is tempest-tossed. Yes, one of the Phrygians is a hero.
    There is bravery in our fighting.   250
    Where is the Mysian*
    who scorns me as an ally?

What man of the Achaeans will the earth-pacing killer
    stab in the huts, as he mimics a wild beast
    treading the ground on all fours?
    May he slay Menelaus and kill Agamemnon
    and bring his head to Helen's hands,
    bring her tears for her vicious brother-in-law   260
    who came to our city,
    came to the land of Troy
    with his fleet of a thousand ships.

Enter a MESSENGER.*

MESSENGER. My lord, I hope that in time to come I may prove

a messenger of such news to my masters as I bring you now.

HECTOR. What great stupidity infects the minds of country-folk! It looks as if you have come with news of your flocks for your masters when they are engaged in war. This is not the place for such information. Don't you know my house or my father's palace? It's there that you should have taken 270 the news that your flock is thriving.

MESSENGER. We herdsmen are stupid, I do not deny it. But none the less I am bringing you welcome news.

HECTOR. Stop telling me how things are going in your farmyard. We carry in our hands the burden of battles and spears.

MESSENGER. I have come with information of that kind myself. A man who commands an army of vast might is on his way. He is a friend to you and an ally to this land.

HECTOR. What is his native land? What country has he left unprotected?

MESSENGER. The land of Thrace. He is called the son of Strymon.*

HECTOR. Are you saying that Rhesus has set foot in Troy? 280

MESSENGER. You have understood my message and spared me the telling of half of it.

HECTOR. How is it that he has veered from the broad highway over the plain and is coming towards the pasture lands at the foot of Mount Ida?

MESSENGER. I do not know for sure, but it is possible to make a guess. It is no small matter to march in an army during the night when one has heard that the plain is full of enemy troops. He scared us countryfolk who live among the crags of Ida in our land's primeval dwellings, as he came through the woods, the haunts of wild beasts, in the night. For the Thracian army came streaming on with great shouts.* In 290 our astonishment and panic, we drove our flocks to the heights in case any of the Argives were coming to destroy or plunder your folds, but then our ears caught their language. It wasn't Greek and so we stopped being afraid. I went to question the scouts who were leading the commander on his journey and I spoke to them in Thracian.* 'Who is your general, and whose son is he, the man who is coming to our city as an ally to Priam's people?'

After I had heard everything I wanted to learn, I stood   300
there. And I saw Rhesus standing like a god on his horse-
drawn chariot. The yoke beam which joined the necks of the
team of colts was of gold, and they gleamed more dazzlingly
white than snow. On his shoulders his shield blazed with
images inlaid with gold.* Bronze Gorgons as on the goddess's
aegis* were set upon the horses' foreheads and clanged forth
fear with their many bells. Not all your arithmetic would
help you to count the number of the army, so overwhelm-   310
ing was it to look upon with its many horsemen, its many
ranks of targeteers,* its many archers, and with them all an
enormous troop of slingers dressed in their Thracian attire.*
   Such is the man who has come as Troy's ally, one that
the son of Peleus will not be able to escape whether he runs
away or stands to face him with his spear.

CHORUS. When the gods stand firm for our citizens, then fortune's current flows directly to success.*

HECTOR. Many are the friends I shall find, now that my spear
   has proved triumphant and Zeus is with us.* But we have   320
   no need of allies who have not laboured with us all the long
   time that the winds of war drove us off-course with their violent blasts and rent the canvas of our ship of Troy. Rhesus
   has shown to us what a friend he was to this land. No, he
   has come to the feast though he did not share in the struggle with the hunters whose spears took the quarry. No, he
   was far away.

CHORUS. You are right to criticize such friends and hold them
   in low esteem. Even so, I urge you to welcome those who
   want to help the city.

HECTOR. There are enough of us, the men who have been
   keeping Ilium safe for so long.

CHORUS. Are you confident that you have now destroyed the   330
   enemy?

HECTOR. Fully confident. The light of tomorrow's dawn will
   prove it.

CHORUS. Beware of the future. The god often reverses things.

HECTOR. I hate the man who comes to help his friends too late.
   However, since he has come, let him stay here not as an ally
   but as our guest as the guests' table. He has forfeited the
   gratitude of Priam's people.

CHORUS. My lord, to reject your allies causes bad feeling.
MESSENGER. Simply by appearing he would terrify our enemies.
HECTOR (*to* CHORUS). You advise me well. (*to* MESSENGER) And
    you were keeping your eyes open at the right time.*

      In view of what the Messenger says, let Rhesus, the lord   340
of the golden armour, stand with us as an ally of this
land.

The MESSENGER *goes out.*

CHORUS (*sings*).
    May Adrasteia, the daughter of Zeus,
    keep my mouth free from presumptuous talk.*
    For I shall say all that my soul
    finds it delightful to express.
    You have come, O son of the river-god, you have come,
    you have approached the hall of the Friendly God,*
    our welcome guest, sent here so late
    by your Pierian mother* and the river
    with its lovely bridges,*   350

    Strymon, who eddying once in watery form
    through the virgin inlet
    of the sweet-singing Muse,
    was father to your manly prowess.
    You have come to me, a Zeus, the bringer of light,
    driving your chariot with its dappled mares.
    Now, O Phrygia my fatherland,
    now by the favour of the god you may call him
    Zeus the deliverer.*

    Shall ancient Troy ever again   360
    drink all day long in revelling companies,
    while they sing love songs,
    out-drinking each other
    as the cups circle and the brain reels,
    when the sons of Atreus have gone
    from the shore of Ilium
    over the sea to Sparta?
    Rhesus my friend, I pray that you may bring these
        things to pass
    through your spear's might
    and reach your home again.

Come, show yourself, confront Achilles,   370
flashing your golden shield in his face
as you raise it aslant
along the chariot's branching rail,
urging on your horses and brandishing your two-
    pronged javelin.*
No one who resists you
shall ever dance on the plains
of Argive Hera.*
No, he shall lie a welcome burden
on this land,
killed by a doom from Thrace.

Enter RHESUS.

CHORUS (*chants*). Ah, ah,   380
    hail, great king. This cub which you have nurtured, O
        Thrace,
    has majesty in his look.
    See his mighty body clad in gold,
    hear the boastful clanging of the bells
    which ring out from his shield straps.*
    He is a god, O Troy, a god, Ares himself,
    this son of Strymon* and the songstress Muse,
    whose coming revives you.
RHESUS. Greetings, noble son of a noble father, Hector, ruler
    of this land. I am speaking to you when the day is old. But   390
    I am happy that you have met with success and are camped
    by the enemies' towers.* I have come to join you in demol-
    ishing their walls and burning the hulls of their ships.
HECTOR. Son of one of the Muses, a melodious mother, and of
    the Thracian river Strymon, it is my custom always to speak
    the truth. I am a straightforward man. Long, long ago you
    should have come to share with this land in its toils. You
    ought not to have left Troy to fall beneath the Argives'
    attack, for all you cared. For you cannot say it was because
    your friends did not summon you that you stayed away and
    failed to come to our defence. How many heralds, how many   400
    senior Phrygians went to charge you to defend our city?
    What splendid gifts did we neglect to send you? You are a
    barbarian of a kindred race to ours, but you betrayed us,

your fellow barbarians, to the Greeks. That was what you
did. Yet it was this hand of mine which raised you from a
petty kingdom and made you the Thracians' great ruler,
when around Pangaeus and the Paeonians' land I fell upon
the Thracians' chiefs and face to face I broke their shields.* 410
I made the people slaves and handed them over to you. You
have spurned your debt of gratitude for these favours and
when your friends are in trouble you rush to our help too
late. But others, men who are not related to us in any way,
have been here long since. Some of them have fallen and lie
in grave-mounds*—no small proof of their loyalty to our
city—while others stay here in arms by their horse-drawn
chariots patiently enduring the winds' chill blasts and the
sun-god's thirsty flame,* not like you lying on soft bedding
as you drained many a toast of wine.

To leave you in no doubt that Hector speaks his mind, 420
that is what I blame you for, and I charge you to your
face.

RHESUS. I too am like this. I speak directly and to the point. I
am a straightforward man. My heart was more distressed,
more unsettled by sorrow than yours, over the fact that I
was not here in this land. But the Scythian people, whose
country borders mine, made war on me when I was on the
point of crossing over to Ilium. I had got as far as the shore
of the inhospitable sea* to ferry across my Thracian army.
There the spear drained the liquid blood from Scythian and 430
Thracian corpses alike and the land soaked it up. It was that
catastrophe which stopped me from reaching the plain of
Troy and coming here as your ally. But when I had smashed
them, I took their children as hostages and set them an
annual tribute to bring to my home. And now I have come
here after crossing the Thracian Bosporus on ship and the
remaining frontiers of your country on foot. You are wrong
to tax me with draining toasts of wine or languishing on
beds in golden palaces. No, I know what kind of frozen blasts 440
lie heavy on the Thracian sea and torment the Paeonians, I
and this soldier's cloak, from bitter experience in the sleep-
less night.

And yes, I have come late in the day, but I am in good
time nevertheless. This is now the tenth year that you have

been fighting and you have achieved nothing as day suc-
ceeds day while you dice with the Argives in the game of
war. But a single span of sunlight will be enough for me to
destroy the towers, fall on the fleet, and kill the Achaeans.
On the day after that I shall leave Ilium and go home, hav-   450
ing cut short your labours. Let no one among you lift his
shield in his hand. I shall smash the Achaeans and put an
end to their loud boasting, even if I have come at the
eleventh hour.*

CHORUS (*sings*). Ah, ah,
   your words show your friendship, you are a friend sent by
     Zeus.
   Only may Zeus, god supreme, keep away from those words
   the divine anger that cannot be resisted.
   No ship from Argos
   has ever brought here
   a greater hero than you. Tell me,   460
   how shall Achilles withstand your spear,
   how shall Ajax?*
   May I behold the day, my lord,
   on which you exact requital for murderous deeds
   with your spear-point!

RHESUS. Such feats shall I perform for you, to make up for my
long absence. But I shall speak with Adrasteia in mind.* And
when we have liberated this city from its enemies and you
have picked out the choicest spoils for the gods, I want to   470
march with you to the Argives' land and ravage all of Greece
with the spear when I get there, so that they in their turn
may know what suffering means.

HECTOR. If I were to win release from the curse that afflicts us
now and rule a Troy restored to its former security, I would
certainly feel enormous gratitude to the gods. But the country of Argos and the meadow-lands of Greece are not as easy
to ravage with the spear as you say.

RHESUS. Don't they tell us that the Greeks who have come
here are their best men?

HECTOR. Yes, and we cannot fault them. But we have enough
to do in driving them away.   480

RHESUS. So when we have killed these, we shall have completed our work?

HECTOR. You must not look into the future at the cost of our immediate needs.

RHESUS. You seem to think it enough to suffer—not to act.

HECTOR. Yes, for here in Asia I rule over a sufficiently vast kingdom.* But you can either provide our left wing or our right or set your targeteers in the middle of the allies and station your army there.

RHESUS. I want to fight the enemy alone, Hector. But if you think it shameful not to join with me in burning the sterns of their ships after your sufferings over all these years, posi- 490 tion me face to face with Achilles and his army.

HECTOR. It is not possible to lift a spear in fury against him.

RHESUS. But I heard that he had sailed to Ilium.

HECTOR. He did, and he is here. However, in his rage against their generals, he refuses to lift his spear to help them.*

RHESUS. Who in their army comes second to him in reputation?

HECTOR. In my view Ajax* is in no way inferior. Neither is Tydeus' son. And then there is that most wily chatterbox Odysseus. His spirit is bold enough and he has done more 500 damage to this land than anyone else. He came to the shrine of Athena in the night, stole the goddess's image and carried it off to the Argives' ships.* And just recently, disguised as a vagabond in beggar's rags, he entered our walls and called down many curses on the Argives—when he had been sent to spy on Ilium.* After he had killed the guards and the gates' defenders, he slipped out. He is always to be found sitting in ambush close to the altar of Apollo Thymbraeus near the city.* It's a vile pest that we have to wrestle with there.

RHESUS. No man of noble spirit would think it right to kill his 510 enemy by stealth.* No, he meets him face to face. I'll capture this fellow who you say plots his schemes and lurks in hiding like a thief, and impale his living body by the road out of the city gates, setting him there for the winged vultures to feast on.* He is a robber who pillages the temples of the gods, and that is a fitting death for him.

HECTOR. Now make your camp, for it is night-time. I shall show you a place where your army is to spend the night sep- 520 arately from our array. 'Phoebus' is our watchword* in case

you need it. Now that you have heard it, remember it and
pass it on to the Thracian army.

(*to the Chorus*) You must go out in front of our lines to
keep wakeful watch and receive Dolon, our spy on their
ships. For if he is safe, he is approaching the Trojan camp by
now.   HECTOR and RHESUS *go out.*

CHORUS (*sings*).
   Who is on guard duty next? Who is taking over from me?
   The first constellations of the night are setting
   and the seven journeying Pleiades are above the horizon.   530
   The Eagle flies in the middle of the sky.*
   Wake up! Why are you delaying? Leave your beds
   and come to your duty.
   Don't you see the bright moon?
   The dawn! The dawn comes near
   and this star is one of the day's harbingers.*
(*chants*)
   —Who was allocated the first watch?
   —The word is, Mygdon's son, Coroebus.*
   —Who came next?—The Paeonian army   540
   roused the Cilicians, and the Mysians roused us.

   —Then is it not time that we went to rouse
   the Lycians to take the fifth watch,
   according to the rota which the lot decreed?*
(*sings*)
   Listen, I hear her—the nightingale, killer of her son,
   sitting on her blood-stained nest by Simois,*
   sings her sorrowful song
   from her throat with all its many tones.   550
   Already they are grazing their flocks on Mount Ida.
   I hear the voice of the pipe
   sounding through the night.
   Sleep casts its spell over my eyes,
   for it falls most sweetly on their lids towards dawn.
(*chants*)
   —Why ever is the scout not coming our way,
   the man Hector sent to spy on the ships?
   —I am alarmed, for he has been gone a long time.

—Can he have fallen into a hidden ambush   560
and been killed? Perhaps so. I am afraid.*

—I propose that we go to rouse
the Lycians to take the fifth watch,
according to the rota which the lot decreed.

The CHORUS *goes out.*

ODYSSEUS *and* DIOMEDES *enter.*

ODYSSEUS. Diomedes, did you not hear the clatter of arms? Or
is the noise that drops on my ears a delusion?   570
DIOMEDES. No, it's the harness which hangs from the rails of
horse-drawn chariots sounding its clang of iron. Fear swept
over me too before I realized that it was only the rattling of
horse trappings.
ODYSSEUS. Be careful that you don't meet their sentries in the
night.
DIOMEDES. Even when stepping in the darkness I shall be on
my guard.
ODYSSEUS. But if you should rouse them, do you know their
army's watchword?
DIOMEDES. It's 'Phoebus'. I know that watchword since I
heard it from Dolon.*
ODYSSEUS. But look! I see that this place where the enemy
were sleeping is deserted.
DIOMEDES. Yes, Dolon said that Hector was lying hereabouts. It was to kill him that I have drawn this sword of
mine.
ODYSSEUS. What does this mean? Surely he hasn't gone off
somewhere with his company?
DIOMEDES. Perhaps he's gone to set up some stratagem
against us.
ODYSSEUS. Yes, Hector is bold now that he is winning, bold
indeed.
DIOMEDES. What should we do then, Odysseus? We have   580
failed to find the man sleeping here and have been cheated
of our hopes.
ODYSSEUS. Let's go towards where the ships are stationed as
quickly as we can. The god who is making him successful is
protecting him. We must not push our luck.

DIOMEDES. Shouldn't the two of us move against Aeneas or
  Paris, the most hated of the Phrygians, and cut off their
  heads with our swords.

ODYSSEUS. How will you be able to search for these men in
  the dark through all the enemy lines and kill them without
  terrible risk?

DIOMEDES. But it would be disgraceful for the two of us to
  return to the ships of the Argives with no startling achieve-   590
  ment to score up against the enemy.

ODYSSEUS. But you *have* achieved something! Did we not kill
  Dolon, that spy on our ships' stations, and have we not kept
  these spoils?* Do you expect to devastate their whole camp?

DIOMEDES. You convince me. Let us go back. May fortune
  smile on us!

ATHENA *appears above the stage building.*

ATHENA. Where are you going off to from the Trojan lines
  with sorrow gnawing at your hearts if the god does not
  allow you to kill Hector or Paris? Have you not heard that
  a man has come to Troy in grand style as its ally?* It is
  Rhesus, and if he lives through this night till tomorrow, nei-   600
  ther Achilles' nor Ajax' spear could stop him razing the
  Argives' walls, laying all flat before his spear as he rushes
  inside the gates, and destroying all your shipways.* If you
  kill him, you have everything. So forget about finding where
  Hector is sleeping and cutting off his head. His death will
  come from another hand.*

ODYSSEUS. My mistress Athena, I recognize the familiar sound
  of your voice.* For you always stand beside me in my trou-   610
  bles and protect me. Tell us where the man has bedded
  down. Where has he been stationed in the barbarians'
  camp?

ATHENA. He is stationed nearby, separately from the rest of
  the host. Hector has allocated him a place outside the lines
  to sleep until night gives place to day. Close by, his white
  mares are tethered to his Thracian chariot* and they gleam
  through the darkness, shining like the wing of a river-swan.
  Kill their master, the two of you, and take these off. They
  will be a most beautiful trophy for your homes. For nowhere   620
  on earth is there such another team of chariot horses.

ODYSSEUS. Diomedes, you must either kill the Thracians or let me do so while you see to the horses.

DIOMEDES. I shall do the killing and you can manage the horses.* You are an old hand with your sly ideas, a quick-witted trickster. A man should be given the task where he can help the most. *ODYSSEUS goes out.**

ATHENA. Look, I see Alexandros* there coming towards us. He has heard unconfirmed rumours from one of the watchmen that the enemy have come here.

DIOMEDES. Is he coming with others or on his own? 630

ATHENA. On his own. It looks as if he is going to where Hector is sleeping to tell him that some men have come to spy on the army.

DIOMEDES. Then shouldn't he be the first to die?

ATHENA. You cannot do more than fate has decreed. It is not right that this man should die at your hand.* No, make haste against the one to whom your visit brings his doom of death. This fellow will think that I am his ally Cypris* standing by to help him in his troubles and I shall speak treacherous words as I converse with him. And although I have told you all this, my victim has not taken it in. 640 Though he was near when we were talking, he did not hear anything.

DIOMEDES goes out.

ALEXANDROS enters.

ALEXANDROS. You, Hector, our general and my brother, are you sleeping? Shouldn't you be awake?* One of the enemy has come close to our army. Either it's marauders or spies.

ATHENA. Have no fear. I am here to protect you, Cypris, your friend. I care about your part in the war. I am not unmindful of the honour you paid me, and I thank you for treating me so graciously.* Now I have come bringing to Troy's army in its hour of triumph a man who is a great friend to you, 650 the son of the songstress, the divine Muse. He is called the son of Strymon.

ALEXANDROS. You always show favour to our city and to me, and I claim that by deciding in your favour I won for the city the greatest treasure that I ever brought her or ever shall. I have come here because I heard confused reports—a

rumour had started up among the watchmen—that Greek
spies have come. One man who did not see them talks of
them, and another who saw them after they had arrived can
say nothing about them. That is why I came to where   660
Hector is sleeping.

ATHENA. Do not be afraid. There is nothing untoward happening in our army. Hector has gone to show the Thracian
army where to sleep.

ALEXANDROS. You convince me. Your words give me confidence and I shall go to guard my post. You have freed me
from fear.

ATHENA. Off with you. Be assured that I am concerned with
everything about you. I want to see my friends triumphant.
Yes, you too will appreciate my concern.*

ALEXANDROS goes out.

(*to* ODYSSEUS *and* DIOMEDES) I call to you, you over-eager pair,
Laertes' son, give your sharp swords a rest. For the Thracian   670
general lies dead and we have his horses, but the enemy
have heard and are coming against you.* You must flee as
quickly as you can to the shipways. Why do you delay? The
enemy's thunderbolt is hurtling towards you. Save your
lives.   *ATHENA goes off.*

ODYSSEUS *enters, pursued by the* CHORUS. *The* CHORUS, ODYSSEUS,
and the CHARIOTEER *chant or sing until* 754 (*except in the short
passage marked 'speaking'*).

CHORUS. You there! You there!
Strike! Strike! Strike! Stab! Stab! Stab!
Who is the man?
Look, I mean him.
Over here, everyone, over here.   680
I have them,* I have seized them.
They are marauders who are disturbing our army in the
darkness.
What is your company? Where have you come from?
What country are you from?

ODYSSEUS. I cannot tell you that. CHORUS. If you don't tell
us, you will die today for your evil handiwork.
Won't you say the watchword before my spear pierces
your chest?

ODYSSEUS. Stop, have no fear. CHORUS. Come near, every-
one. Strike away.*
Did you kill Rhesus? ODYSSEUS. Don't strike me. Strike
someone who wants to kill you.
Wait, everybody. CHORUS. No, we shall not. ODYSSEUS.
Hey! Do not stab a friend.
CHORUS. And what is the watchword? ODYSSEUS. 'Phoebus'.
CHORUS. Correct. Let each man hold back his spear.
Do you know where the men have gone? ODYSSEUS. I saw
them somewhere over here.*   ODYSSEUS slips out.
CHORUS. Track them down, everyone, or should we raise the   690
alarm cry?
But it is dangerous to startle the allies from their sleep
with an alarm.

Who was the man who has gone?
What great bold fellow is going to boast
that he escaped my grasp?
Where shall I find him?
Who can I say he looks like,
the man who has run on fearless foot in the darkness
through our lines and watchposts?
Is he a Thessalian
or a man who lives in a coastal city of the Locrians?*   700
Or does he lead a lonely life on a distant island?*
Who was he? From where? What is his fatherland?
Which god does he declare supreme?*

—Whose work is this? Is it Odysseus'?
Yes, if we can judge by his previous actions. Of course.
—You really think so? —Of course I do!
—Certainly he has been a bold enemy to us.
—Whose courage are you praising? Whose? —Odysseus.
—Do not praise a robber who fights by trickery.

Before now he came into our city,*   710
his eyes bleared with tears,
his body wrapped in rags,
a sword hidden
under his cloak.
Begging in order to keep life and soul together, he crept
around, a vagabond menial,
his head begrimed with dirt and dust.
He poured abuse
on the royal house of the sons of Atreus,

for all the world as if he hated the commanders.
May he die, die as he deserves, 720
before he can trample the Phrygians' land beneath his
    feet!

—Whether it was Odysseus or someone else, I am still afraid,
for Hector will put the blame on us guards.
—Saying what? —Angry . . .
—That we've done what? What are you afraid of?
—That there passed by us . . . —Who?
—Those who came into the Trojan camp during the night.
CHARIOTEER (*off-stage*). Oh, oh!
What a heavy blow of fate! Alas, alas!
CHORUS. Watch out!
Crouch down in silence, everyone. Perhaps somebody is 730
    coming into the snare.
CHARIOTEER (*off-stage*). Oh, oh!
What overwhelming catastrophe for the Phrygians!
    CHORUS. It is one of the allies who is lamenting.

Enter the CHARIOTEER, *wounded in his side and bathed in blood.*

CHARIOTEER. Oh, oh!
Calamity has fallen on me and on you, king of the
    Thracians.
Oh, my king, you looked on Troy, that most hated of
    cities,
and then what an end you met with!
CHORUS (*speaking*). Which of our allies are you? My vision is
    blurred in the darkness and I cannot make you out
    clearly.
CHARIOTEER. Where can I find one of the Trojan chiefs?
Tell me, where does Hector
sleep the night in arms? 740
To which of the army's captains should I tell
what we have suffered, what someone has done to us
unseen in the night and then vanished?—yet all too visible
is the web of sorrow that he has spun.
CHORUS. Some disaster is falling on the Thracian army.
There's no escaping it, if this man's words mean anything.
CHARIOTEER. Our army has been massacred, our king has
    fallen,

the victim of a treacherous blow. Ah, ah, ah, ah!
What agony courses through my body   750
from the pain of this bloody wound.
If only I could die!
Was it fated that, the moment he had reached Troy as
    your ally,
Rhesus and I should die so ingloriously?

CHORUS. He uses no riddling words to let us know of this cata-
    strophe. He tells us plainly that our allies have been destroyed.
CHARIOTEER. Ill work has been done, ill and most shameful
    too. Yet this doubles the ill. For to die a glorious death if one
    must die is bitter, I think, for the man who dies—how could
    it be otherwise? Even so, it gives the survivors good reason   760
    to boast and adds to the glory of the house.* But we have
    died as fools die and there is no fame for us. For when Hector
    had pointed us to where we were to lie and told us the
    watchword, we went to sleep in exhaustion after our march,
    and no night guards were set for our army. We did not place
    our armour in good order or hang the goads over the horses'
    yokes,* since our king had heard that you were winning and
    besieging the sterns of the ships. No, we simply flung our-
    selves down and slept.
        But my heart-felt concern for the horses broke off my   770
    slumbers, and I gave them their feed in generous measures
    since I expected to yoke them for battle at dawn. Then I saw
    two men prowling around our army through the murky
    darkness. But when I stirred, both of them crouched down
    and moved off again. Believing that some marauders from
    the allies were approaching, I shouted out to them not to
    come near our army. They made no response, and I said no
    more. I returned to my resting place and went back to sleep.
    And in my sleep a vision appeared to me. As in a dream I   780
    seemed to see two wolves which had climbed up onto the
    backs of the horses that I tended and used to drive as I stood
    beside Rhesus. Mounted there and lashing the horses' hides
    with their tails, they drove them, and the mares snorted,
    breathing rage from their nostrils, and reared up in their
    panic.* And while I was trying to protect them from the
    beasts, I woke up, for my night terror startled me from sleep.

I lifted my head and heard the moans of dying men.* And a   790
hot jet of newly-shed blood hit me as I lay close to my
slaughtered master, now in the agony of death. I leapt up
but had no spear in my hand, and as I looked around hunting for one, there stood beside me a sturdy fellow who struck
me in the side of my belly with his sword. I felt his strength
in the violence of the blow as he ploughed the wound's deep
furrow in my body, and I fell headlong, while they took the
chariot and horses and ran off in flight.

    Ah! ah! The agony wears me down and the pain stops me
from standing upright any more. Though I am an eye-   800
witness of the catastrophe, I am not able to say how those
who are dead met their end or who killed them. But I can
guess this much. It was our friends who inflicted these torments on us.

CHORUS. Charioteer of the Thracians who has suffered this terrible fate, do not torment yourself over that, for it is the
enemy that did these things.

    But Hector himself has been told of the disaster and is
coming to sympathize, I think, with your sufferings.*

Enter HECTOR.

HECTOR (*to the Chorus*). You here, you who are responsible for
this calamity, how did the enemies' spies get past you unob-
served? You are disgraced and the army has been massa-   810
cred. Why didn't you beat them back either when they were
coming into our camp or when they were leaving it? (*To the
Chorus Leader*) Who shall be punished for this if not you? For
you, I say, stood guard over our army. They have gone off
unscathed, with many a jeer at the Phrygians' cowardice
and at me, the commander.

    Be sure of this, then—I swear it by father Zeus—either
flogging or beheading lies in store for you for what you have
done. If I do not carry out my threat, you can think of
Hector as a cipher and a coward.*

CHORUS (*sings*). Oh, oh,   820
    †O lord of our city, mighty, mighty in my judgement,
    they must have arrived when I came
    to announce to you† that fires were blazing round the ships.
    For my eyes were wakeful in the night

with no slumbering or drowsing—
I swear it by Simois' streams.
Do not be angry with me, my lord,
for I am altogether innocent.
If you find out later
that I have done or said anything wrong,   830
bury me alive. I ask for no mercy.

CHARIOTEER. Why do you threaten these men, and, a barbarian yourself, undermine the way I, your fellow barbarian,
see things, as you weave your web of words? It was you who
did these things. There is no one else whom we the wounded
or the dead would even consider as the guilty party. You will
need to make a long and cunning speech to persuade me
that you did not kill your friends. It was the horses you
longed for. It was because of these that you constantly urged
your allies to come, because of these that you killed them. 840
They came—they are dead. Paris' violation of hospitality
looks less shameful than yours in this murder of your allies.*
No, do not say that one of the Argives came and massacred
us. For tell me, who could have got past the Trojan companies and reached us without being noticed by them? You
were camped in front of us. So was the Phrygians' army.
Which of your other allies was wounded, which killed, when
the enemy you speak of came? But we have been wounded
and those who suffered worse no longer see the sunlight.* 850
    To put it plainly, we blame none of the Achaeans. For
which of our foes could have made their way through the
darkness and discovered the ground where Rhesus was
sleeping unless one of the gods had informed the killers?*
They didn't even know that he had come. No, this is a plot.

HECTOR. We have now had dealings with our allies for all the
time that the Achaean host has been in this land and I am
not aware that we have heard any harsh words from them.
But it looks as if such criticism is to start with you.* May I
never conceive such a passion for horses that I kill my 860
friends! This is Odysseus' handiwork. Who else of the
Argives would ever have plotted or done such a deed? I am
afraid of him, and something else troubles my heart. Has he
met Dolon and killed him? He has been gone a long time
now and has not reappeared.

CHARIOTEER. I don't know these Odysseuses of yours that you
  speak of.* Our wounds were inflicted by no enemy.
HECTOR. You believe that then if it's what you think!*
CHARIOTEER. O my fatherland, if only I could die on your soil!
HECTOR. Do not talk of dying. We have enough dead men   870
  already.
CHARIOTEER. What refuge can I find now that I have lost my
  master?
HECTOR. My house will take you in and heal you.
CHARIOTEER. What sort of care may I expect from murderers'
  hands?
HECTOR. Can't this man stop harping on the same theme!
CHARIOTEER. My curse on the man who did this! I do not aim
  these words at you as you claim so loudly. But Justice under-
  stands.*
HECTOR. Take him up. Bring him to my house and look after
  him in such a way that he will have no cause for complaint.
  But you must go to Priam and the elders on the wall* and   880
  tell them to bury the corpses by the public roadway.*
                              The CHARIOTEER *is carried off.*
CHORUS (*chants*). Why does some new divinity lead Troy back
  after its great triumph, back to sorrow?
  What fate does it bring to birth?

The MUSE *appears above the stage building carrying the dead*
                    RHESUS *in her arms.*

  Look! Look!
  What god appears overhead, O my king,
  holding the new-slain corpse in her arms
  as on a bier?
  I feel fear as I look upon this tragedy.
MUSE. You may look at me, Trojans. For I whom you see here   890
  looking upon this, my dear son, piteously killed by enemies,
  am the Muse honoured among poets, one of the sisters. The
  man who murdered him, tricky Odysseus, shall pay due
  punishment in time to come.*
(*sings*)
  In an unpremeditated dirge
  I lament you, my son,
  your mother's grief, for the voyage

you made to Troy.
Though I said no, though your father entreated you,
you went from us in defiance   900
on your ill-starred voyage of sorrow.
Alas I cry for you, my dear, dear son,
my child, alas!
CHORUS. As far as one who is no relative may, I pity your
son for his cruel death.
MUSE (*sings*). My curse on Oeneus' grandson,
my curse on Laertes' son*
who has robbed me of my boy,
the best child that a mother ever bore!
My curse on Helen too, who left her Greek home   910
and sailed here to a Phrygian bed!
She has killed you beneath Ilium,* fighting for Troy's sake,
my dearest son, and she has emptied numberless cities
of their bravest men.
(*speaks*) Thamyris, son of Philammon,* you wrung my heart
often when you lived and often when you went to Hades.
For what caused me to bear this unhappy son was the arro-
gance which tripped you up when it led you to challenge us
Muses. As I crossed over the river's streams, I was drawn to
Strymon's fertile bed of love—when we came to craggy   920
Pangaeus where the soil is gold,* we Muses who had practised our instruments to perfection, to compete in music-
making with the skilful Thracian poet, and we blinded
Thamyris who had often slighted our skill. And when I had
given you birth, I cast you into your watery father's eddy-
ing stream, feeling shame before my sisters because of my
lost virginity. Then Strymon gave you to no mortal hands
but to the nymphs of the springs to nurse.

  After your fine upbringing by those maidens, you ruled   930
Thrace and were the first of men, my child. And as long as
you fought your bloody battles in your native land I had no
fear that you would die. But I tried to tell you never to make
the journey to Troy since I knew your doom. However,
Hector's embassies, for ever treading on each other's heels,
persuaded you to go there and help your friends.

  Athena, it is you alone who are the cause of this doom.
Odysseus and the son of Tydeus did nothing—it was you

who did the deed, and do not imagine that I am blind to this. 940
Yet we sister Muses honour your city above all others with
our presence in your land. Orpheus ordained the torch pro-
cessions of your mysteries and he was the cousin, yes the
cousin, of this corpse, your victim. Musaeus, your revered
citizen who reached the peak of artistry, was trained by
Phoebus and us sisters.* And as my reward for this, I hold
my son in my arms and weep for him. I shall call no other
to sing the dirge.*

CHORUS. So the Thracian charioteer was mistaken, Hector, 950
when he savaged us for having plotted this man's death.

HECTOR. I knew it. We needed no seers to tell us that this man
died through the schemes of Odysseus. But when I saw the
Greeks' army encamped on this soil, was it not inevitable
that I would send heralds to my friends begging them to
come and help our land? Yes, I did send them. And he was
under an obligation to help me and came here. I take no joy
in his death, no, none at all.

Now I am ready to make a tomb for him and to burn with
him splendid robes without number too.* For he came as our 960
friend and a cruel fortune has taken him from us.

MUSE. He shall not go down into the dark earth. I shall pray for
this much from the bride below, the daughter of Demeter,* the
goddess of fertility—that she shall send up his soul from the
dead. She has an obligation to show that she honours the
relations of Orpheus.* And although to me he will be as a dead
man who no longer looks upon the light of day—for he will
never meet me again or see his mother's face—he will lie con- 970
cealed in the caves of this silver-bearing land,* a man-god
beholding the light, a prophet of Bacchus who lived on rocky
Pangaeus,* the deity revered by those who understand.

I shall bear the grief of the sea goddess Thetis more lightly
now. For her son* too must die. We sisters shall sing our
dirges first for you, my son, then later for Achilles in Thetis'
time of grief. Pallas who killed you will not save him, so fatal
is the arrow that Apollo's quiver holds in reserve for him.
Alas for the sufferings of mothers, for human woes! All who 980
take good account of such pain will live without children.
They will not give them life and then bury them.*

The MUSE goes off.

CHORUS. It is the task of Rhesus' mother to see to his funeral
  rites. As for you, Hector, if you wish to lay your hand to
  what lies before us, now you can. For the day is dawning.*
HECTOR. Go, order the allies to arm themselves at once and to
  harness the necks of their horses. With torches in hand, they
  must await the blare of the Tyrrhenian trumpet. For I am
  confident that we can get over the ditch and the walls of the   990
  Achaeans and fire their ships. Yes, the rays of this rising sun
  herald the day of freedom for the Trojans!

                                         HECTOR *goes out.*

CHORUS (*chants*).
  Obey our lord. Let us put on our arms
  and march in order. And let us tell our allies
  to do this. Perhaps the god who fights on our side
  will give us victory.*   *The* CHORUS *go out.*

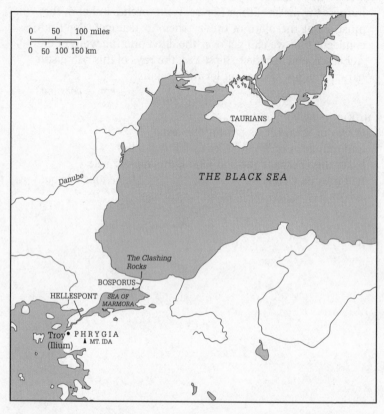

Map of the Black Sea (after E. C. Kennedy, *Scenes from Euripides'* Iphigenia in Aulis *and* Iphigenia in Tauris (Macmillan, 1954))

EXPLANATORY NOTES

IPHIGENIA AMONG THE TAURIANS

1   *s.d.*: the Taurians lived in the south-west Chersonese (now the Crimea) on the north of the Black Sea at or near the modern Balaclava, a region which Lena Yermolajeva of St Petersburg University (who was born nearby) assures me fits the geographical 'facts' of Euripides' play (see 107, 262–3, 1391–3 and n. at 40).

1–2   *Pelops . . . Oenomaus*: Pelops had to beat Oenomaus, king of Pisa in Elis (in south west Greece), in a chariot race to gain the latter's daughter Hippodamia in marriage. He won the race by flagrant cheating and fraud which led to the deaths of Oenomaus and his charioteer. (However, a different version of the story is given at 823–5. In this Pelops engages in a heroic fight with Oenomaus.)

6–9   *My father slaughtered me . . . dark-blue sea*: Helen, the wife of Menelaus, king of Sparta, had run off to Troy (in the north-west corner of modern Turkey) with the Trojan prince Paris, and the Greeks assembled at Aulis to sail on an expedition to get her back.

    Euripus is the windy and narrow strait, famous for its frequent changes of current, separating the island of Euboea from the coast of Boeotia where Aulis was situated. This town stood on a small promontory with a bay on each side, one of them facing north, the other south.

10   *a thousand ships*: the 'canonic' number of the Greek ships which sailed to Troy. (See Christopher Marlowe, *Doctor Faustus*: 'Was this the face that launched a thousand ships . . .?') Homer gives the number as 1,186, and Thucydides a round total of 1,200.

13   *Achaeans*: used by Euripides, following the example of Homer, of the Greeks generally.

16   *Calchas*: a Greek seer from Mycenae or Megara, he could interpret the future, as well as knowing the past and present.

20–1   *For you vowed . . . the year produced*: the goddess of the moon is Artemis. In the year of Iphigenia's birth (presumably about fifteen years before the Greeks assembled at Aulis), Agamemnon, king of Argos, had made the vow referred to here, perhaps to propitiate the goddess. The 'most beautiful thing' of course

proved to be his daughter (23). Cicero gives this as an example
of a promise which it is wrong to fulfil. Agamemnon 'ought to
have broken his vow rather than commit so foul a wrong' (*De
Officiis* 3.25.95).

32–3   *He got . . . were wings*: there is a certain absurdity in this Greek
         etymology for the name of a barbarian king, but the Greek tragic
         poets were enthusiastic about such plays on words and *thoas*
         actually does mean 'swift' in Greek.

40   *I begin the ritual of his slaughter*: the Greek historian Herodotus
         describes the customs of the city (4.103.1–3): 'They sacrifice to
         the virgin goddess [i.e. Artemis] both shipwrecked men and any
         Greeks they take through piracy. They follow this procedure:
         after beginning the sacrificial rites, they hit the victim over the
         head with a club. Some say that they throw the body down from
         the cliff (for the temple stands on one) and place the head on a
         pole. Others agree about the head, but say that the body is not
         thrown over the cliff but buried in the earth. The Taurians them-
         selves say that this deity to whom they sacrifice is Iphigenia, the
         daughter of Agamemnon. As for the enemies they overcome,
         this is what they do. Each man cuts off the head, takes it away
         to his home, and then fixes it on a long pole and sets it high
         above his house . . . They say that these heads are set on high
         to guard the whole house.'
           E. Hall (*Inventing the Barbarian* (Oxford, 1989), 111 f.) gives
         an admirable analysis of Euripides' considerable debt to
         Herodotus (not just to 4.103 but to 4.99 as well) in *IT*. She con-
         cludes by saying that the 'coincidence of language and material
         in the two writers is far too great for it to be supposed that
         Euripides was not enormously indebted to the historian; indeed,
         it is most likely that the poet's barbarous Taurian society con-
         stituted a dramatic bringing to life of chapters in Herodotus, and
         was therefore entirely new to tragedy'. (See her Introduction,
         pp. xvi–xvii.)

42–3   *I shall tell to the air . . . any healing*: to tell the sun a bad dream
         was viewed as a cure, since the sun was supposed to have the
         power to neutralize the influences of night.

59–60   *And I cannot . . . death day*: these lines are clearly un-Euripidean.
         They assume that Iphigenia does not realize that things may
         have changed since she was whisked off to the Taurians.
         Pylades, Strophius' son, is in fact soon to appear. Strophius had
         married Iphigenia's aunt and Pylades is thus her cousin
         (917–19).

67–71   *Take care . . . Orestes*: Iphigenia believes that Orestes is dead (56, etc.). After she leaves the stage two men enter. One of them calls the other 'Pylades' (69): he was celebrated as the friend of Orestes. The speaker then goes on to say that they had sailed from Argos (70): this was Orestes' home town. Then (71) Pylades addresses his collocutor by name: it is Orestes. The dramatic irony here is handled with some subtlety.

72   *And this is the altar*: in the Greek world, the altar, which had to be accessible to the whole population, was outside the temple, which was itself viewed as the private house of the god.

74   *And do you see the heads*: the word I have translated 'heads' in fact means 'spoils' and so could refer to armour stripped from the victims. However, I feel that my translation is justified in view of the passage from Herodotus quoted in the n. at 40.

79–81   *Troop upon troop . . . track*: Phoebus Apollo, god of prophecy, had instructed Orestes to kill his mother in revenge for her killing of his father Agamemnon. However, Orestes' act of matricide had called up the Furies (spirits of vengeance, especially for crimes within the family, and embodiments of a guilty conscience) from the Underworld and they had pursued him relentlessly. The imagery here is probably from the chariot race, in which the charioteer would double back in the direction he had come after turning sharply round the turning post. The word 'spinning' in 82 continues the metaphor, for it is used of chariot wheels.

113–14   *Look there . . . to let ourselves down*: Pylades points out to Orestes the space between the temple's triglyphs (grooved tablets above the columns) through which they could climb. In later temples, these hollows were filled in by metopes.

124–5   *the two Clashing Rocks . . . the inhospitable sea*: these two rocks guarded the entry to the Black Sea ('the inhospitable sea') at the Bosporus. After Jason's ship, the Argo, had successfully managed to get through them without being crushed as they clashed, they remained fixed in place.

The Black Sea is called inhospitable on a number of occasions in the play (218, 253, 341, 395, 1388). There is a play on words here. The sea's name in Greek meant 'hospitable', an attempt to make it so by avoiding reference to the bad weather conditions for which it was notorious. In recording the truth about the inhospitable reception that this sea gave to strangers, Euripides shows it as essentially un-Greek, for hospitality to strangers was a key ingredient of Greek social behaviour.

127–8   *O daughter of Leto, Dictynna, goddess of the mountains*: Leto's two
          children were the divine twins Apollo and Artemis. Dictynna is
          a cult name for the latter, either derived from the Greek word
          for 'hunting or fishing net', or from Mount Dicte in Crete.

128–9   *to your halls . . . lovely columns*: M. Platnauer ((ed.), *Euripides:
          Iphigenia at Tauris* (Oxford, 1938), n. at 129) quotes Milton,
          Paradise Lost 1.713–15:
          > Built like a temple, where pilasters round
          > Were set, and Doric pillars overlaid
          > With golden architrave.

137   *Here I am*: Iphigenia had made it plain to the audience that she
          wished to see the Chorus at 64–5.

166   *which are poured to soothe the spirits of the dead*: milk, wine,
          honey (163–5) and water were poured upon the ground as
          offerings to the dead, who, it was hoped, would send up bless-
          ings from the Underworld to the survivors.

174   *I shall not bring my golden hair*: as a sign of mourning a lock of
          hair was normally cut off and placed on the tomb. This was a
          safe symbol of shared severance from life.

180   *the barbarian dirge of Asian women*: the Chorus of Greek hand-
          maidens plan to demonstrate the intensity of their sorrow by
          singing in the Mysian or some other Asiatic mode (musical
          style). Euripides was very conscious of the different emotions
          associated with the various modes. Plutarch tells the story that
          he rebuked a chorus member for laughing when the poet was
          singing in the plaintive Mixolydian mode (*de Audiendo* 46b). See
          Hall, *Inventing the Barbarian*, 82.

189–90   *Who of Argos' . . . now*: I have followed Badham's reading of
          these corrupt lines.

192:      ⟨*upon the house, causing the Sun's*⟩ *winged mares to veer round*: a
          very corrupt passage in the Greek. I have supplied the words in
          brackets. The reference seems to be to the occasion when Atreus
          served up his brother Thyestes' children to him in a stew. So
          appalling was this act that the Sun did not complete his chariot
          ride through the sky but simply turned round and went back
          down again. Cf. *Electra*, 727–36.

196   *because of the golden-fleeced lamb*: the origin of the feud between
          Atreus and Thyestes (see n. at 192) was their rivalry for pos-
          session of a gold-fleeced lamb which marked its owner out as
          King of Argos. Cf. *Electra*, 699–726.

200   *Tantalus' descendants*: Tantalus was the grandfather of Atreus
        and Thyestes and thus an ancestor of Iphigenia. A perjurer and
        the murderer of his son Pelops (though the latter was brought
        back to life), he is for ever punished in the Underworld for his
        sins.

210   *The unhappy daughter of Leda*: Zeus fell in love with Leda, the
        wife of Tyndareus, king of Sparta. The god disguised himself as
        a swan in order to make love to her incognito, and she laid two
        eggs, from which emerged two pairs of children: Clytemnestra
        (the daughter referred to here) and Polydeuces, and Helen and
        Castor. Polydeuces and Castor were known as the Dioscuri (the
        sons of Zeus) or the heavenly twins because they became a con-
        sellation in the sky (Gemini in Latin).

217   *for the son of the daughter of Nereus*: Nereus' daughter was the
        divine sea-nymph Thetis. Her son was Achilles, who emerged as
        the greatest of the Greek heroes.

221   *to Hera, the goddess of Argos*: Argos was a key centre of the wor-
        ship of this goddess, who remarks in Homer's *Iliad* (4.51–2) that
        her three favourite cities are Argos, Sparta, and Mycenae.
        Several cults of Hera are actually attested at Sparta. On the hill
        dominating the Argive plain was her most famous sanctuary,
        and a temple stood there perhaps from the eighth century BCE.
            In this line and in 222–4, which relate to life in Attica (the
        country whose main city was Athens), Iphigenia is lamenting
        that she cannot join in civic worship as a female citizen of a civ-
        ilized Greek state. (It is interesting that the Attic Euripides makes
        his Argive heroine take Attica as her model.) She is trapped in
        the murderous rituals of a cruel tribe which totally fails to
        understand the Greek concept of hospitality to strangers
        (225–8).

223–4   *an image of Athenian Pallas and the Titans*: at the Panathenaea (a
        great annual Attic festival) the *peplos* (a sacred robe) was carried
        in procession to the temple of Pallas Athene, goddess of Athens.
        On this robe was woven a picture of the battle of the gods
        against the Titans (the older gods) and of Athena's victory over
        the Giant Enceladus.

225–6   *but I stain . . . doom*: see n. at 344–7. C. S. Jerram (ed., *Iphigenia
        in Tauris* (Oxford, 1900)) comments (n. at 225–6): 'Observe how
        each item in the description serves to point the contrast between
        Iphigenia's present and former condition; dying shrieks and
        groans instead of festal song and the whirring loom, blood-
        stained altars for the gay colours of embroidered tapestry.'

241   *the dark-blue Clashing Rocks*: Jerram (n. at 241) suggests that the
          adjective may be due 'to their hazy appearance when
          approached by sea'.

245–55   *Where are they from? . . . the sea-water*: stichomythia. See
          Introduction, p. xxxvi.

263   *where the purple-fishers shelter*: purple dye could be obtained
          from the purple-shellfish. The purple-fishers would shelter in
          such hollows as the broken cliff (262–3) while watching the
          floats of their traps.

270–4   *O son of the sea-goddess . . . Nereids*: who, the pious herdsman
          wonders, can these two figures be? Ino, to escape the fury of her
          mad husband, jumped into the sea with her infant son
          Melicertes. Poseidon, the sea god, transformed mother and son
          into the sea deities Leucothea and Palaemon respectively.
          Perhaps those two are the pair in the cave. Or perhaps they are
          Castor and Polydeuces, the Dioscuri (see n. at 210), who became
          a constellation in the sky which was extremely useful to
          mariners and thus gave them associations with the sea. Or can
          they be two grandsons of Nereus, the old man of the sea and the
          father of fifty daughters (see n. at 217)?

284   *like a hunter*: the idea seems to be that of the hunter surprised
          by the sudden appearance of some wild beast and crying for help.

344–7   *O my unhappy heart . . . in your grasp*: the play seems to speak
          with different voices about whether Iphigenia had sacrificed
          Greeks in the past or not (38–9, 72, 225–6 (yes she has) *but*
          258–9 (no she hasn't)). Platnauer comments here (n. at 346):
          'This passage surely supplies convincing proof that Greeks *had*
          already been sacrificed; that Iphigenia *wept* does not mean she
          did *not* sacrifice.'

348–50   *Now, however, because of the dream . . . who have come here*:
          'Wecklein justly notes the tragic irony involved in making
          Iphigenia steel her heart against the unknown Orestes, on
          account of her love for Orestes himself' (Jerram, n. at 350).

352   *the more fortunate*: has something gone wrong with the text
          here? It is hard to see Orestes and Pylades as numbering among
          'the more fortunate' of men. Perhaps Euripides in fact wrote 'the
          more *un*fortunate'.

354   *not a breath of wind from Zeus*: Zeus was, among other things,
          the weather god.

372–3   *And as I looked . . . bridal veil*: Iphigenia looks back to the time
          she set out from Argos dressed for her wedding. Her mother

Clytemnestra had stayed at home (365–7) while in Euripides' *Iphigenia at Aulis* she insisted on escorting her daughter to Agamemnon at the Greek camp.

387–8   *the feast which Tantalus gave. . . . a boy's flesh*: Tantalus chopped up his son Pelops and served him up to the gods as a stew. In fact the gods realized what was going on and did not touch the flesh, with the exception of Demeter who, rendered absent-minded by her distress at the loss of her daughter, ate one of the boy's shoulders before she realized what it was. The gods rearticulated Pelops, gave him an ivory shoulder in place of the one Demeter had eaten, and brought him back to life.

389–91   *My view is that . . . evil*: here Euripides makes Iphigenia 'openly reject the Taurians' identification of their savage goddess with Artemis, her own Hellenic heavenly patroness' (Hall, *Inventing the Barbarian*, 184).

392–6   *Dark, dark blue . . . for Asia's soil*: the straits referred to are the Bosporus (which links the Sea of Marmara to the Black Sea). Io, a priestess in Argos, was seduced by Zeus, who transformed her into a cow in an attempt to disguise this liaison from his wife Hera. Hera sent a horsefly to torment her in her cow form and, driven by this insect, she fled from Argos and crossed the Bosporus (which in fact means 'cow crossing') from Europe into Asia.

400–1   *the Eurotas . . . streams of Dirce*: Eurotas flowed through Sparta and Dirce was a river of Thebes. The Chorus speculate about what Greek city the strangers may be from.

411–12   *Are they eagerly competing to increase their houses' wealth*: the Chorus wonder whether the two strangers are merchants.

423–4   *the unsleeping coast of Phineus*: Phineus was the king of Salmydessus. The coast of this country (between the promontory of Thynias and the Bosporus) was famously stormy.

425   *Amphitrite*: 'Amphitrite, as the wife of Poseidon, personifies the restless motion of the billows' (Jerram, n. at 425).

435–7   *the land of many birds . . . Achilles runs*: the island of Leuce (modern Phidonisi), on which stood a temple to Achilles, is opposite the mouth of the Danube. The name means 'white' (cf. ' with its white coast', 436), and it was so called either because of the white birds which abounded there or because of its white cliffs. The ghosts of Achilles and other dead heroes were supposed to have run races there.

439–42   *If only . . . Helen would leave the city of Troy and come here*: the Chorus do not know about Helen's return to Greece. Iphigenia, however, appears to have been told that the Trojan War is over and that she has gone back to Menelaus (519–21).

494–569   *This man . . . So you were nothing then*: stichomythia. See Introduction, p. xxxvi.

499   *And you, what name were you given by* your *father*: Orestes avoids giving a direct answer to this question. Iphigenia does not in fact discover his identity until more than 300 lines later. This, combined with Orestes' ignorance of who she is, gives fertile ground for dramatic irony.

502   *If I were to die without a name, no one could mock me*: knowledge of someone's name gives power over that individual to the person who discovers it. Nobody can exult over the death of Orestes if he maintains his anonymity.

510   *Yes, from Mycenae*: Mycenae is some six miles from Argos, and the Greek tragedians use the names of the cities interchangeably, usually preferring Argos.

512   *But I both wanted and did not want to go*: Orestes wanted to go in so far as he was not exiled from Argos and hoped to find an end to his troubles through his journey to the Taurians' land (85–92); he did *not* want to go inasmuch as he was driven out by the Furies. Aristophanes satirizes Euripides for such verbal paradoxes at *Acharnians* 395–6:

            DICAEOPOLIS. Is Euripides at home?
            SERVANT. He is at home and not at home, if you get my meaning.

522   *And her return has brought no good to one member of my family*: i.e. to Agamemnon. His victory in the Trojan War had brought about Helen's return—and naturally his own. His wife Clytemnestra killed him when he arrived back. The 'one member of my family' could alternatively be Iphigenia, who Orestes believes has been sacrificed to secure Helen's return.

532   *He died*: according to Strabo (14.1.27), the seer died of grief at being beaten in a soothsaying competition by Mopsus, grandson of Teiresias, at a grove sacred to Apollo at Colophon in Ionia.

533   *how just that is*: for Calchas had demanded Iphigenia's sacrifice (16–24).

548   *he destroyed another*: Orestes here refers to himself.

568   *He lives, poor creature, everywhere and nowhere*: E. B. England (ed.), *Iphigenia in Tauris* (London, 1886), n. at 568, aptly quotes a letter of Sir Thomas More to Erasmus: 'The heretic Tyndale . . . who is in exile nowhere and everywhere.'

573-5   *One thing alone . . . who have experienced it know*: in this corrupt and suspect passage, Orestes expresses his bitterness at the living death he is enduring.

584-5   *a letter which a prisoner wrote out of pity for me*: a woman of the heroic age would have been illiterate, though Phaedra writes a letter herself in *Hippolytus* (856 ff.).

588-90   *For I had no one whom I could keep alive*: one of a pair of strangers can be spared; but the man who wrote the letter for Iphigenia must have been on his own, and thus it was impossible for her to save him.

612-13   *For I have a brother . . . I cannot see him*: Iphigenia is still thinking of Orestes and Pylades as brothers (cf.497), despite the fact that she knows that they are not. Orestes, of course, had said that they were brothers in love (498). This passage is richly ironical since a genuine pair of siblings is on stage.

616-27   *Who will sacrifice me . . . corpse for burial*: stichomythia. See Introduction, p. xxxvi.

626   *A gaping chasm in the rock, full of holy fire*: Diodorus of Sicily (20.14.6) thinks that Euripides took this idea from a horrendous Carthaginian ritual: 'There was in their city [Tyre] a bronze statue of Cronus [Baal-Moloch], extending its hands, palms up and sloping towards the ground, so that a child placed upon it rolled down and fell into a chasm full of fire.'

677   *the Phocians' many valleys*: the country of Phocis in central Greece was Pylades' native land. It contained the southern spurs of the great Parnassus mountains and thus was well-endowed with valleys.

697-8   *my family's name would live . . . never be erased*: 'The importance to a Greek of having his family continue is a matter of religion; for naturally where there are no descendants there can be no ancestor-worship' (Platnauer, n. at 697).

700   *Argos, famed for her horses*: a stab of poignancy as Orestes, apparently about to die, recollects the pastures of his homeland where the horses graze.

709   *my foster-brother*: Orestes had been brought up with Pylades in the house of the latter's father Strophius in Phocis (see n. at 677) after he had been taken to safety there from Argos in the aftermath of his father's murder at his mother's hands.

727   *the many folding leaves of my tablets*: such tablets consisted of two or more small wooden boards, the surfaces of which were indented over most of their area. The indentations were filled

with wax, and messages were written on the wax with a metal pen. The boards might be hinged together. They could be tied up with string, the knot of which might be sealed.

735–54   *What do you want then . . . if it is helpful*: almost all in stychomythia. See Introduction, p. xxxvi.

791–2   *Look, I am carrying . . . your sister here*: in a fine *coup de théâtre*, Pylades walks a few paces across the stage to deliver a message which Iphigenia had assumed would involve a veritable odyssey.

805–21   *Your brother is not there . . . for my cenotaph at Argos*: almost all in stichomythia. See Introduction, p. xxxvi.

810   *No, you must speak and I shall listen*: Iphigenia is afraid that if she asks the questions she may give away information which will lead Orestes to the right answers.

811   *First I shall tell you something that I heard from Electra*: Orestes was only a baby when Iphigenia left Argos to go to Aulis. Euripides is careful to make it plausible that he should know things which Iphigenia can remember.

812   *You know that a feud arose between Atreus and Thyestes*: see notes at 196 and 192. These notes explain 813 and 816 as well.

814   *Do you remember weaving this feud in your fine-textured web*: Iphigenia has chosen appalling episodes from her family's history to portray in her weaving (see also 816). This is scarcely suprising in a household where the maiden's quarters are seen as an appropriate place to display a grisly man-slaying spear (823–6). The descendants of Atreus have a warped view of life. But perhaps there is a universal theme here. In the *Iliad* we find Helen blithely weaving 'many battles of the horse-taming Trojans and the Achaeans with their bronze tunics, battles which they were enduring for her sake at the hands of Ares [the god of war]' (3.125–8). Women in the heroic age are portrayed as deeply conscious of the savagery raging outside their secluded quarters.

818   *the nuptial water*: it was the custom for Greek brides and bridegrooms to bathe ceremonially on the morning of their marriage, if possible in water from a sacred spring, e.g. at Athens from the fountain of Enneacrounus, formerly called Callirrhoë (Thucydides 2.15.5).

824–5   *This he brandished in his hand when he killed Oenomaus*: a variant of the usual story which is told in the n. at 1–2.

831   *And I hold you, the girl men thought dead*: while Iphigenia sings, Orestes sticks doggedly to the spoken language throughout the recognition scene (827–99).

845-6   *O hearth of the Cyclops-built palace . . . Mycenae*: the walls of Mycenae were built of such huge masses of rough-hewn stone that it was thought that mere humans could not have constructed them. The gigantic Cyclopes must have performed the task.

898   *the two of us, the last of Atreus' descendants*: Iphigenia forgets for a moment about Electra—in whose fate she in fact proves to be extremely interested (912-14)—perhaps unsurprisingly in view of the fact that she and Orestes are alone together on the verge of the civilized world.

900-1   *I saw this with my own eyes . . . words can express*: the Chorus use theatrical language to reinforce the emotional impact of the recognition scene. They 'saw' it, rather than hearing it through a 'messenger' speech (there are two of these in this play (260-339, 1327-1419). They tell us that words cannot express how wonderful it was.

912   *You won't stop me asking my questions*: in a less politically correct age (date of publication, 1900) Jerram comments (n. *ad loc.*): 'Iphigenia, with a woman's pertinacity, insists on completing her information about the family.'

915-39   *She lives with my friend here . . . keep silence*: stichomythia. See Introduction, p. xxxvi.

918   *Is he the son of Atreus' daughter*: the daughter was Anaxibia. Obviously she was the sister of Agamemnon and the aunt of Iphigenia.

935   *Yes, they forced a blood-stained bit into my mouth*: Jerram (n. at 935) comments: 'The persecution of Orestes by the Furies is compared to the driving of a horse with a rough bit which makes its mouth bleed.'

942-4   *Next Loxias . . . the nameless ones*: Loxias is a name for Apollo. It means either 'the Ambiguous' or 'the Speaker'. Both would refer to his oracular function.

   the nameless ones: men were reluctant to name the Furies, those terrifying goddesses of vengeance (see n. at 79-81). Indeed, in an attempt to soften their vindictive rage, they often called them 'the Kindly Ones', hoping thus to make them so. (Cf. n. on 124-5 on the Black Sea.) However, Orestes in point of fact calls them Furies three times in the course of this speech.

945-6   *For there is a holy tribunal . . . act of pollution*: Ares had killed Halirrhothius, son of Poseidon, for the rape of his daughter Alcippe. The tribunal took place on the Areopagus ('Hill of Ares') in Athens, which derived its name from this trial.

949–54   *those who did have a sense of duty . . . took their pleasure thus*: as
          the playwright obligingly causes him to inform us (958–60),
          Orestes' reception in Athens is the mythical explanation of the
          Athenian feast of Choes (Wine-jugs). At this feast every partici-
          pant had his own table and a separate cup in place of the com-
          munal mixing bowl.

962   *myself standing on one platform, the eldest of the Furies on the other*:
          Pausanias informs us (1.28.5) that there were two stone blocks
          on opposite sides of the Areopagus court, one for the accuser
          called 'the stone of implacability' and one for the accused, 'the
          stone of criminality'.

965–6   *when Pallas' hand . . . equal*: as president of the trial, Pallas
          counts the votes and, finding them to be equal, declares that
          Orestes is acquitted. The rule that an equal number of votes
          meant acquittal was observed in classical Athens.

968–9   *All of the Furies . . . of the voting*: the temple of the Furies was
          an underground passage on the lower slopes of the Areopagus,
          approached by a long chasm and with a spring of water at the
          bottom.

972   *to Phoebus' holy ground*: i.e. to Delphi.

976–7   *Then Phoebus . . . tripod*: to deliver his prophecies, Apollo worked
          through his priestess, the Pythia. Crowned with laurel, she sat
          on a tripod (a three-legged stand), became possessed by the god,
          and prophesied under divine inspiration.

1014   *the city of Pallas*: there is clearly a gap in the text after these
          words. The clauses which I have enclosed in brackets may well
          represent the basic meaning of the original but that would prob-
          ably have been decidedly longer.

1020–48   *Would we be able to kill the king . . . without the king's knowledge*:
          stichomythia. See Introduction, p. xxxvi.

1021   *This is a fearful thing you have suggested—that visitors should kill
          their host*: for the Greeks the concept of hospitality was
          supremely important. Guests and hosts were expected to treat
          each other with consideration and respect. Orestes had earlier
          complained about the hospitality he himself had received at
          Athens (947–56), but here shocks Iphigenia by his highly un-
          Greek suggestion that they should kill their host. She jibs at
          doing to their Taurian host what the Taurians do to their Greek
          guests.

1048–9   *It is your job to see to everything else*: i.e. to getting on board the
          ship and sailing away.

1068-70 *You I beseech . . . knees*: Iphigenia 'supplicates' various members of the Chorus. This process consisted of touching some part of the body (preferably the chin and/or knees) of the person from whom you wanted to gain a favour. That person would then feel under considerable pressure to grant it. Words could substitute for the actual gesture, and, as England writes (n. *ad loc.*), 'these customary formulas of entreaty do not necessarily imply that Iphigenia goes down into the orchestra to touch the limbs, etc., mentioned.'

1086-7 *But be gracious to us . . . Athens*: Iphigenia's hope is that Artemis will quite literally come to Athens in the embodiment of her image. The play remains interestingly opaque about whether the goddess actually wishes to leave the land of the Taurians or not.

1089-94 *You halcyon bird . . . easily understand*: Alcyone married Ceyx and they were so happy in their marriage that they compared themselves to Zeus and Hera. Enraged at this, those gods transformed them into birds, a diver and a halcyon respectively. The halcyon's cry could be easily understood because it made the noise 'ceÿx', i.e. her former husband's name. (The bird referred to is in point of fact a kingfisher, but to translate it so is to lose the resonant associations of the name 'halcyon'.)

    A famous verse translation of this play by Gilbert Murray (1910) is seen at its best in the opening of this Chorus:

    Bird of the sea rocks, of the bursting spray,
      O halcyon bird,
    That wheelest crying, crying, on thy way;
    Who knowest grief can read the tale of thee:
    One love long lost, one song for ever heard
      And wings that sweep the sea.

1096- *as I long . . . pay service to the Muses*: the Chorus think back
1105 nostalgically to Greece, where they were captured in war and sold into slavery. The description specifically refers to the island of Delos (in the middle of the Aegean sea) which they came from. It is interesting that in 422 BCE, as Thucydides tells us (5.1) 'the Athenians removed the Delians from Delos [to Asia]; they now thought that at the time when they had been consecrated they were impure because of some ancient offence'. In fact, the Athenians soon brought them back because Pythian Apollo told them to, and we may think here of Iphigenia's promise to restore the Delian women to Greece (1067-8). It is certainly possible that this episode may lie behind Euripides' choice of this particular nationality for his Chorus. More significantly, Delos stood

at the heart of the Greek world, midway between the cities of Ionia (on and near the coast of modern Turkey) and those of the mainland. These echt-Greek maidens provide an extreme contrast with the barbarian land at the edge of the world where they now find themselves. At the same time, the focus on Delos—with its international associations ('the festival gatherings of the Greeks', 1096) and its situation at the heart of the Athenian empire—assists the shift of focus from Argos, the actual homeland of Iphigenia and Orestes, to their destination of Athens.

The palm tree was 'dear to Leto in her travail' (1102) because the goddess is said (Theognis 1.5) to have supported herself by the branches of the tree while giving birth to Apollo (and presumably Artemis). This birth was accompanied by the singing of swans (1104–5—Callimachus, *Hymn to Delos* 249–52). The circular lake (1103–4) has been drained by French archaeologists.

1121–2   *To fall to grief from happiness—that makes life grim for mortals*: compare Dante, *Inferno* 5.121–2:

> Nessun maggior dolore
> Che ricordarsi del tempo felice
> Nella miseria.

(There is no greater grief than to remember a happy time when plunged in misery.)

1128–31   *And Phoebus the seer . . . the gleaming land of the Athenians*: Phoebus Apollo is the god of music. It was a function of a seer to forecast the ship's course. 'Gleaming' was an adjective notoriously applied to Athens. Aristophanes makes his Chorus say in *Acharnians* (639–640): 'And if someone wanted to fawn on you and called Athens 'gleaming', he could win anything from you just through that word 'gleaming'—when he's actually lauding you with an honour fit for sardines.'

1155   s.d: Iphigenia carries on the image of the goddess. By constantly referring to its pedestal, the playwright suggests that it is of a certain size. However, the evidence of an ancient wall painting and various friezes suggests that the statue actually used as a prop may have been fairly small (Iphigenia in *Lexicon Iconographicum Mythologiae Classicae* (Zurich and Munich, 1990), pls. 61, 73, 76, and 83).

1159–
1221   *My lord, stay where you are in the portico . . . I join you in that prayer*: stichomythia. See Introduction, p. xxxvi.

1161   *I avert the evil omen*: what Iphigenia actually says is 'I spat it out'. However, rather than actually spitting, one could simply use this expression when one wished to avert a sight or remark of evil omen.

1171   *They killed their mother*: it is necessary for Iphigenia to pretend that Orestes and Pylades are actual brothers.

1193   *The sea washes away all that is bad from men*: this fine line summarizes the ancient belief in purification by water. Such a belief is referred to in Shakespeare's *Macbeth* (ii.ii.61–4), where, however, it proves inoperative:

> Will all great Neptune's ocean wash this blood
> Clean from my hand? No, this my hand will rather
> The multitudinous seas incarnadine,
> Making the green one red.

Diogenes Laertius (3.6) tells how Euripides quoted this line to extol the virtues of bathing in the sea, by which Euripides had once been cured when he fell sick during a visit to Egypt with the philosopher Plato.

1203–33 *Let me have what you know I need . . . and to you too, goddess*: the metre changes from the standard iambic rhythm of Greek tragic dialogue to the trochaic. This reflects Iphigenia's growing excitement, an emotion which is reinforced by the fact that the stichomythia is conducted in divided lines from now until 1221.

1214   ⟨*IPHIGENIA. A natural conclusion.*⟩: I have filled what is plainly a gap here.

1231   *you will dwell in a pure temple*: this will prove to be at Halae in Attica. See n. at 1450–63.

1234–82 *Son of a glorious mother, Leto's son . . . with all its visitors*: the Chorus here vindicate the oracle of Apollo at Delphi (on the slopes of Mount Parnassus in central Greece) after the doubts voiced by Orestes.

     The first possessor of the Delphic oracle, which was situated at the centre of the world and close to the purifying waters of the Castalian spring, had been Earth and next had come her daughter Themis. The Python, another child of Earth, defended the shrine for his mother and sister. Apollo slew the Python and took possession of the oracle, banishing Themis. For the operation of the oracle, see n. at 976–7. The vapour which inspired Apollo's priestess to her divine responses emerged 'from beneath' his shrine (1256).

     Euripides may have invented the story of how Earth interfered with Phoebus' *modus operandi* in revenge for the banishment of Themis. The older gods communicated through dreams, and their dream-oracles were consulted by clients sleeping on the ground at the shrine (hence 'the dark earth-beds', 1266-7). When Zeus shakes his locks (1276) at the young Apollo, he is showing his customary sign of assent. He endorses Apollo's monopoly to prophetic truth through his responses (given in hexameter verse—hence 'chants', 1283—composed by Apollo's priests on the basis of the priestess's ravings).

1293-4   *But the king . . . from the temple*: the Chorus show their loyalty to the Greek escapees by misleading the Messenger. Cf. the superbly vacuous 1296-7.

1342   *oar-pins*: these were pins in the side of the ship to which the oars were secured by leather hoops dropped over them.

1350   *catheads*: a beam projecting almost horizontally from each side of the bows of a ship for raising and carrying the anchor.

1355-6   *tried to drag . . . the stern-holes*: 'The [stern-holes] were two holes in the stern bulwarks, one on either side, through which the [steering-oars] passed.' (Platnauer, n. at 1356). Lucian (*Toxaris* 6) refers to a picture of the scene in a Scythian temple in which the Taurians are portrayed hanging from the rudders and trying to get on board, but having no success.

1406   *But the ship kept moving closer, closer to the rocks*: it is interesting that Artemis does not respond favourably—rather the opposite—to Iphigenia's appeal and the sailors' chant (1398-404). Interesting too is the fact that it is Athena, not Artemis, who appears (1435) as the *deus ex machina*. What Artemis feels about the theft of her image is left worryingly opaque. Cf. n. at 1086-7.

1414-17 *Revered Poseidon . . . prey*: Poseidon, who built the walls of Troy with Apollo, is seen as hostile to Orestes as the son of Agamemnon who had destroyed that city.

1429-30 *fling them over the rugged crags or impale their bodies on stakes*: E. Hall (*Inventing the Barbarian*, 158) comments that 'although the Greeks regularly threw criminals off cliffs, the impalement even of corpses or parts of them was denounced by Herodotus' Pausanias as a barbarous act unfit for Greeks (9.79). But the Thoas of the *IT* is made to plan not just to stick his victims' heads on stakes, but to impale them bodily.'

1449   *Athens, that god-built city*: built, in fact, by Athena herself after she had won the contest with Poseidon over who was to be the city's protector.

1450-63 *there is a place . . . the holy meadows of Brauron*: Halae Araphenides was in the east of Attica, on the coast opposite the hills above the town of Carystus in the south of the island of Euboea across the Euboaean Gulf. At Halae there was an ancient temple of Artemis Tauropolis, and at Brauron, a little South of Halae, the goddess was worshipped as Artemis Brauronia. Euripides puts the image at Halae and Artemis at Brauron.

The 'naming' (1454) refers to the Artemis *Tauropolis* (Tauropolos in Euripides), the latter word having a false etymology foisted on it by the playwright, who derives it from the Tauri and from 'pol' which is part of the Greek word for 'wander' (i.e. here referring to Orestes' wanderings).

1472   *when the votes are equal the defendant is acquitted*: see n. at 965–6.

1484   *I shall stop the spearmen I am sending against the foreigners*: the Greeks used a single word for 'guest', 'host', 'stranger', and 'foreigner', subsuming all these identities under the important concept of hospitality. Thoas now embraces this concept. Indeed he espouses it with a fullness of spirit that the tricky Greeks of the play do not themselves display. See notes at 124–5, 221, 1021.

1497–9   *O most reverent Victory . . . crown me*: the playwright prays for victory in the drama competition in an ending identical with those of his *Orestes* and *Phoenician Women*.

BACCHAE

1 *s.d.*:   the smouldering tomb may be off-stage.
The god Dionysus, who speaks the prologue to give us the necessary background information, may wear a smiling mask (439). He is disguised as a mortal (4, 53–4) and is unique among Euripides' prologists in that he is a god who participates in the action.

3   *in a birth precipitated by the lightning flame*: the myth tells how Hera, jealous at Zeus' affair with the Theban princess Semele, who was now pregnant by him, persuaded her to ask him to come to her in his divine form. Zeus, who had sworn to grant any request, appeared to her as the god of thunder and lightning. Thus Semele was incinerated, but Zeus snatched the baby Dionysus from her womb and sewed him in his thigh (cf. 286–97).

4   *Dirce . . . Ismenus*: the rivers of Thebes.

10–11   *Cadmus who has forbidden men to tread on this ground*: places struck by lightning were viewed as having been touched by the

15

24–5

30

37–8

40

45

55

59

60

63

supernatural. By this edict Cadmus shows a characteristic combination of reverence and family feeling.

Bactra: the capital city of Bactria, a country made up of what are now parts of Afghanistan, Uzbekistan, and Tadjikistan.

fastening a fawnskin . . . in their hands: the fawnskin was the holy garment (138) traditionally worn by bacchae; the thyrsus (see the glossary at the head of the translation) is to be horrifically transformed into a 'weapon' (762–3, 1099).

clever idea: the play frequently debates where true wisdom lies. See especially the enigmatic choral lyrics at 877–912. Cf. notes at 179, 200, 395, 641, 877, 1005–10, 1150–2.

Mixing with the daughters . . . roofless rocks: Dionysus' cult is essentially democratic. These lines also bring out the contrast between the women's safe homes in the ordered city and their present unconventional dwelling in the wild.

that it is still uninitiated in my bacchanals: initiation into the Bacchic mysteries is an important theme of the play. See R. Seaford, Euripides, *Bacchae* (Warminster, 1996), 39–44: 'Although the Dionysiac mysteries might take various forms, basic seems to have been a rite of passage centred around an extraordinary (sometimes death-like) experience that effected a transition from outside to inside the group . . . and from anxious ignorance to joyful knowledge, a transition in which the initial attitude of the initiand is likely to be ambivalent' (p. 39).

fights against the deity: Pentheus' hubristic folly is expressed in a military metaphor (cf. 325, 1255). The metaphor is reflected in the reality of the play's action in the literal armed force with which he attacks Dionysus and his followers (52, 628–36, 761–4).

Mount Tmolus: the holy ridge of mountains which forms the backbone of Lydia and dominates Sardis. Cf. 65 and 462.

mother Rhea: the mother of Zeus and other gods, and assimilated to the Asiatic mother goddess Cybele. See n. at 79.

Here to this royal palace of Pentheus: this is the only occasion in extant Greek tragedy when the Chorus is summoned into the theatre. Seaford (p. 28) comments that the chorus 'are, as embodying the threatened cult, unusually central to the action, while retaining the typical choral function of providing moral and emotional comment on it'.

Cithaeron: a mountain range near Thebes, and a resonant name in the tragic tradition, above all in Sophocles' *Oedipus the King*.

66   *Bromius*: a title for Dionysus meaning 'roarer' and referring to his manifestations as bull-god, lion-god, and earthquake-god; his kettle-drums roar also (156).

68–9 *Who is on the street . . . come outside*: all Thebans, whether out of doors or at home, are invited to witness the worship of Dionysus. As J. Diggle observes (*Euripidea* (Oxford, 1994), 4) the Lydian Chorus are 'active proselytizers'.

79   *Cybele*: the cult of this Asiatic mother goddess arrived in Greece in the sixth century BCE or possibly before, and was introduced into the Athenian agora some time in the fifth century.

100   *the bull-horned god*: for Dionysus as bull, cf. 1017,1159 and notes at 618, 918–22.

101–4 *he garlanded . . . beast-born prey*: the handling of snakes was a genuine feature of certain forms of Dionysiac cult.

108   *bryony*: an evergreen creeper with clusters of white flowers and scarlet berries.

112–13 *white-haired curls of braided wool*: in its ritual use, wool may be a substitute for the lamb as a sacrificial victim. Seaford (n. at 112) suggests that 'the maenadic rejection of working wool (118–19)' is 'conceivably relevant here'.

117–18 *stung to frenzy from their looms and shuttles*: working at the loom was the main activity of Greek women and it defined their role.

120–34 *O secret chamber . . . Dionysus rejoices*: the myth of the origin of the *tympanon* (the 'circle of stretched hide'). Zeus was hidden from his father Cronos (who would have eaten him if he had found him) in a cave on Mount Dicte in Crete. In order to drown his infant cries, which might have attracted Cronos' attention, the Couretes (= youths), identified by Euripides with the Corybants (male ministers of Cybele), invented the *tympanon* to supply a covering noise. This was then borrowed from the rites of Cybele (identified with Rhea—see n. at 59) for use in Dionysus' festivals.

The satyrs were horse-men or goat-men with a long thick tail and a huge permanently erect penis. They attended Dionysus.

135   *He*: either Dionysus himself or a participant representing Dionysus.

139   *the joy of eating raw flesh*: we do not know whether this was an actual feature of Dionysiac worship. See n. at 1184.

141   *Euoi*: this ecstatic cry is inscribed (as *euai*) on a mirror of the late sixth century BCE found at Olbia.

154   *glittering pride of Tmolus, its river awash with gold*: i.e. the
       Chorus, who come from the region of Mount Tmolus (see n. at
       55). 'Glittering pride' suggests 'the showy trappings of the ori-
       ental women' (E. R. Dodds, Euripides, *Bacchae* (Oxford, 1960),
       n. at 152–4).
       The river Pactolus brought gold-dust down from Mount
       Tmolus.

170   *s.d.*: The blind Teiresias is probably led on by a boy.

171–2 *Agenor's son who left the city of Sidon*: Cadmus left the
       Phoenician city of Sidon where Agenor was king in order to
       search for his sister Europe after her abduction by Zeus.

175–7 *what I agreed with him . . . shoots of ivy*: what is the mood of this
       scene? Seaford (n. at 170–369) feels that it is 'not comic but fes-
       tive'. 'The participation of old people was a striking and heart-
       ening expression of the all-inclusiveness of the festival.' Seaford
       also draws attention to the comprehensive nature of Dionysiac
       worship: 'Everybody must join in, young and old, without dis-
       tinctions.' (See esp. 206–9.) Teiresias and Cadmus 'embody the
       participation of *males* (the females, young and old, are already
       participating: 35–8, 694), specifically of *old* males . . ., dressed,
       like the maenads, with fawnskin, crown, and thyrsus (176–7)'.

179   *the wise voice of a wise man*: the 'What is wisdom?' theme. Cf.
       notes at 30, 200, 395, 641, 877, 1005–10, 1150–2.

188–9 *How delightful it is to have forgotten that we are old*: for the reju-
       venating effect of Dionysiac ritual, see Aristophanes, *Frogs*
       354–8 and Plato, *Laws* 665–6.

190–200 *For I am young too . . . eyes of the gods*: stichomythia: see
       Introduction, p. xxxvi.

200   *In the eyes of the gods we mortals have no wisdom*: the 'What is
       wisdom?' theme. Cf. notes at 30, 179, 395, 641, 877,
       1005–10, 1150–2.

214   *How excited he is*: as Dodds observes (n. at 214), a hint to the
       director. 'Pentheus is characterized throughout by lack of self-
       control, in contrast with the supernatural [calm] of Dionysus.
       His behaviour in this scene is, as Murray says, that of a typical
       tragedy-tyrant.' Seaford (n. at 214) has a different emphasis,
       relating Pentheus' 'fluttering, nervous excitement' to that of
       mystic initiands. 'Pentheus is characterised by the first of his
       many experiences reflecting initiation into the Dionysiac mys-
       teries.' For a discussion of this see Seaford, pp. 39–44. Cf. my n.
       at 40.

225   *they put Aphrodite before Bacchus*: while Pentheus' belief that the maenads indulged in drunkenness and sex may be justified (despite the messenger's denial at 686–8), his emphasis on sex may not be without psychological significance. Dodds writes (n. at 222–3), 'His attitude to the Bacchanal women is not one of simple repulsion: unlike Hippolytus, he is the dark puritan whose passion is compounded of horror and unconscious desire, and it is this which leads him to his ruin.'

228   *I shall hunt down*: here there is launched a series of metaphors taken from the language of hunting. Those who know the myth—or know how drama works—will be aware that the intention to hunt is expressed by the hunt's eventual victim. Seaford (n. at 228) says that on an item of Greek pottery in Heidelberg 'roughly contemporary with *Bacchae* Pentheus sets out with hunting-spears and net'.

229–30   *Ino and Agave . . . Autonoe, I mean*: this short passage is almost certainly interpolated. Whether or not it is Euripidean, it is telling to have a mention at this early stage—and from this speaker's lips—of Actaeon, whose fate foreshadows that of Pentheus. Artemis, because Actaeon had boasted that he was better at hunting than her (the better known version is that he had seen her bathing naked), transformed him into a stag, whereupon he was torn to pieces by his own hounds. Cf. 337–40, 1291.
     Ino and Autonoe are Agave's sisters and Pentheus' aunts.

235–6   *his fragrant hair . . . in his eyes*: there is something feminine about Dionysus' powerful sexuality. And his ruddy complexion is suitable for the god of wine.

241   *by cutting his head from his body*: a brutally tyrannical declaration. The threat, however, is not to be fulfilled. On the contrary, it is Pentheus who will be decapitated.

250   *what a laugh*: this crudely insensitive reaction shows up the blind folly of Pentheus.

255–7   *You want . . . burnt offerings*: seers such as Teiresias would interpret the future from the flight of birds (cf. 'wonder-watcher', 248) and the entrails of sacrificial victims. Others would, of course, have to tell the blind Teiresias about these. The kings in Greek tragedy who level a charge of venality against this particular seer, such as Creon (*Antigone* 1050) and Oedipus (*Oedipus the King* 388), come to disaster, and so will Pentheus.

264   *Cadmus who sowed the earth-born crop of men*: Cadmus killed a dragon, the offspring of Ares and the god's ancient guardian of

the place. Athena gave him half of its teeth to sow, and, when he did this, 'Sown Men' sprang from the ground. They then slaughtered each other. Only five survived, one of them being Echion, Pentheus' father, and together with Cadmus they built the citadel of Thebes.

275-6   *The goddess Demeter—she is Earth*: in cult these two goddesses were in fact always distinct. Earth was viewed as a cosmogonic element while Demeter, the divinity of agriculture, is essentially the goddess of corn (or grain).

280-4   *which puts an end . . . their daily round of cares*: cf. *Macbeth*, II.ii.37-41:

> the innocent sleep,
> Sleep that knits up the ravell'd sleave of care,
> The death of each day's life, sore labour's bath,
> Balm of hurt minds, great nature's second course,
> Chief nourisher in life's feast.

286-97: *Do you mock him . . . new story*: this odd passage cannot be rendered satisfactorily in English. The idea is that the Greek word for 'thigh' (*mēros*) became confused with the word for hostage (*homēros*) and this led to a new version of events. However strange this may appear to us, it reflects an attitude to myth current in Euripides' time (Seaford, n. at 286-97).

307   *over the upland between the two peaks*: i.e. the stretch of wild but fairly level country above the Phaedriades (= the shining rocks) which tower over Delphi.

334-6   *And you should tell a lie . . . family*: Cadmus here shows his characteristic family solidarity. (Cf. notes at 10-11, 1308-12.) He may not, however, be as cynical a manipulator of the truth as these lines could suggest. He may simply feel that this is an approach which might work with Pentheus.

337-40   *You have seen . . . than Artemis*: see n. at 229-30.

350   *wool ribbands*: the hanging up of these consecrated Teiresias' seat as a place of divination.

356-7   *meet his punishment of death by stoning*: the carrying out of this form of execution involves a number of citizens, and thus the community validates the sentence. It is an unwise threat for an isolated tyrant figure to make. Cf. Creon in Sophocles, *Antigone* 36.

367   *Pentheus does not bring sorrow*: *penthos* is the Greek for 'sorrow'. Thus the name Pentheus offers an opportunity for a play on words. Cf. 508, 1112-13.

370   *Purity*: 'it refers mainly to purity or scrupulousness in ritual, but also sometimes—as here—has a moral dimension' (Seaford, n. at 370).

384–5   *males*: the Chorus responds to Pentheus' charge about the drunkenness of women in the Bacchic rites (260–2).

395   *Mere cleverness is not wisdom*: in this important statement of the 'What is wisdom?' theme, the 'cleverness' is that of Pentheus. Cf. 266–9, 311, 332, 655–6 and notes at 30, 179, 200, 641, 877, 1005–10, 1150–2.

402–16:   *May I come . . . hold their rites*: the 'escape prayer' is frequent in Euripides (e.g. *Hippolytus* 732–51, *Helen* 1478–86), and the *Va pensiero* theme finds him at his most evocative. Aphrodite was born from the foam of the sea and soon came to Cythera and then to Paphos in Cyprus. 'The barbarian river with its hundred mouths' must be the Nile, but how does it fertilize Cyprus? Dodds writes (n. at 406–8), 'I am tempted to guess that Euripides is alluding to the belief, held to-day by Cypriot peasants and reported as far back as 1816 by the Turkish traveller Ali Bey, that the island's numerous, rather brackish springs are fed not by local rainfall but by water which has passed under the sea (Unger-Kotschy, *Cypern*, 70; Hill, *History of Cyprus*, i.6).' Pieria, the famously beautiful hill-country on the Northern side of the Olympus *massif*, is the traditional birthplace of the Muses.

419–20   *Peace . . . who rears children*: in the Staatliche Antikensammlungen und Glyptothek in Munich is a Roman copy of a Greek statue by Cephisodotus dating from around 375 BCE. This shows Peace holding a baby (Wealth) in her left arm. The idea behind the image is that 'Peace is the nurse of Wealth; that if nurtured by Peace, Wealth will flourish and grow—a fact of life much appreciated in basically agricultural communities' (S. Woodford, *An Introduction to Greek Art* (London, 1986), 152).

441–2   *Stranger . . . who sent me*: the isolation of Pentheus is stressed.

453–6   *Well, physically . . . laden with desire*: R. P. Winnington-Ingram (quoted by Dodds, n. at 453–9) remarks that 'the sensual appearance of the Stranger is precisely the form in which Dionysus should and could reveal himself to the suppressed sensuality of Pentheus'.

It would be imprudent for a wrestler to wear his hair long since it would give his opponent a hold. In Euripides' Athens, long hair was a mark of aristocratic young men, and this caused resentment. Seaford (n. at 455–6) suggests that 'Pentheus himself may have long hair, but held up in a band' (cf. 831).

463–508 *I know of it . . . fit to sorrow for*: stichomythia. See Introduction, p. xxxvi.

491 *the bacchant*: the Greek words here could equally well mean Bacchus—an appropriate touch in an encounter laden with irony.

498 *The god will free me whenever I wish*: Dionysus is the god of liberation. A Roman name for him is Liber (= free).

507 *I am Pentheus, the son of Agave and of my father Echion*: Pentheus insists on his identity, which is soon to fragment.

508 *You have a name fit to sorrow for*: see n. on 367.

514 *as slaves at the loom*: weaving is a polar opposite to maenadism. Cf. n. at 117–18.

519 *Achelous*: the largest river in Greece, and, according to the scholiast T on *Iliad* 21.195, 'the source of all the others'.

526 *Dithyrambus*: this is the name of (*a*) a Dionysiac choral performance, (*b*) a member of the Dionysiac company, and (*c*) (as here) Dionysus himself.

538–41 *He reveals . . . Echion begat*: see n. on 264.

556–9 *Where then on Nysa . . . Corycian peaks*: Nysa is an imaginary mountain associated with Dionysus. The Corycian heights are Mount Parnassus, where was the famous Corycian cave.

561–4 *where Orpheus once . . . wild beasts*: Orpheus was the 'type' of the musician and poet. His singing was so beautiful that wild beasts would follow him and trees and plants would bow to him.

569–71 *the swift-flowing Axios and the river Lydias*: these are rivers in Macedonia which Dionysus will cross on his way (apparently from Thrace) to Pieria.

574 *a land of fine horses*: Macedonia, by the capital of which (Aegae) the Lydias flowed. This reference may have been intended by Euripides as a compliment to Archelaus, the king of Macedonia, at whose court he may have written this play.

587–8 *Soon the palace of Pentheus will . . . collapse*: we know nothing about how the earthquake would have been suggested by the staging. See S. Goldhill, *Reading Greek Tragedy* (Cambridge, 1986), 277–84 for a discussion of this.

618 *a bull*: the bull is a Dionysiac animal. R. P. Winnington-Ingram (*Euripides and Dionysus* (London, 1997), 84) suggests that 'in binding it with effort and strain Pentheus is performing the futile task of constraining the animal Dionysus within himself'. Cf. notes at 100, 918–22.

641   *A wise man should always keep a balanced and easy temper*: the 'What is wisdom?' theme. Cf. notes at 30,179, 200, 395, 877, 1005–10, 1150–2.

647–55   *Stand still . . . I am so*: stichomythia. See Introduction, p. xxxvi.

651   *The one who grows the rich-clustered vine for men*: it seems likely that one or more lines, in which Pentheus insults Dionysus, have fallen out of the text after this one.

668–74   *I want to hear . . . just men*: we see two sides of Pentheus here, first his tyrannical aspect, and secondly his belief in free speech and his sense of justice.

693   *a marvel of good order to look upon*: this order is soon to be violently disrupted.

704–11   *And one of them . . . streams of honey*: like that of Moses, Dionysus' rod can draw water from the rock. Wine, milk, and honey are also miraculously produced.

717   *And someone who had tramped the town and was a glib speaker*: it is a city slicker, an urban demagogue, not one of the pastoral figures, whose advice leads to disaster.

729   *And I jumped out, eager to snatch hold of her*: it is the threat of violence that unleashes the violence of the maenads. Left to themselves, they are wondrously peaceable.

736   *They held no iron weapons in their hands*: the bacchae are endowed with supernatural strength. Cf. 1104, in the lead-up to the mutilation of Pentheus ('with crowbars not of iron').

754–7   *They seized children . . . bronze or iron*: the frenzied bacchae possess a perfect sense of balance. Dodds quotes Nathaniel Pearce's account of ecstatic dancers in Abyssinia (n. at 755–7): 'I have seen them in these fits dance with a bruly, or bottle of maize, upon their heads without spilling the liquor, or letting the bottle fall, although they have put themselves into the most extravagant postures.'

780–1   *the Electran Gate*: on the south side of Thebes where the road from Cithaeron came in.

781–5   *Order all . . . the bacchae*: Pentheus is incapable of learning. He does not seem to have taken in that arms are useless against the bacchae.

800   *I am locked together . . . and can find no escape from the hold*: a metaphor from wrestling, suggesting that the somewhat feminine Dionysus is in his way a wrestler after all (cf. 455), and perhaps carrying erotic overtones as Pentheus wrestles with the god.

802-41   *Sir, it is still possible . . . I shall lead the way*: stichomythia. See Introduction, p. xxxvi.

810   *Ah*: the turning point of the play. Dionysus, his offer of help scornfully rejected, now establishes a powerful ascendancy over Pentheus, who becomes his increasingly degraded plaything.

821   *Then put fine linen clothes around your body*: there is no need for Pentheus to dress as a woman. Dionysus wishes to degrade him, as he makes explicit in 850-6.

829   *spectator*: a word appropriate to the theatre fits well with this discussion of the costume which Pentheus will assume. It is significant that tragedy originated in the cult of Dionysus and was in Athens performed at his festivals.

831   *First I shall make your hair hang long on your head*: either by putting a wig on Pentheus, or by letting down his hair if it is tied up in a band. Cf. n. at 453-6.

843   *Let us go . . . seems best*: the dots reflect the fact that something may have fallen out of the text here.

845-6   *Either I shall march . . . advice*: Pentheus deludes himself in the belief that he still has freedom of choice.

877   *What is wisdom?* this important theme is here given a motto-like encapsulation. Cf. notes at 30, 179, 200, 395, 641, 1005-10, 1150-2.

915   *in female get-up as a maenad, a bacchant*: 'no mere pleonasm,' notes Dodds (n. at 915-6), 'but a climax of cumulative scorn; Pentheus is dressed as a woman, as a madwoman [the literal meaning of 'maenad'], as a Dionysiac woman.'

918-22   *How strange . . . a bull*: Pentheus hallucinates: he sees double. But the vision of Dionysus as a bull reflects the genuinely bull nature of Dionysus. See notes at 100, 618.

933   *But hold your head upright*: Pentheus may have flung his head back in a Bacchic pose.

938   *Yes . . . the tendon*: Pentheus looks over his shoulder at the back of his left leg, having bent the left knee and raised the left heel.

941-2   *Will I be more . . . in this one*: vase paintings suggest that there was in fact no rule about this.

945-6   *Would I have the strength . . . on my shoulders*: 'Like the old men in Scene I, Pentheus feels himself filled with magical strength; but with him this consciousness takes the form of megalomaniac delusions . . .' (Dodds, n. at 945-6).

951-2   *You really mustn't destroy . . . where he plays his pipes*: the Nymphs are female deities, the spirits of the fields and woods and of nature in general. Pan is a god of shepherds and flocks, half man, half goat.

962-3   *Escort me through the middle . . . who dares this deed*: now Pentheus invites the publicity he had shunned at 840. He is blind to any sense of shame. Dressed in female clothes, he insists on his masculine daring.

972   *Through these you will find a glory that towers to heaven*: there is a hideous foreshadowing of Pentheus mounted aloft on the fir (1064, 1073).

977-   *On, swift hounds of Frenzy . . . maenads' drove*: the Greek metre
1023   which predominates in the electrifying original of this Chorus is the dochmiac, called by Dodds (n. on Stasimon 4) 'the metre of maximum excitement'.

977   *Frenzy*: this horrendous goddess—who actually appears in Euripides, *Heracles* (922-1015) to cause Heracles to kill his family—hunts with a pack of hounds.

990   *the race of Libyan Gorgons*: the Gorgons, who lived in the far West (hence Libyan), had snakes for hair and their penetrating gaze turned men to stone.

1002-7   *death is an ungainsayable teacher . . . beautiful*: the Greek text here is incurably corrupt. Any attempt to reconstruct its meaning becomes, as in my version, perilously close to guesswork.

1005-10   *I do not begrudge the wise their wisdom . . . honour the gods*: the limitations of wisdom are now stressed in an interesting development of the 'What is wisdom?' theme. Cf. notes at 30,179, 200, 395, 641, 877, 1150-2.

1024-6   *O house . . . in the ground*: see notes at 171-2 and 264.

1035   *Do you think the men of Thebes so spineless ⟨that they will not punish you⟩*: some words seem to have fallen out of the manuscript here. Their meaning must have been something on the lines of the bracketed clause.

1039-40   *it is not proper, women, to exult over horrific deeds*: this sentiment finds emphatic expression in Homer's *Odyssey* (22.412): 'It is not holy to boast over men killed.'

1056   *like fillies released from the patterned yoke*: yoking was a standard image for marriage, and this the unyoking symbolizes the dislocation of the marital home. (See Seaford's n. at 1056.)

1064   *Laying hold of the topmost, heaven-piercing branch of a fir*:
         Dionysus appears to grow supernaturally in height.

1066-7   *a rounded wheel . . . peg*: a peg is fastened to a surface. Attached
         to the peg is a string with its other end attached to a piece of
         chalk. When pulled round, the piece of chalk traces a wheel-like
         circle.

1084-5   *The sky fell silent . . . wild beast's cry*: Dodds comments (n. at
         1084-5) that these lines 'describe wonderfully the hush of
         nature at the moment when the pent-up forces of the supernat-
         ural break through . . . Stillness is the traditional response of
         nature to a divine epiphany.'

1096-   *they first climbed . . . their target*: B.Seidensticker (in 'Sacrificial
1100:   Ritual in the *Bacchae*' in G. W. Bowerstock *et al.* (eds.)
         *Arktouros. Hellenic Studies presented to Bernard M. W. Knox on
         the occasion of his 65th birthday* (Berlin and New York, 1979))
         relates everything that happens to Pentheus from his assuming
         female dress onwards to the pattern of animal sacrifice. The
         pelting of Pentheus here, for example, is seen as the equivalent
         of the pelting of the victim with barley groats. As Seaford com-
         ments (n. at 1096-100), 'The collective violence that in the
         normal sacrificial pelting is symbolic has against Pentheus
         become real, with the result that he resembles the scapegoat
         pelted with stones.'

1107-8   *this climbing beast and stop him reporting*: Agave sees Pentheus
         both as a beast and as a man. There is a striking irony here, for
         despite the killing of Pentheus, we are at this very moment lis-
         tening to a *messenger reporting* the activities of the bacchae.

1115-16 *he flung the band from his head*: as he returns to sanity, Pentheus
         rejects his female attire.

1117-18 *he touched her cheek*: a traditional gesture of supplication.

1120-1   *I have done wrong*: Pentheus dies repentant, making use of the
         Greek word *hamartia* (a factual and/or moral error) which is a
         key element in Aristotle's theory of tragedy (*Poetics* 1453ᵃ8). Cf.
         Cadmus' admission at 1344.

1150-2   *Moderation and piety . . . the truest wisdom*: the Messenger
         answers the Chorus's motto-like encapsulation of the 'What is
         wisdom?' theme at 877. Cf. notes at 877, 30, 179, 200, 395,
         641, 877, 1005-10.

1157   *the sure fennel-rod, the weapon of Death*: the thyrsus was part of
         Pentheus's dress for death, his funeral attire (cf. 835, 857).

1167   *s.d.* When the play was performed at the Parthian court in 53
        BCE, the actor carried the head of the Roman general and politi-
        cian Marcus Licinius Crassus, who had just been killed in the
        disastrous Roman defeat at Carrhae. It is probable that in the
        earliest performances Pentheus' mask was used to represent his
        head.

1170   *this new-cut tendril*: here Agave seems to think that her prey is
        a plant, presumably ivy.

1184   *Why should I join you, poor creature*: 'The invitation to a feast—
        presumably with Pentheus' remains as the principal dish—is too
        much for the nerves of the Chorus: their attitude of forced
        approval breaks down' (Dodds, n. at 1184).

1205:   *the Thessalians' thonged javelins*: according to Xenophon (*Hell.*
        6.1.9) the Thessalians were almost all javelin-throwers, and
        they may indeed have been thought to be the inventors of that
        weapon. The thong facilitated throwing by imparting a twist
        which helped accuracy.

1214–15 *nail to its entablature the lion's head*: it was customary for Greeks
        to attach the heads of the victims of sacrifice and perhaps of
        hunting to their buildings. The part of the entablature referred
        to is the horizontal band above the columns.

1227   *Actaeon*: see n. at 229–30.

1236–7 *I abandoned . . . bare hands*: a striking expression of the disloca-
        tion of the conventional role of women that has taken place in
        Thebes.

1264–301 *What is wrong . . . fell upon Pentheus*: stichomythia, except for
        1269–70 where Agave has a pair of lines. See Introduction,
        p. xxxvi. Drawing on his psychiatric experience, A. Devereux
        (summarized in R.Seaford, n. at 1264–97) argues that Euripides
        has given us a condensed picture of the process of insight-and-
        recall-oriented psychotherapy. Indeed, it is the first surviving
        record of a psychotherapy.

1277   *in your arms*: the idea of a child in its mother's arms is sug-
        gested here.

1300   *Is every limb laid decently by limb*: Agave's question is not
        answered, and it appears that something must have fallen out
        of the text here. But how much? In the third century CE Apsines
        wrote that in Euripides Agave, 'having been freed from madness
        and having recognised her own child torn apart, accuses herself
        and evokes pity . . . (Euripides wished to evoke pity for Pentheus)
        for his mother taking each of his limbs in her hands laments

over each one of them.' Presumably this lament occurred at this
point. (See Seaford's n. at 1300–1. I have given his translation
of Apsines.)

1308–12 *It was through you . . . give due punishment*: Cadmus' estimate of
the dead Pentheus may seem over-generous in view of the character we have been shown earlier. This may be the result of the
de mortuis nil nisi bonum principle. But it is significant that
Cadmus tells us that his grandson 'struck terror into the city'
(1310); and in his very first speech Pentheus was protective of
Cadmus, accusing Teiresias of leading him astray (255, cf.
345–6). Seaford (p. 47) summarizes: 'Crucially, Cadmus' funerary encomium (1302–26) for Pentheus praises him not for any
civic role but as defender of the royal household and as such
[striking terror into the city].' Cf. notes at 10–11, 325–6.

1313   *But now I shall be a dishonoured exile from this house*: Cadmus fore-
sees the banishment that Dionysus will later prescribe for him.

1329   *my fortunes have changed . . .*: there is a gap in the text of at least
50 lines. It seems certain that Dionysus appeared, unmistakably
a god, above the palace. He probably announced the establish-
ment of his cult at Thebes. He may have reproved the Thebans
for rejecting him and described their consequent expulsion from
the city (Seaford (n. at 1329–30) considers this most unlikely).
He almost certainly predicted the fate of each individual. Agave
and her sisters must leave Thebes (1363, etc.). The text starts
up again with Dionysus' description of the exile of Cadmus. (The
evidence for this is in the Hypothesis (the plot summary) of the
play and a Christian text, possibly of the eleventh or twelfth century, called *Christus Patiens*, which is clearly influenced by
Bacchae.)

1332   *Ares*: the god of war.

1336   *the oracle of Loxias*: Loxias is Apollo; his most important oracle
was at Delphi.

1341–2   *If you had known how to be wise when you were unwilling*: the
'you' here (and at 1345) is plural. Cadmus has most assuredly
tried to be reverent and wise, but the royal family in general
have not.

1344–51: *Dionysus we beseech you . . . what necessity decrees*: stichomythia.
See Introduction, p. xxxvi. It is possible, indeed tempting, to take
these lines as a Euripidean attack on the gods, but it may be
more appropriate to see here a clear-sighted assessment by the
poet of the vindictiveness of slighted divinity.

1361–2 *the downward-plunging river Acheron and find peace*: this river in
North West Greece flows through an impenetrable gorge. It was
thought to plunge down into the Underworld.

'Cadmus finds in his eventual translation to Elysium only a
culminating cruelty. That is psychologically right: the god's
mortal victims have nothing left for comfort but their mortality
. . . and the tired old man sees himself robbed even of that.
(Dodds, n. at 1360–2).

1381–92 *The divine will . . . has happened here*: the 'stock' ending of four
or, with a variation in the first line, five of Euripides' plays.

IPHIGENIA AT AULIS

1   *s.d*: the stage building must do duty for a tent—as will be suggested by a speaker (12). The stage-building, which is imposing
enough to do service as a palace in many plays, has in fact left
its mark in 2—where the word I have rendered by 'tent' really
means 'house'.

Like Euripides' *Electra*, this play, performed by day in bright
Athenian light, opens in darkness, again evoked by the speakers
(6–8, etc.). The Old Man's sluggish entry is presumably somewhat delayed.

1–48   *Old man, come here . . . dowry long ago*: among Euripides' extant
plays, only *Rhesus* and *Iphigenia at Aulis* (IA from now on) begin
with lyrical (here chanted) poetry. The authorship of the present
passage and the whole of *Rhesus* are in doubt.

7–8   *near the Pleiades on their seven paths*: the Pleiades were the seven
sisters who became the seven stars of the constellation of that
name.

10–11   *The winds are hushed . . . Euripus*: Euripus is the strait which sep-
arates the island of Euboea from Boeotia in mainland Greece (see
map). The audience begins to discover about the setting of the
play. We discover the exact location, Aulis (now disfigured by a
cement factory), in 14.

In Euripus the current changed seven times a day (Strabo
1.3.12); and the name was used proverbially of an unstable
man (Aeschines 3.90). The sea is quiet now, but it is to prove a
highly appropriate background for the extreme shifts in the protagonist's decisions.

12   *Why are you darting about outside your tent*: Agamemnon's
insomnia is an index of a guilty conscience.

16-18   *I envy any man . . . I envy less*: the theme of the ordinary man's
          ease of spirit in contrast with the anxieties that torment a king
          is one that Shakespeare communicates with particular expres-
          siveness, as in *2 Henry IV*, III.i.26-31:
                Canst thou, O partial sleep, give thy repose
                To the wet sea-boy in an hour so rude,
                And in the calmest and most stillest night,
                With all appliances and means to boot,
                Deny it to a king? Then happy low, lie down!
                Uneasy lies the head that wears a crown.

34-5   *You have lit a lamp*: is there a table (on which Agamemnon can
          constantly erase what he has written on his tablet, 37) with a
          torch on it on stage? Or is the lamp simply suggested by the
          words (see n. at 1 s.d.)? Menelaus can, after all, mime the era-
          sure standing up.

39   *pine tablets*: two (or more) wooden tablets were covered with
          wax (which was kept in place by a raised border) on which mes-
          sages would be scraped with a stylus. They could also be
          smoothed over and thus erased. These tablets would be hinged
          to each other so that they could be shut together like a modern
          book, and then sealed.

39-40   *shedding a big rich tear*: the phrase is Homeric, one of many ref-
          erences in *IA* to this great epic poet—after all, it is a kind of pro-
          logue to the story of the *Iliad*.

46-8   *Tyndareus . . . long ago*: Tyndareus, the husband of Leda, was
          Menelaus' predecessor as king of Sparta. The Old Man's history
          makes him the perfect go-between for Agamemnon and his wife.

49-107   *Leda . . . Menelaus and myself*: the Prologue proper—in which
          the audience is given the information it needs in order to under-
          stand the action. The conventional nature of such prologues is
          often in conflict with naturalism, perhaps above all in this
          instance when the Old Man would surely know all that
          Agamemnon tells him in 49-85.

69   *the sweet winds of love*: the stillness of the actual winds (10-11,
          88) is in contrast with the potent winds of love and the shifting
          currents of human motivation in *IA* (see n. at 10-11).

71-2   *this man who had judged the goddesses*: Paris, the son of King
          Priam of Troy and an oxherd on Mount Ida behind Troy (76),
          awarded a golden apple as a prize for beauty to Aphrodite, god-
          dess of love, who had offered him the most beautiful woman in
          Greece if she won. (This of course proved to be Helen.) The two
          goddesses who lost were Hera and Pallas Athena.

73–4   *dazzling in the finery . . . luxury of the east*: this talk of oriental luxury with its overtones of effeminacy and decadence is common in classical literature, but none the less expressively scornful for that.

89   *Calchas the seer*: he could interpret the significance of the flight of birds and knew the past, present and future. He had been given this gift of prophecy by his grandfather Apollo.

91   *Artemis who dwells in this place*: gods are imagined as inhabiting the areas where they are worshipped. Artemis was the goddess of hunting.

95   *Talthybius*: one of Agamemnon's heralds.

100–3   *Achilles . . . Phthia*: Achilles, the greatest of the Greek warriors, came from Phthia in Thessaly (the capital of which was Pharsalus) where his father Peleus was king. His mother was the sea goddess Thetis (see 134). *Achaeans* is Homer's collective noun for the Greeks.

112   *Argos*: where Agamemnon was king. See n. at 152.

121   *sheltered Aulis*: the bay at Aulis offers protection from the currents of Euripus.

152   *the Cyclops' palace*: it was the popular belief that the walls of Mycenae were made of such immense stones that only the huge Cyclopes (one-eyed giants) could have built them. Mycenae and Argos were both by tradition Agamemnon's capital cities, in Homer always the latter. In Greek tragedy they are referred to interchangeably.

156–8:   *The glimmering dawn . . . the sky here*: day has arrived.

162   *s.d.*: the excited curiosity of these sight-seeing day-trippers is conveyed with appealing vivacity. These are youthful (615), eager married (176) women. From any realistic standpoint, their presence at Aulis must be highly improbable, but these sympathetic young wives, poised in age between the maiden Iphigenia and the motherly Clytemnestra, prove dramatically apt observers for the action of *IA*.

170   *Arethusa*: a popular name for a fountain. The most celebrated of these was at Syracuse in Sicily, and among several others was the one at Calchis.

174   *red-haired Menelaus*: Menelaus is given one of his Homeric epithets (adjectives). Cf. n. at 39–40.

178–9   *Eurotas*: the river which flows through Sparta.

184   *the Cyprian goddess*: Aphrodite was born from the foam of the
          sea and landed first on the island of Cythera and then on
          Cyprus—hence 'Cyprian' here, and the name Cypris by which
          she was also known.

182   *by the dewy waters of a spring*: in Euripides, *Andromache* 284–5,
          the goddesses are described as bathing in a woodland spring
          before going to Paris to be judged.

192–4   *the two Ajaxes . . . Salamis*: as is implied here, Ajax the son of
          Telamon—who came from the island of Salamis near Athens—
          was a far greater fighter than Ajax the son of Oileus, who, as
          well as being inferior to his namesake, was a bad character.

194–5   *Protesilaus*: the first Greek to be killed at Troy, he was struck
          down by Hector as he leapt from his ship.

196   *draughts board*: the game was a kind of backgammon, combin-
          ing skill with chance. A famous vase by Exekias dating from
          540–530 BCE (in the Vatican in Rome) shows Achilles and Ajax
          (the son of Telamon) sitting playing this game.

203–4   *the son of Laertes from his mountainous island*: i.e. Odysseus from
          Ithaca.

206–9   *And I saw . . . Chiron trained to perfection*: 'swift-footed' is one of
          the key epithets (adjectives) used of Achilles in Homer's *Iliad*. He
          was brought up by the civilized centaur (half man, half horse)
          Chiron.

224   *sweeping close round the turnings of the race-track*: too wide a turn
          at the ends of the race course would waste valuable time.
          Euripides may have written an ode (quoted by Plutarch at
          Alcibiades 11.2) in celebration of Alcibiades' victory in the char-
          iot race in the Olympic Games of 416 BCE.

232   *to see something wondrous*: the word for 'see' here is part of the
          Greek word for 'theatre'. The theatre audience watches the
          Chorus watching the Greek army. Both Chorus and audience are
          in fact spectators (cf. n. at 628–9) as Homer's catalogue of ships
          (from *Iliad* 2.484–877) becomes living drama.
                 The Greek word for 'wondrous' literally means 'beyond even
          a god's power to express'. It is a Homeric word, used in tragedy
          only here, and so plays its part in Euripides' conjuring up of
          Homer's world.

239–40   *the Nereid goddesses*: the Nereids were sea-deities, the daughters
          of Nereus and the granddaughters of Oceanus. In most accounts
          they numbered fifty, which conveniently allows one per ship.
          Achilles' mother Thetis was one of them.

244–5   *Mecisteus' son . . . brought up*: the son of Mecisteus and grandson of Talaus was Euryalus.

248–9   *the son of Theseus*: in Homer the leader of the Athenian contingent is Menestheus, and he is the son of Peteus and an enemy of Theseus. Euripides must here be referring to either Acamas or Demophon, the two sons of Theseus.

256–9   *Cadmus . . . earth-born Leitus*: for the Theban myth which explains Cadmus, the dragon and the earth-born men, see *Bacchae*, n. at 264.

261   *And from the land of Phocis*: something has fallen out of the text here. The words supplied in brackets aim to do no more than make sense.

265–6   *from Cyclops-built Mycenae the son of Atreus*: for *Cyclops-built*, see n. at 152. The son of Atreus is Agamemnon; his brother is, of course, Menelaus.

274   *Gerenian*: from Gerena or Gerenon, a city in Messenia in South Greece near Pylos where Nestor ruled—a Homeric epithet.

275–6   *the river Alpheus, their neighbour, footed like a bull*: the Alpheus flowed through Pylos (hence 'neighbour'). It is common for rivers to be typified in the form of a bull. Ancient writers suggest that this is because of the noise the rivers make and their bends, which are called horns.

287   *inhospitable to sea-faring men*: the Taphians had a reputation for piracy. (See Homer, *Odyssey* 15.427.)

288–93   *And Ajax . . . supremely manoeuvrable vessels*: this is a problematic passage. However, it certainly establishes that Ajax was at one end of the line of ships and thus, like Achilles at the other end (235–7), in one of the two positions most exposed to danger (since they alone were exposed on one flank). This positioning was repeated on the shore at Troy.

301–2   *And I heard . . . which I keep in my mind*: the Chorus here makes it plain how it knows so much about the fleet. It could scarcely have deduced all it has told us from mere visual observation. This is an extraordinarily bathetic conclusion to the Chorus' delightfully animated song.

303   *Menelaus*: a Victorian editor of the play, E. B. England (*Iphigeneia at Aulis* (London, 1891)), remarks at this point: 'It is with a sigh of relief that every student must turn from the perplexities of the prologue and the doggerel navy list at the end of the parados [opening Chorus], to a scene of definite intelligible action, and of genuine Euripidean stamp.' Many may feel that

England does far less than justice to the passages of which he is so scornful.

303–33   *Menelaus . . . a hateful thing*: are almost entirely in stichomythia. See Introducton, p. xxxvi.

309   *someone else*: i.e. Agamemnon.

317–401   *What's going on . . . in good order*: a new metre—called 'trochaic'—starts up at 317 in the Greek and is sustained for 84 lines. England (n. ad loc.) remarks: 'The livelier metre not only suits a rapid appearance [for Agamemnon] on the stage, but also the hasty tempers of the interlocutors in the following scene.'

321   *Do you think that Agamemnon, son of Atreus, is going to tremble and not look you in the eye*: there is a play on words here in the original which gives the line its point. The Greek word for 'untrembling' and the name Atreus are similar in sound.

332   *No, for your thoughts are crooked, shifting with every moment*: the flux of Agamemnon's thoughts, set against the background of the shifting currents of Euripus (see n. at 10–11), is clear from 84–110. There is irony here too. Menelaus' thinking is to undergo an extreme sea-change later in the play.

333   *What a fine gloss you have put on your base deed*: the base deed is presumably the interception and opening of private correspondence, with a glance at the rough treatment of the Old Man.

339–45   *you know how humble you were . . . rarely to be seen*: Athenian politicians of the fifth century BCE seem to have been more consistent in their behaviour towards the voters than Agamemnon, as portrayed here by Menelaus. Cimon (Plutarch, *Cimon* 10.1–2) removed the fences from his estates so that anyone could take the produce, gave dinner to all who wanted it (or at least to the members of his deme), and tactfully dispensed money hand-outs and free clothes. Pericles and Nicias on the other hand kept out of the public eye (Plutarch, *Pericles* 7.4, *Nicias* 5.1).

359–62   *your heart rejoiced . . . Achilles*: Menelaus gives an extremely different version of what happened from Agamemnon's account at 93–7. Both are highly plausible psychologically.

370   *Unhappy Greece*: an important statement of what W. Stockert calls the 'Panhellenic motif' (*Iphigenie in Aulis* (Vienna, 1992), n. at 410). The Greeks have united to fight the barbarians, but here are two of their leading figures quarrelling violently with each other.

402   *What you have just spoken is different from what you said before*: Agamemnon is now stating his determination not to kill his

daughter with unhesitating, indeed superb confidence. The Chorus base their comment on the shifts—and shiftiness—of Agamemnon of which Menelaus has spoken (334–75).

At this line, the metre now moves back to the iambic, the regular metre of dramatic dialogue.

403   *But it is good to hear you talk of sparing your child*: the Chorus of young women is naturally sympathetic to Iphigenia's plight. Ennius in his Latin adaptation of *IA* used a Chorus of soldiers instead. While this may have seemed decidedly more realistic, the galumphing, down-to-earth quality of the fragment of Ennius' writing for them which survives underscores the fine dramatic judgement of Euripides in his choice of observant women with a finely-tuned sensibility for this fundamentally important role.

410   *Do you not think it right to share in the efforts of Greece*: the Panhellenic motif (see n. at 370). Agamemnon's duty to the assembled Greeks is in conflict with his love for his daughter.

413   *O king of all the Greeks*: these words form the second half of a line which Menelaus has begun. C. E. S. Headlam comments (*Iphigeneia at Aulis* (Cambridge, 1886), n. at 414) that, though it is 'a general rule in tragedy that a line is not divided between a person already on the stage and a fresh arrival', the fact that this happens here is justified by the hurried entry of the messenger, impatient to spill out his news.

422   *women and fillies alike*: Headlam suggests (n. on 420 ff.) that the travellers walk 'on the grass round a spring' while the horses stand in its waters—presumably before being turned loose in the fields (422). But why shouldn't Clytemnestra and Iphigenia be allowed to wet their feet?

433   *They are consecrating the young girl to Artemis*: England (n. at 433) calls this a 'clumsy attempt at tragic irony'. 'This very significant hint of Iphigenia's fate,' he continues, 'is dragged in "by the head and shoulders".' This is unreasonable. Artemis was one of the goddesses to whom offerings were made before marriage. The army's ignorance of the true situation is given poignant emphasis.

435   *bring the baskets*: in these was the barley meal to be sprinkled over the victim and the altar.

446–9   *Men of low birth . . . unhappiness*: England (n. at 446–9) quotes Beaumont and Fletcher, *The Maid's Tragedy* v.2: 'But such the misery of greatness is, They have no time for tears.'

454   *what shall I say to my wife*: Agamemnon had hoped that
           Clytemnestra would stay at home and send Iphigenia to Aulis
           without her. It is Clytemnestra's decision to accompany her
           daughter that has given Agamemnon the *coup de grâce*, for now
           that the army knows that Iphigenia is here, her sacrifice seems
           inevitable. The presence of the wife will not only make the deed
           far more problematic to encompass but will add greatly to the
           emotional trauma of putting it into effect.

460–1   *why . . . virgin . . . marry her*: Agamemnon finds the word 'vir-
           gin' grimly inappropriate since he believes that his daughter will
           be violated by her marriage to the god of the Underworld.

473   *I swear by Pelops*: some have felt that this apparent recantation
           of Menelaus is false, designed to ram home, behind a façade of
           sincere fraternal support, the true dangers Agamemnon would
           face if he did not kill Iphigenia. For the writer of these notes, a
           violent shift in Menelaus' view of the situation seems entirely
           characteristic of this play (see n. at 10–11), and I take the
           speech at face value. However, Pelops and Atreus, the father
           and grandfather of Agamemnon and Menelaus, are famously
           treacherous characters in Greek mythology, and this could cer-
           tainly foster some suspicion about the words of a man who
           swears by them so eagerly (Pelops here, Atreus in 474).

477–8   *When I saw . . . tears for you in my turn*: Greek actors wore
           masks, which denied them changing facial expressions.
           Agamemnon may have suggested weeping through his voice,
           while Menelaus may have mimed it by, e.g., putting his hands
           up to his eyes. This play is remarkable for the weeping which is
           said to take place on stage, i.e. at 39–40, 496–7, 650, 683–4,
           888–9. The characters, especially Agamemnon, seem to be seek-
           ing to drown the stage in tears.

488   *win Helen*: there is a play on words here which cannot be repro-
           duced in English. The Greek word for 'win' contains the first syl-
           lable of the name Helen.

504   *words, worthy of Tantalus*: Tantalus, another ancestor of Aga-
           memnon and Menelaus (see n. at 473), was father of Pelops and
           founder of the dynasty, and received a famous punishment in
           the Underworld because of his evil dealing on earth. The blithe
           approval of this notorious figure by the Chorus here may
           awaken further doubts about the sincerity of Menelaus' speech.

508   *Strife between brothers*: Agamemnon is no doubt thinking of the
           murderous conflict between his father Atreus and Atreus'
           brother Thyestes.

513–27   *What is this . . . that possesses him*: stichomythia. See Introduction, p. xxxvi. The convention comes under some strain at 522–3.

519   *Not if he dies first*: Menelaus chillingly suggests that they arrange the murder of Calchas, and Agamemnon does not seem shocked by this.

521   *Yes, hateful and useless—while alive*: I have followed Nauck's reading of this corrupt line.

524   *The vile son of Sisyphus*: Odysseus is usually regarded as the son of Laertes. The tradition which describes him as the son of Sisyphus is insulting to him since it makes him out to be a bastard and tarred with his father's criminality.

543–57   *Happy are they . . . in full force*: the female Chorus in Euripides, *Medea* (627 ff.) express very similar sentiments.

553   *Cypris*: i.e. Aphrodite. See n. at 184.

556–7   *may I have my part . . . when she comes in full force*: cf. Racine, *Phèdre*, I.iii: 'Vénus toute entière à sa proie attachée.'

576–8   *imitating the Phrygian pipe of Olympus*: the Olympus who invented the pipe was a mythical personage who lived in Mysia before the Trojan War. A real-life Olympus who invented the enharmonic scale and established the pipe by the side of the lyre in Greek music flourished *c*.650 BCE. In Greek literature the two figures are often merged. 'Phrygian' may simply mean 'Trojan' here. Alternatively—or in addition—it may refer to the Phrygian mode with its 'mournful and passionate strains'. (See Headlam, n. at 576.)

590–1   *Ah! Ah! Great is the happiness of the great*: the Chorus, who know the mortal danger in which Iphigenia stands, greet the new arrivals with extraordinarily fulsome strains. It seems probable that the whole of this ecstatic welcome (590–606) is not by Euripides. O. Taplin (*The Stagecraft of Aeschylus* (Oxford, 1977), 77) comments that 'it is best to regard the lines as hurriedly composed pastiche'.

614   *your weak, delicate, and dainty feet*: the feminine fragility of Iphigenia is stressed. Yet *iphi* is Homeric Greek for 'strongly', 'mightily'. Her name in fact proves a true guide to her personality as it ultimately emerges in this play.

621–2   *And take this child . . . son*: the presence of the baby Orestes is a poignant touch. F. Jouan (*Iphigénie à Aulis* (Paris, 1983), n. at 627) remarks: 'It has sometimes been considered that the verses about little Orestes are excessively extended and sacrifice too much for the effect of *pathos*. But this scene of family tenderness must appear piquant to an audience which knows that 'little Orestes' will later kill his mother!'

626   *Nereus' daughter*: the sea-goddess Thetis.

628–9   *give these foreign women a picture of my happiness*: Clytemnestra wants to demonstrate her joy by posing with her children in a happy family group (an effective irony). Again the Chorus spectate. Their experience is a reflection of that of the theatre audience. Cf. n. at 232.

631–7   *Mother, I shall outrun . . . Don't be angry*: after Clytemnestra has greeted her husband rather formally, 'Iphigenia throws herself into her father's embrace . . . and as he turns to respond to the queen's greeting Iphigenia would have him yet spare all his attention to herself, asking pardon for the importunity of her affection. The repetition of words has caused this passage to be held unsound, but it is in the situation a very natural and pathetic touch' (Headlam, n. at 631–6).

634   *we have come in obedience to your commands*: in fact, as we have seen (100), Agamemnon never sent for Clytemnestra, only for Iphigenia, and it is his wife's presence that has reduced him to his *impasse*. Cf. n. at 454.

640–76   *My father . . . altar, father*: stichomythia. See Introduction, p. xxxvi. This scene is full of poignant irony.

662   *Phrygians*: i.e. Trojans.

665   *you will come to the same place as your father*: i.e. either the altar where her father is to sacrifice her, or the Underworld, or both.

654   *I shall talk nonsense then if that will make you happy*: this line, with its intimacy and playfulness, evokes the loving closeness of the relationship between father and daughter.

667   *A voyage yet lies in store for you as well and on it you will forget your father*: this is the voyage to the Underworld. The text is corrupt, and the word 'forget' is speculative.

675   *the holy water*: needed for purification for the sacrifice.

681   *o this blond hair*: in Homer blond hair is customary for princes and young women. In Euripides all young people are blond.

697–738 *Asopus . . . Do what I say*: stichomythia. See Introduction, p. xxxvi.

703   *Zeus, who had the authority to do so, betrothed her to him and gave her away*: in Athenian society all women had a man in authority over them. According to the myth, Zeus wanted to marry

Thetis himself, but the goddess Themis prophesied that the son of Thetis would be more powerful than his father. Thus Zeus was content to marry her off to Peleus, which she was in fact extremely reluctant to do.

705   *Chiron*: see n. at 206.

708   *Did Thetis or his father bring up Achilles*: Achilles, of course, is not famous yet, but there is surely a certain humour in the total ignorance about him which Clytemnestra displays here. Agamemnon imparts a great deal of information, but—another humorous touch?—omits the birth of Achilles.

715   *That will be the business of the master who has won her*: a fine irony: Agamemnon is referring to the god of the Underworld.

717   *At the time of the full moon*: the full moon was an auspicious time for weddings.

739   *by the sovereign goddess of Argos*: i.e. Hera, goddess of marriage.

740   *while I look after everything indoors*: C. Luschnig (*Tragic Aporia: A Study of Euripides' Iphigenia at Aulis* (Victoria, 1988), 18) remarks: 'We meet Clytemnestra as a happy housewife, stubborn perhaps over the proprieties due to family affairs, but no killer.' By the end of the play, Luschnig suggests, the tragic events have set her on the path to becoming one.

751-800 *There will indeed come to Simois . . . empty fiction*: Simois was a river on the plain of Troy, whose waters according to Homer, were 'swirling'. Ilium and Pergamum were other names for Troy. Phoebus Apollo, the god of prophecy, was on the side of the Trojans, whose walls he had helped to build, in the Trojan War. Cassandra was his wild prophetess. Ares was the god of war. He in fact supported the Trojans, but is here viewed as a symbol of war and all its troubles. The Dioscuri were Castor and Polydeuces, who formed a constellation. The Lydians were Asians, presumably Trojans here; the Phrygians were the Trojans, as always in Euripides. Myth had it that Zeus came to Leda in the form of a swan, whereupon she gave birth to two eggs, out of which sprang two pairs of children, Polydeuces and Clytemnestra, and Helen and Castor—in which case Tyndareus, Leda's husband, would not have been their father.

Now that Iphigenia is here, the Chorus know that war is an inevitability. They visualize its horrors and conclude by casting doubt on the myth that makes Helen the miraculously-born offspring of Zeus. Apart from her dazzling beauty (which is not stressed in this play), the woman who has brought all this destruction in her wake may just be an ordinary mortal.

804   *The fact is . . . circumstances*: Achilles is here, and elsewhere in the play (see e.g. 965–7), concerned with the well-being of the whole Greek force. His speech here conveys well the idea of *waiting* (804, 813, 815). There is an irony in the fact that he thinks of himself as a bachelor (805–6) at a time when we have heard much false news about his imminent wedding.

814   *Myrmidons*: the followers of Achilles.

821   *O lady Modesty*: England calls this 'an almost comically outspoken expression of surprise' (n. at 821). Certainly the moment raises a laugh in Cacoyannis' film of *Iphigenia*. It appears that Achilles, who tries to escape from Clytemnestra at 830, has not had much experience of women (cf. 802). This initial bashfulness adds depth to his subsequent relations with Iphigenia and her mother.

851   *Goodbye*: it was Achilles who wanted to get away at 430. Now Clytemnestra wishes to flee in embarrassment. Such shifts and echoes are characteristic of *IA*.

855–916 *Stranger . . . we are lost*: the metre now shifts back to the trochaic (see n. at 317–401). This rhythm 'corresponds to the exciting nature of the old man's communication' (England, n. at 855).

881   *Dardanus*: the first king of Troy.

885   *He wanted you to be happy to bring your child here to marry Achilles*: this is mistaken. Agamemnon very much did *not* want his wife to come to Aulis. See n. at 454.

900   *I shall feel no shame in falling at your knees*: by the process called supplication, the person seeking a favour would fall to his or her knees before the person asked to give it. He or she would touch the other's body—the knees and chin (909) were the most effective areas—and this would make it extremely difficult to reject the entreaty.

902   *She is my child. She comes first. I must fight for her*: England comments (n. at 902): 'This is one of the Euripidean lines which touch hearts of all times.'

952–3   *Or Sipylus . . . draw their descent*: Mount Sipylus, in the area of Mount Tmolus in Lydia, was where Tantalus, great-grandfather of Menelaus and Agamemnon, came from. Any settlement in this barbarian region would be regarded by the Greeks as a mere collection of dwellings of semi-savages.

955   *barley*: see n. at 435.

963-4   *It was mainly . . . in marriage*: this is wrong, though Clytemnestra is happy to encourage Achilles in this belief (986–7). It is clear that she knew next to nothing about him.

965-7   *I would not have refused . . . comrades in arms*: in this disconcerting variation of the Panhellenic motif (see notes at 370 and 410), Achilles makes it clear that he has no moral objection to human sacrifice to further the Trojan War or indeed to lending his own name to assist a fraudulent scheme. It is simply that Agamemnon has insulted him by not asking him first (961–3)!

1019-21   *I should become . . . by force*: readers of Homer's *Iliad* will be surprised by an Achilles who is hoping to preserve, indeed enhance, his friendship with Agamemnon and is fearful of criticism from the Greek army. Clearly the temperate values his teacher Chiron had instilled in him (920–7) have had their effect on Euripides' characterization.

1031   *Tyndareus*: the husband of Clytemnestra's mother (see n. at 751–800). Achilles here speaks as if he, and not Zeus, were her father.

1036   *the Lybian lotus pipe*: the Libyan lotus was often used for making pipes.

1045   *Mount Pelion*: a mountain in Thessaly not far from Phthia.

1053   *Ganymede the Phrygian*: Zeus fell in love with the boy Ganymede while he was tending his father's flocks in the mountains near Troy. The god metamorphosed into a eagle and carried him off to Olympus to be his wine-steward. Zeus had presumably brought him to the wedding of Peleus and Thetis to perform that function there.

1054-7   *And along the bright white sands . . . dance*: being sea-goddesses, the Nereids could only dance at the sea's edge. They could not attend their sister's wedding. See n. at 239–40.

1058   *their staffs of silver fir*: these were, in fact, the traditional weapons of the centaurs.

1064   *Phoebus*: Phoebus Apollo, god of prophecy.

1067-75   *He will come at the head . . . Thetis who bore him*: Hephaestus was the god of fire and made two sets of divine armour for Achilles. The second set was the one given to the hero by his mother. Achilles' intention may have been 'to burn the famous land of Priam to ashes' (1069–70), but he was to be killed before Troy was taken and sacked.

1078   *the Nereids*: i.e. the daughters of Nereus. See n. at 239–40.

1080   *you*: i.e. Iphigenia.

1089   *a son of Inachus*: i.e. descended from a river god in the Argolid, and therefore 'an Argive' (the meaning here).

1122–3   *My child . . . in front of your eyes*: England (n. at 1122 f.) remarks: 'There is no longer the glad greeting which met Agamemnon in the former scene (640 ff.). The heroine's head is bowed down, and her face covered in sign of grief.'

1127   *all*: presumably Clytemnestra, Iphigenia and Orestes.

1139   *This mind of yours is no mind at all*: Clytemnestra is referring to Agamemnon's pretence of ignorance.

1150   *Tantalus*: not Agamemnon's ancestor but his cousin. Euripides is the first to give the version of the marriage of Clytemnestra and Agamemnon continued in the lines which follow (1151–6).

1151   *And you wafted my baby to your share of captives*: an alternative reading means: 'You dashed my baby living to the ground.' This could well be preferable, since, if Agamemnon had spared the child, he would scarcely have provoked the vengeance described in 1153–4.

1153   *The two sons of Zeus, my brothers*: Castor and Polydeuces. See n. at 751–800.

1161   *happy when you went away*: i.e. happy at the thought that he had a chaste wife who was increasing the value of his property back at home.

1180   *the father who has left such a motive for hatred in the house*: this line is corrupt and I have given a plausible, though quite possibly incorrect meaning. However, what I have led Clytemnestra to say here does sum up an important implication of 1171–84. Clytemnestra can see that, if the killing of Iphigenia proceeds, she will be nursing her bitter feelings against her husband as she waits at home for the whole duration of the Trojan War. The subtext in this passage seems to be her awareness that she will be transformed from a loving mother into a killer. See n. at 740. Luschnig (*Tragic Aporia*, 32) writes: 'One of the great losses in this tragedy is the conversion of Clytemnestra from the perfect wife to her opposite. She could have been another Penelope. Learning comes through suffering, but what it teaches is not always forgiveness or justice. Clytemnestra had forgiven her husband once. But he did not learn from her suffering . . .'

1201   *Hermione*: the daughter of Menelaus and Helen.

1211   *Orpheus*: Orpheus, the 'type' of the singer, musician, and poet,
        made such sweet music that animals would follow him, trees
        and plants would bow to him, and the wildest of men would be
        tamed.

1216   *a suppliant's branch*: a branch of olive wood with strands of wool
        twined round it, carried by suppliants. For the conventions of
        supplication, see n. at 900.

1220   *I was the first to call you father*: we discover that Iphigenia was
        Agamemnon's eldest child. The two younger daughters, not
        mentioned by name in *IA*, were called Electra and Chrysothemis.

1250-2 *The light of day . . . to die nobly*: like others by the strait of
        Euripus with its shifting currents (see notes at 10-11 and 332),
        Iphigenia is going to reverse her present view of things radically
        (see esp. 1375-85, 1503).

1253-4 *Cruel-hearted Helen . . . their children*: the characteristic banality
        of the Chorus' comment here stimulates Headlam to a com-
        monsensical discussion of their role when commenting within
        the dramatic scenes on the views of the protagonists (n. at 1253
        f.): 'when an actor has been able to excite and maintain the
        keen interest of his audience during a speech of any length,
        there follows upon its close a slight restless movement through
        the house as people recover themselves from the sustained effort
        of attention. There is therefore a brief interval in which the effect
        of any weighty utterance would be weakened or lost. It is by the
        help of the chorus that this interval is bridged; and the modes
        of expression which they adopt, together with the range of sen-
        timents to which they generally confine themselves, are there-
        fore worthy of remark. We find them at these critical moments
        interposing a short sentence, which designedly contributes noth-
        ing either striking or novel or essential to the development of the
        action . . . Often, as here, they simply repeat in a quiet manner
        the "note" of the situation; or they touch upon the moral issues
        at stake, viewing them however, as suits their character of spec-
        tators of the action, not so much with reference to the individ-
        ual case as in connexion with the abiding principles by which
        the world is ordered. We thus perceive that on both the artistic
        and moral sides their position is in living accord with the aims
        of the drama; and so far from being offended by "the common-
        places of the chorus" we should in this very characteristic recog-
        nize an economy of the most discerning and effective nature.'
            The reference to 'a great struggle' which 'has come to the
        sons of Atreus and their children' may evoke the *Oresteia* (458

BCE), the trilogy in which Aeschylus deals with the horrors which afflict this family after the Trojan War. It may be that this resonance rescues these lines from the charge of banality.

1264   *desire*: my translation of the Greek name 'Aphrodite'. Aphrodite is the goddess of sexual passion. The Greeks are on fire with love of war. There is an irony here too, for Aphrodite caused the Trojan War by causing the love between Paris and Helen.

1271   *Greece*: 'Agamenon chooses, now for the last time, to be not a man but an identity, to be the leader and, therefore, the apologist for the greatest common event in Greek history' (Luschnig, *Tragic Aporia*, 31). For the Panhellenic theme, see notes at 379, 410, 965-7.

1275   *through force*: is there a strong trumpery element in Agamemnon's patriotism? Paris did not—according to Agamemnon (75), the Chorus (585-6), and indeed most sources in Greek literature—use force to abduct Helen. In fact, the person who did win a wife by force was Agamemnon himself (1149—see Luschnig, *Tragic Aporia*, 51).

1284-9 *Snow-beaten valley . . . Paris*: Paris, also known as Alexandros (1292-3), was the second son of Priam, king of Troy, and Hecuba. As he was about to be born, Hecuba dreamed that she gave birth to a torch which set fire to Troy. This dream was interpreted as signifying that Paris (the torch) would destroy the city, and so he was abandoned at birth on Mount Ida where it was intended that he should die. He survived, however, was brought up by shepherds and became an oxherd. He was called the child of Ida (1289-90) because that was where he had been exposed and reared.

1304   *vain*: the Greek word for which this stands is (T. Stinton, *Euripides and the Judgement of Paris* (London, 1965), 33-4) 'an untranslatable word implying pride, luxury and sexual forwardness'.

1320   *sterns*: ships were drawn up on the beach and anchored by the stern.

1338-   *My mother . . . we are free*: we return to the trochaic rhythm (cf.
1401   notes at 317-401, 855-916) which reflects extreme agitation, and perhaps lends a note of hysteria to Iphigenia's great patriotic speech (1368-401). This agitated effect is enhanced in 1341-68 when the lines are divided between Achilles and Clytemnestra, thus creating an extraordinary sense of excitement, tension and pressure.

1352   *All the Greeks*: the Panhellenic theme: cf. notes at 370, 410, 965-7, 1271.

1360   *Well, I shall have my reward*: meaning either 'a chivalrous action is its own reward' (Headlam) or 'I *shall* have a reward': i.e. 'I shall win the bride'.

1362   *What, the son of Sisyphus*: see n. at 524.

1368   *Mother*: in this great speech, Iphigenia proudly asserts a completely different view of life. This is the last—and the most extraordinary—of the shifting attitudes and decisions of the characters as they stand by the shifting straits of Euripus (cf. notes at 10-11, 332, 1250-2). Aristotle accused Euripides of inconsistency here 'since the girl who beseeches is in no way like her later self' (*Poetics* 1454ª), but we may disagree, feeling that the playwright has paved the way for this conversion. See also n. at 1402-3.

1371   *the stranger*: Achilles has, in his own mind, almost succeeded in making Agamemnon's invented marriage plan a reality. Iphigenia will not go along with this. She maintains a distance between herself and Achilles, and she never addresses him by his name.

1378   *Greece in all its greatness*: from now until the end of Iphigenia's speech, the Panhellenic theme (cf. notes at 370, 410, 965-7, 1271, 1352) blares forth superbly. The Chorus, however (see n. at 1402-3), and Achilles (especially at 1424 and 1428-30) cannot see the matter with the heroine's single-minded clarity of vision.

1402-3   *The part you play . . . sickness lies*: the Chorus admire Iphigenia but even so they see that something fundamental is very wrong indeed. Are they here making a comment on the play's behalf, 'in living accord with the aims of the drama', to use Headlam's words (see n. at 1253-4)? I certainly accept what they say in these lines. I feel that Euripides endows Iphigenia with a kind of heroism when she makes a coherent pattern out of her own life in the cruel and anarchic world of *IA* where humans are at the mercy of malevolent or chaotic forces whether divine or human. I also believe that the high patriotic ideals adopted by Iphigenia are viewed by Euripides as false ones. I believe this especially in view of the fact that this play was written as the Peloponnesian War neared its end—a war in which the Greek city states had torn each other apart and the fighting had lost any sheen of glamour or nobility. Spartans and Athenians may be moored in alliance with each other around the bay at Aulis (247-9,

265–7) in our play, but, in historical fact, within two or three years of its composition Sparta finally defeated and occupied her hated rival Athens (see Chronology, pp. xlix–xlx). So much for Panhellenism! Even so, we must surely admire the way in which Iphigenia finds within herself the strength to construct an identity which holds a valid meaning for her, and she goes off to die with this identity fully intact.

1430   *a foolish impulse*: Achilles disconcertingly advances this possible view of Iphigenia's decision to die. His words here run completely counter to the spirit of his uncompromising 1421–3.

1433   *why these tear-filled eyes*: tears again, this time from Clytemnestra. Cf. n. at 477–8. The passage starting from this line and continuing till 1465 is almost completely in stichomythia. See Introduction, p. xxxvi.

1436   *Do not make a coward of me*: by causing me to weep in sympathy with you.

1437   *Then do not cut off a lock of your hair*: she refers to the lock of hair customarily laid on the grave. Since the head and the hair signified strength and life, the cutting of the latter symbolized submissive grief. And the cut hair replicated safely the hair cut from the victim before sacrifice (1478).

1440   *I have been saved and through me you shall win glory*: dramatic irony, not only since in the play as we have it Iphigenia *is* saved, but also because Clytemnestra is to win the opposite of glory through her subsequent actions.

1442–4 *No, no . . . memorial*: Iphigenia shows the clairvoyance with which Euripides sometimes endows doomed or dying characters in his plays.

1455   *He must run a terrible race because of you*: presumably this refers to Agamemnon's subsequent murder by Clytemnestra. Note the athletic image.

1457   *But it was by a foul trick, unworthy of Atreus*: since Atreus killed the three sons of his brother Thyestes and served them up to their father in a stew, this comment of Clytemnestra's proves disconcerting. In fact, Agamemnon's family had a history of infanticide.

1466   *I forbid you to let fall a tear*: Iphigenia tries to put an end to the play's copious weeping, but she proves unsuccessful. See notes at 477–8, 1433, 1549–50.

1471–2 *and let my father . . . right*: a ritualistic movement put into practice at 1568.

1500–1   *Are you calling on the city . . . Cyclopian hands*: Perseus is said to have founded Mycenae (Pausanias 2.3.16). For the Cyclopian hands, see n. at 152.

1503   *a light for Greece*: cf. Achilles at 1063.

1507–9   *a different life . . . beloved light*: These poignant lines come from a poet who may have been shortly to die himself. Headlam (n. at 1507 ff.) suggests that the word 'different' is here employed euphemistically, 'contrasting the free vigorous life beneath the sun with the feeble shadowy existence in the underworld'.

1510–14   *Ah! Ah! . . . goddess divine*: to supremely poignant effect, the Chorus, whom Iphigenia has told to sing a propitious song (1467–8), simply mimic her own utterance (1475–82) until their hymn of praise to Artemis veers into a welter of blood (1515–7).

1549–50   *he groaned loudly . . . in front of his eyes*: a contemporary of Euripides called Timanthes (of Cynthus, later of Sicyon) painted a celebrated picture of the sacrifice of Iphigenia which may (or may not) have been inspired by this speech. Cicero (*Orator* 22.74) commented of Timanthes' work (now lost) that 'the painter saw that, since at the sacrifice of Iphigenia Calchas was sad, Ulysses [i.e. Odysseus] was sadder, and Menelaus was grieving, Agamemnon's head had to be veiled because that supreme sorrow could not be portrayed by the brush'. A famous wall painting from Pompeii (in the National Archaeological Museum, Naples) shows Agamemnon standing, his head veiled, his right hand before his eyes. We have here the final outburst of tears in the play, though, of course, it is only reported. See notes at 477–8,1433 and 1466.

1563   *Talthybius—whose office it was*: Talthybius is a herald of the Greeks. Cf. n. at 95.

1570–1   *O daughter of Zeus . . . darkness of the night*: Artemis is addressed here as the goddess of hunting on earth and of the moon in the sky. Are we intended to think also of her identification with the death goddess Hecate (see Aeschylus, *Suppliants* 676)?

     Achilles, who speaks these words, now appears to accept the inevitability of Iphigenia's death (cf.1425–30).

1581   *I stood there, my head drooping*: The sons of Atreus and the whole Greek army are looking down at the ground (1577). The messenger now lowers his head. Thus nobody apart from Calchas can see what happens.

1601-2   *When the whole victim had been burnt to ashes*: normally some of
          the sacrificial victim would be kept for human consumption. In
          this case, the entire victim is burnt for Artemis.

1626   *May all go well with you*: Clytemnestra does not respond to
          Agamemnon's conciliatory and buoyant words. Her silence is
          pregnant indeed. See notes at 740 and 1180.

RHESUS

General notes

1. Though it has proved convenient in these notes to refer to the author
of *Rhesus* as Euripides, there is considerable doubt about whether he in fact
wrote the play. See W. Ritchie, *The Authenticity of the Rhesus of Euripides*
(Cambridge, 1964) and E. Fraenkel, *Gnomon* 37 (1965), 228-41 for the
arguments for and against his authorship.

2. While nearly half of the Greek tragedies which have come down to
us relate to the capture of Troy and the events surrounding it, *Rhesus* is the
only one in which the action coincides with events in Homer's *Iliad*, the so-
called Doloneia (Book 10). There is a question mark over the authorship of
this part of the *Iliad*, and it is a curious coincidence that similar doubts
should arise over both the Doloneia and the play which tells the same story.
    On the question of the authorship of *Iliad* 10, an ancient commentator
wrote as follows: 'The ancient critics say that this rhapsody was a separate
composition by Homer, and not included by him in the *Iliad*, but added to
the epic by Peisistratus [an Athenian tyrant of the sixth century BCE].'
Certainly, the episode is entirely self-contained and could be removed from
the poem without leaving any trace; and there are differences both in language and in style between Book 10 and the rest of the epic. But, as
M. Willcock says in his admirable summary of the debate (*A Companion to
the Iliad* (Chicago, 1976), pp. 113-15), 'this does not preclude the view
that the book's insertion [in the *Iliad*], and any modifications that were necessary for that purpose, were the work of the *Iliad* poet himself'. Certainly,
the episode adds a new dimension to the poem, showing a chilling interro-
gation (of the captive Dolon) and a contemptible display of cowardice (by
Dolon), as well as a night-raid with its horrific blood-stained slaughter of
defenceless sleepers. The fact that these grim aspects of warfare are unique
to this part of the poem can surely be seen as an argument for its retention
within the fabric of an epic whose 'subject is war and the pity of war'.

3. The situation in Homer and Euripides: in the tenth year of the Trojan
War, the Achaeans (Greeks) have had a disastrous day's fighting. This is in
fact due to the intervention of Zeus who wishes the Trojans to be dominant
for the time being. But Hector, the Trojan commander, had been misled by

his success into a dangerous and presumptuous self-confidence which clouds his judgement. See n. at 52-5.

4. I quote liberally from the *Iliad* in these notes. B. Fenik may be right to argue that 'the *Rhesus* is not based primarily upon *Iliad* 10, but upon a non-Iliadic version of the Rhesus story . . .' (*'Iliad X' and the 'Rhesus'* (Brussels, 1964)). However, it remains likely that the spectators' reactions would have been affected by their knowledge of the story as told in the *Iliad*. This is the version that is almost certain to have been by far the most familiar to them as they watched Euripides' play.

1	*s.d.*: the Trojans, in their new-won self-confidence, are camping outside their city on the plain close to the Achaean camp for the first time in the ten years for which they have been under siege.
1-51	*Come to where . . . against me*: this is one of only two of Euripides' plays to begin with chanted poetry. The other is *Iphigenia at Aulis*.
5	*of the night*: uniquely in Greek drama, the action of this play, performed in the bright Athenian light, takes place entirely at night. This is established by the language. The word 'night' is often repeated, occurring five times before 22.
8	*your frightening gaze*: the Greek I have translated 'frightening' in fact means 'gorgon-faced'. There is a reference here to *Iliad* 8.349 where Hector is described in the previous day's fighting 'glaring with the eyes of a Gorgon or of Ares, the curse of men'. The Gorgon's gaze turned men to stone; Ares was the god of war.
12	*What is the watchword? Say it*: the Chorus never do say it. There is a feeling of confusion in this opening scene in the dark with its agitated metre, which looks forward to the start of *Hamlet* with its similar sense of dislocation as one guard takes over from another in the night. See n. at 521.
28-9	*Panthus' son or Europa's*: Panthus' son is either Euphorbus or Polydamas; Europa's son is Sarpedon.
30	*the interpreters of the victims' entrails*: i.e. the soothsayers who would make predictions about the future from studying the the innards of sacrificial victims.
32	*Phrygians*: the Phrygians in fact lived to the south-west of the Trojans, but in tragedy they are usually identified with them.
36	*from Cronos' son Pan*: Pan was a rustic deity who could cause sudden terror (hence 'panic'). Said to be the son of Cronos here, he is generally described as the son of Zeus (the son of Cronos).

41   *Argive*: i.e. Greek (not simply from Argos in southern Greece where Agamemnon, the Greek commander-in-chief at Troy, was king).

43   *The moorings . . . torches*: in the *Iliad* (at the end of Book 8), it is the Trojans who light innumerable fires as they camp in the plain. There is no mention of Greek fires.

52–5   *For those men . . . in the night*: in fact, when Agamemnon had suggested to the Greek leaders that they sail home in *Iliad* 9, he was greeted by an appalled silence and then scathingly criticized by Diomedes. The Greeks have no intention of leaving Troy, and Hector's immediate assumption that they do smacks of over-weening self-confidence. F. A. Paley (*Euripides*, i (London, 1872)) sums up his character (*Rhesus*, n. at 52): 'a vaunting, hasty, impetuous chieftain, proud of his recent successes, and much too confident in his own conclusions.'

59–60   *If the bright beams of the sun had not failed*: there is textual corruption here, but this translation probably conveys the right meaning. Homer describes the previous day's sunset as follows: 'And the bright light of the sun sank into Ocean, drawing black night over the grain-giving ploughland' (8.485–6, translated by M. Hammond (Penguin Classics, 1987)—as are all other further translations of the *Iliad*).

62   *Achaeans*: i.e. Greeks.

72–3   *so that our enemies . . . blood*: cf. *Iliad* 8.512–15 where Hector says, 'No, they must not be allowed to board their ships as they please, without struggle, but let some of them take a wound back with them to nurse at home, hit by an arrow or sharp spear as they jump to their ships.'

74–5   *or be captured . . . fertile soil*: Shakespeare puts similarly vain-glorious optimism in the mouths of the French leaders on the eve of the Battle of Agincourt (*Henry V*, III.7).

78–84   *If they aren't . . . arm against the enemy*: stichomythia: see Introduction, p. xxxvi.

86   *s.d.*: Aeneas is Hector's cousin, a member of the royal family of Troy but from a cadet branch and thus with less influence than his relative.

100–1   *As they flee . . . by my spear's might*: cf. 72–3.

105–8   *I wish that you were . . . sensible plans*: cf. Polydamas' comments to Hector at *Iliad* 13.727–34: 'Because god has granted you excellence in battle, this makes you want to outdo others in the mind's work too—but you cannot choose of your own will to have all gifts together. God gives one man skill in battle, and to another he gives dancing, and to a third the playing of the lyre and song: and in another man's breast wide-seeing Zeus puts wisdom, which brings benefit to many men and is the saving of many too, as he knows best of all.'

110–11   *So you intend to lead your army over the ditches*: in *Iliad* 7 (337–43) Nestor advises the building of a wall as a defence for the Achaeans. 'And close outside it we should dig a deep ditch all the way round, which could keep back chariots and men, should the proud Trojans' fighting ever press hard on us.' His advice is taken and the ditch is built with stakes fixed in it (7.441).

117–18   *Tell me . . . their chariots' axle-boxes*: cf. *Iliad* 12.61–74 where Polydamas advises Hector: 'it is folly for us to drive our fast horses across the ditch. It is very hard to cross—there are sharp stakes set at its edge, and the Achaeans' wall is close beyond them . . . But if they round on us in counter-attack from the ships, and we are fouled in the ditch they have dug, then under the rally of the Achaeans I doubt that even one man would get back to the city with the news.'
          The axle-boxes are the boxes in which the axles turn.

120   *He will not let you set fire to the ships*: at *Iliad* 9.650–3 Achilles says: 'I will not think of bloody warfare until . . . Hector has killed his way through the Argives right up to the Myrmidons' huts and ships, and has set the ships smouldering with fire. But at my hut and my black ship I think that Hector will be stopped, however much he lusts for battle.'

128   *if this lighting of beacons is leading us into some trap*: a famous instance of night fires being used for trickery in warfare is Hannibal's deception of Gallic tribesmen (Livy 21.32).

158–9   *Your tricky name suits you admirably, Dolon*: *dolos* is the Greek word for trick. Dolon is described at *Iliad* 10.315–17 as 'a man rich in gold and rich in bronze, who was ugly in appearance, but quick of foot: and he was the only son among five sisters.' Willcock (*Companion to the Iliad*, n. at 10.317) writes that it is 'not fanciful to see this as information about personality rather than biography. Dolon evidently lacks self-criticism and thinks himself more important than he is; perhaps he has been "spoiled" by his five sisters.'

162   *reward*: Dolon's use of this financial word, soon to be followed by 'profit' in the next line, awakens suspicions of a possibly mercenary nature. In fact, it is not money he wants. He is wealthy enough already (170, 178).

166–81   *I do not desire . . . ask me for*: stichomythia. See Introduction, p. xxxvi.

171   *Ilium's*: Ilium is another name for Troy.

173   *do not ask for the commanders of the ships*: the Greek leaders would be worth vast ransoms.

175   *the son of Oileus*: this is the 'lesser Ajax', the leader of the Locrians, a hero of the second league ('not the great size of Ajax son of Telamon, but much smaller' (*Iliad* 2.528–9)). The greater Ajax is referred to at 462 and 497.

182   *Achilles' horses*: described at *Iliad* 16.149–51: 'Xanthus and Balius, horses that flew swift as the blowing of the winds: they were born to the west wind Zephyrus by Podarge the Storm-mare, as she grazed in a meadow beside the stream of Ocean.' At 23.277–8 Achilles says: 'they are immortal horses, given by Poseidon to my father Peleus, and he then handed them to me' (cf. 185–6). To wish to possess these immortal horses shows appalling *hubris* (presumption) on Dolon's part.

197   *This is a glorious task*: how 'glorious' is a nocturnal spying mission likely to prove?

197–201 *Yet it is a great thing . . . a full reward for you*: the Chorus feel that Dolon would have done well to take up Hector's suggestion of marriage to one of his sisters (167). They sense that he has overreached himself by his *hubris* in demanding the horses.
         what comes from the gods (199): i.e. death or a safe return.

208–12   *I shall fasten a wolfskin . . . disguise*: in Homer (*Iliad* 10.334–5) Dolon merely 'put on a grey wolf's pelt . . . and a cap of marten skin on his head'. The disguise Euripides gives him has been much-ridiculed. However, Porter (Euripides, *Rhesus* (Cambridge, 1929), n. at 210 ff.) quotes F. W. Newman on the use of the same device among the American Indians: 'In their war with the natives several English sentinels were killed, no one knew how; until every sentinel was ordered to fire on whatever approached him. One fired and killed a native warrior who was crawling up to him on all fours, in aspect like a large hog.'
         One may suspect, though, that Euripides is aiming to show the absurd impracticability of Dolon's scheme.

216   *Hermes . . . lord of cheats*: Hermes is, among other things, the god of both travel and robbery.

219–24   *I shall return . . . Tydeus' son*: there is irony here for Odysseus and Diomedes (Tydeus' son, 224) will destroy Dolon. Diomedes in fact chops off Dolon's head (10.455–6).

224-5   *God of Thymbra . . . Lycia*: there was a famous altar of Apollo at
         Thymbra, a town in the Troad (the region of Troy); the god was
         born on Delos, an island in the middle of the Aegean, and had
         one of his two most important cult centres there; he had an ora-
         cle at Patara in Lycia.

230   *Dardanus' people*: Dardanus was the founder of the Trojan race.

232   *who built the ancient walls of Troy*: Apollo built the walls of Troy
         with Poseidon.

237   *Phthia*: the region in Thessaly where Achilles comes from.

251   *Mysian*: the Mysians were allies of the Trojans who lived to the
         SE of the Troad. In the *Iliad* their allies tend to adopt an arro-
         gant attitude toward the Trojans. See n. at 856–9.

263   *s.d.*: the messenger is a countryman, and his humble back-
         ground introduces a non-Iliadic note, for in that poem no char-
         acter of unaristocratic birth is mentioned save for the repellent
         Greek commoner Thersites (2.211–77). This messenger is sym-
         pathetically portrayed. He does not take offence at Hector's
         hasty abuse (266–74). He displays decidedly more military
         awareness than Hector on the subject of Rhesus' arrival
         (284–6). He shows initiative and is a good linguist (296–7—see
         n. at 297). When we may have thought that his function had
         been completed, he intervenes to give Hector sound advice
         which the latter gracefully accepts (335 and 339; see n. at
         339–40). His decency and the unaffectedness of his simple rus-
         ticity add conviction and emphasis to the important passage
         where he communicates the impressiveness of Rhesus and his
         army (301–16). The wonderment is delightfully in accord with
         the characterization. And there is a touch of naïveté here too:
         he thinks that Rhesus is more than a match for the pre-eminent
         Achilles, even visualizing the latter in flight. This view is alto-
         gether unrealistic.

279   *The land of Thrace. He is called the son of Strymon*: for Thrace, see
         map (pp. lii–liii). Strymon is a river god. His river, naturally
         called Strymon, is midway between Greece and Asia and of great
         strategic importance. An Athenian audience would probably
         have thought back to an appalling massacre of 10,000 of their
         citizens by the local Thracians at Drabescus when they had been
         trying to found a colony on the banks of the Strymon in 465 BCE
         (Thucydides, 1.100.3). They did in fact build a colony there in
         437–6 but it surrendered to the Spartans in 424.

290   *with great shouts*: is there a hint at over-confident imprudence
         among the Thracians here?

297   *I spoke to them in Thracian*: Paley asks (n. on 297) how Trojan
       rustics 'came to speak the Thracian dialect'. He answers his
       question by saying that 'there can be little doubt that among
       such close neighbours of common Pelasgic origin there would be
       much also that was common to their respective languages'.

303–6 *The yoke beam . . . inlaid with gold*: modelled on Homer
       10.436–41 where Dolon is blabbing to his Greek captors,
       Odysseus and Diomedes: 'His [i.e. Rhesus'] are the finest horses
       I have seen and the largest—whiter than snow and like the
       winds they run. His chariot is a beautiful work of gold and
       silver. And he has come with prodigious armour made of gold,
       a wonderful sight—such things should not be worn by mortal
       men, but rather by the immortal gods.' See n. at 921–2.

306   *Bronze Gorgons as on the goddess's aegis*: the aegis was a kind of
       breastplate made of goat-skin worn by the goddess Athena (and
       also by Zeus). At its centre was a representation of the Gorgon
       Medusa's severed head. (The real one could turn men to stone.)
       When shaken by the goddess, it struck panic into her enemies.

311   *targeteers*: these were the regular Thracian troops. They carried
       light wicker shields and javelins.

312   *dressed in their Thracian attire*: Herodotus (7.75) informs us that
       the Thracians wore fox skins on their heads, tunics with a
       brightly-coloured long cloak thrown over them, and high boots
       of fawnskin. They fought with javelins, light shields and small
       daggers.

317–18 *When the gods . . . success*: 'The chorus mean that Hector's
       recent success, showing the favour of heaven to the Trojans, has
       now been crowned by this second piece of luck, the arrival of a
       powerful ally' (Paley, n. at 317).

320   *Zeus is with us*: Hector is unaware that Zeus is only supporting
       the Trojans temporarily. The tide of war will turn. See 3 in intro-
       ductory notes.

339–40 *You advise me . . . right time*: Hector may be rash and impulsive,
       but he gives in generously, as at 138. Even so, Porter (n. at
       340 f.) could be right to detect a note of sarcasm in 'the lord of
       the golden armour'.

342–3 *May Adrasteia . . . presumptuous talk*: like Nemesis, Adrasteia is
       a goddess who punishes boastful words. She was originally a
       Trojan mountain deity, and the popular derivation of her name
       led to the meaning of 'the Inevitable One'. The Chorus invoke
       her here in order to avert any harm which may arise from their

glorification of Rhesus. Are they—and the messenger—somewhat over-enthusiastic about the Thracian hero?

345   *the Friendly God*: probably Zeus, god of hospitality.

349   *your Pierian mother*: Rhesus' mother was one of the Muses, who lived on Mt. Pieria just north of Mt. Olympus. We do not know which of them she was.

349-50   *river with its lovely bridges*: excavation has revealed the wooden piles of the bridge at Amphipolis on the Strymon (*Oxford Classical Dictionary* (Oxford, 1996), p.76). The crossing of this bridge by the Spartan general Brasidas in 424 BCE was a key factor in his capture of the city (Thucydides, 4.103-104.1).

358-9   *Zeus the deliverer*: after the Persian War (480-479 BCE), the Greeks set up an altar to Zeus the deliverer, and the poet Simonides composed a famous epigram for it.

374   *your two-pronged javelin*: a dart with two prongs like a fork, which will inflict a double wound.

376-7   *on the plains of Argive Hera*: the goddess Hera was the protectress of Argos in south Greece where she had a famous temple.

383-4   *the boastful clanging of the bells which ring out from his shield straps*: these straps ran round the edge of Thracian shields at a slight distance from it. They were fastened to the shields at intervals by pins. The fighter would slip his forearm through the handle and then grasp one of the loops with his hand.

      For the alarming Thracian bells, cf. 308. (The Trojans too carried bells (Sophocles, Fragment 775).)

385   *this son of Strymon*: the Greek word which I have translated 'son' in fact means 'colt'. There may be a hint that Rhesus is in a sense a magnificent animal like one of his glorious horses (cf. 'cub', 382).

391   *the enemies' towers*: according to the *Iliad* (7.437) towers punctuated the Greeks' defensive wall. See n. at 110-11.

408-10   *around Pangaeus and the Paeonians' land . . . broke their shields*: we know nothing of these services of Hector to Rhesus apart from what we are told here. Pangaeus is a Thracian mountain range famous for its mineral deposits. (See n. at 921-2.) Not far from the coast, it extends some 25 km. from south-west to north-east, and its highest point reaches 1,956 m.

      The Paeonians lived in northern Macedonia.

414   *grave-mounds*: such mounds still exist in great numbers in the region of the Hellespont.

417-18   *patiently enduring . . . thirsty flame*: Euripides here owes a debt
         to Aeschylus, who (*Agamemnon*, 563-6) causes a Greek herald
         to complain of the extremes of temperature on the plain of Troy.

428-9   *I had got as far as the shore of the inhospitable sea*: Rhesus has
         come to the shore of the Hellespont on the Thracian Bosporus.

451-3   *Let no one among you . . . at the eleventh hour*: the *hubris* (pre-
         sumption) of Rhesus knows no bounds, and the Chorus try to
         avert the divine resentment which they fear it may arouse
         (455-7).

462   *Ajax*: see n. at 175.

468   *I shall speak with Adrasteia in mind*: see n. at 342-3. The rest of
         what Rhesus says scarcely bears out the truth of this comment.

484   *here in Asia I rule over a sufficiently vast kingdom*: at *Iliad*
         24.544-5, Achilles comments on the vast extent of Trojan rule
         which held sway 'in all the land contained by Lesbos out to sea,
         where Makar reigned, and Phrygia far inland, and boundless
         Hellespont'.

494-5   *in his rage . . . to help them*: Achilles has withdrawn from the
         fighting because Agamemnon, the Greek commander-in-chief,
         has taken away from him a slave-girl who had been given to
         him as part of the spoils of war (*Iliad* 1). There is a clear refer-
         ence to the *Iliad* here in that the Greek word for 'rage' (494)
         begins that poem.

497   *Ajax*: see n. at 175.

501-2   *He came to the shrine . . . Argives' ships*: the theft of the image of
         Athena belongs to a later stage of the traditional story than the
         arrival of Rhesus. However, as Porter remarks (n. at 501), the
         'description of Odysseus as midnight marauder provides a touch
         of tragic irony for the spectator who thinks of Rhesus' coming
         doom'.

503-5   *And just recently . . . to spy on Ilium*: this episode is based—very
         freely—on Homer, *Odyssey* 4.242-58.

508   *the altar of Apollo Thymbraeus near the city*: see n. at 224-5. An
         ancient critic found fault with the phrase 'near the city' because
         the altar is all of five miles distant from Troy!

510   *No man of noble spirit would think it right to kill his enemy by
         stealth*: there is strong dramatic irony here (cf. n. at 501-2), as
         well as a devastating anticipatory comment on the horrific igno-
         bility of the secret murders to be performed by Odysseus and
         Diomedes.

513-15   *I'll capture . . . to feast on*: E. Hall (*Inventing the Barbarian* (Oxford, 1989), 158) comments that 'the impalement even of corpses or parts of them was denounced by Herodotus' Pausanias as a barbarous act unfit for Greeks (9.79)'.

521   *'Phoebus' is our watchword*: since, as we now discover, there is a watchword, why did not the Chorus respond with it to Hector's challenge at the start of the play (12—see n.)? There is an irony in the use of the name of the sun-god for the watchword in this night-bound play.

529-31   *The first constellations . . . flies in the middle of the sky*: Porter (n. at 528 ff.) quotes Dr A. S. Way: 'Aquila [the Eagle constellation] is high in the southern heavens and the Pleiades are well above the Eastern horizon, at about 3 a.m. in the middle of June.'

537   *this star is one of the day's harbingers*: Way suggests that the star may be Mira Ceti.

539   *Coroebus*: the fiancé of the Trojan princess Cassandra, he is a significant figure in the second book of Virgil's *Aeneid* which describes the fall of Troy.

545   *the rota which the lot decreed*: the rota is as follows: 1. Paeonians under Coroebus, 2. Cilicians, 3. Mysians, 4. Trojans, 5. Lycians.

546-7   *Listen . . . Simois*: the story of Procne's transformation into a nightingale is told at *Odyssey*, 19.518-23: 'You know how Pandareus' daughter, the tawny nightingale, perched in the dense foliage of the trees, makes her sweet music when the spring is young, and with many turns and trills pours out her full-throated song in sorrow for Itylus her beloved son, King Zethus' child, whom she mistakenly killed with her own hand' (trans. E. V. Rieu).
   The Simois is one of the rivers of the plain of Troy.

561   *Perhaps so. I am afraid*: the Greek text is corrupt here. I have translated Headlam's emendation.

573   *I heard it from Dolon*: Euripides leaves Dolon's failure and death to be inferred, and it is through such hints as this (cf. 575-6) that he recalls to the audience's mind the grim Homeric account of the Trojan's capture and death (10.339-459). In the *Iliad* he is spotted by Odysseus and caught by that hero and Diomedes, whereupon he is immediately seized by a gibbering panic. As they interrogate him, Odysseus and Diomedes are vividly characterized, the former appearing sympathetic, the latter proving the 'hard' one. Petrified with terror and desperate to stop at nothing to save his life, Dolon gives far more information than

is demanded from him—and information of an extremely dangerous kind. He says that the allies are leaving the watch to the Trojans. (In Euripides' play, this seems only to be true of Rhesus' station.) His abject blabbing avails him nothing. Diomedes decapitates him.

592–3   *have we not kept these spoils*: either Odysseus or Diomedes is carrying the wolfskin they have stripped from Dolon. In the *Iliad*, Odysseus leaves the spoils from Dolon on a tamarisk bush, marking the spot with a sign (10.465–8), while they perform their work of slaughter in the Thracians' position. They pick them up again on the way back to the Greek camp (10.526–9).

598–9   *Have you not heard . . . ally*: in the *Iliad* Dolon pours out information about Rhesus (10.433–41); in this play Dolon sets out on his mission before Rhesus' arrival.

600–4   *if he lives . . . shipways*: Athena here endorses Rhesus' apparently extravagant boasting at 447–50.

     In talking of Rhesus living through the night till the morrow (600), Athena may be referring to the tradition that Troy could not be conquered if Rhesus' horses had drunk from the waters of Scamander, one of the rivers of the plain of Troy.

607   *His death will come from another hand*: i.e. from that of Achilles (*Iliad* 22).

608–9   *I recognize the familiar sound of your voice*: Athena is presumably invisible to the human characters. Cf. *Hippolytus*, 1395–6 where the dying man recognizes Artemis. In the *Iliad* Athena cheers on Odysseus and Diomedes as they set out on their mission by sending them a heron. 'Their eyes could not see it in the darkness of the night, but they heard its cry. Odysseus was delighted at the omen of the bird' (10.274–7). Odysseus goes on to pray to Athena, and his comment, 'You always stand by me in every kind of danger' (10.278–9) is the source for 609–10.

616–17   *Close by . . . chariot*: presumably it was the noise of the harness of these horses that Odysseus and Diomedes heard at their entry (565–9).

624   *I shall do the killing and you can manage the horses*: in the *Iliad* (10.479–502) Odysseus and Diomedes act as a team. As in the *Rhesus* (622–3), Odysseus offers Diomedes the choice of whether to kill the men or get the horses. While Diomedes kills twelve Thracians, 'resourceful Odysseus behind him would take the body by the foot and drag it clear, his mind thinking of a path for the lovely-maned horses, so they could pass through easily and not be frightened by treading on corpses—they were not used to them' (10.490–3). Willcock (*Companion to the Iliad*, n. at 10.479–502) remarks that Odysseus shows 'his cool intelligence' here. It is a fine touch on Euripides' part to make his Trojans and the Thracian charioteer quite unclear about which of the two did what. They were, of course, ignorant of the details of the night-raid.

626 *s.d.*: the actor playing Odysseus is presumably to re-enter fifteen lines later in the role of Alexandros.

627 *Alexandros*: an alternative Iliadic name for Paris.

635 *It is not right that this man should die at your hand*: according to the *Little Iliad* Alexandros was killed by Philoctetes.

637 *This fellow will think that I am his ally Cypris*: Cypris ('the Cyprian one') is an alternative name for Aphrodite, goddess of love, who was born from the sea and carried by Zephyrs first to Cythera and then to Paphos in Cyprus (hence the name). Paris had judged her the most lovely of a trio of goddesses in a beauty competition—which accounts not only for Cypris' love towards him but also for Athena's hate (639), for she was one of the two goddesses whom Paris had slighted by not awarding them the prize.

643 *Shouldn't you be awake*: in literature responsible leaders tend to be insomniacs. *Iliad* 10 begins (1–4): 'The other leading men of the Achaeans slept the night long beside the ships, mastered by soft sleep. But sleep did not keep its sweet hold on Agamemnon, son of Atreus, shepherd of the people, whose mind was filled with worry.'

647–8 *I am not unmindful . . . graciously*: see n. at 637.

665–7 *Be assured . . . concern*: there is a rich vein of irony in these lines.

671–2 *the enemy have heard and are coming against you*: cf. *Iliad* 10.507–12: 'As godlike Diomedes was thinking this [whether to take Rhesus' chariot or kill more Thracians] over in his mind, Athena stood by him and spoke to him: "Think of going back now to the hollow ships, son of great-hearted Tydeus, so you do not have to return in full flight—some other god might well wake the Trojans." [Apollo does in fact alert a Thracian to what has happened (515–19).] So she spoke, and he heard the goddess' voice.' The implication of the last clause is that Diomedes could hear but not see her. See n. at 608–9.

681 *I have them*: the plural may indicate that they have been chasing Diomedes too. However, it appears that they have caught only Odysseus.

685   *Stop . . . away*: there are insurmountable problems relating to the text and its distribution to the speakers hereabouts. This line and the next are particularly puzzling.

689   *I saw them somewhere over here*: with these words Odysseus points the Chorus on a wrong scent and then makes his get-away. Is there a note of farce here?

700   *Locrians*: the leader of the contingent from Locris in north-east Greece (see map) was the lesser Ajax. See n. at 175.

701   *a lonely life on a distant island*: it was customary to speak of the inhabitants of the Aegean islands, as opposed to mainland Greeks, with contempt. Cf. Euripides, *Andromache* 14. Like the Locrians and Thessalians (699–700), the inhabitants of the Sporades (= 'scattered'), a group of Greek islands, had a reputation for piracy.

703   *Which god does he declare supreme?* Zeus, the supreme god, was worshipped under different names among different peoples.

710   *Before now he came into our city*: See n. at 503–5. As there, the story we are given is very different from that told by Helen in the *Odyssey*.

758–60   *For to die . . . the glory of the house*: this sentiment finds expression elsewhere in Euripides, at *Cyclops*, 201; *Heraclidae*, 533–4; *Trojan Women*, 401–2; and Fragment 734.

765–7   *we did not place our armour in good order or hang the goads over the horses' yokes*: both these actions would have ensured that the equipment was available at a moment's notice. In the *Iliad* both Odysseus and Diomedes observe the latter precaution, at 10.500–1 and 23.510 respectively.

780–6   *And in my sleep . . . panic*: the inclusion of the Charioteer's horrific dream is perhaps suggested by a powerful passage in *Iliad* 10 (494–7): 'But when the son of Tydeus came on the king, he was the thirteenth that he robbed of life's sweetness, and his breath came gasping from him. There was a nightmare at his head that night by Athene's devising—and it was Tydeus' son.' As Willcock observes (*Companion to the Iliad*, n. at 10.496–7), 'We are left uncertain whether Rhesus was breathing heavily because he was having a nightmare or because he was dying and also whether in fact he had a dream at all or whether it is merely a figure of speech. (Dreams are also said elsewhere to stand by the dreamer's head.)' Willcock comments on the 'strangely impressionistic' effect here.

789   *the moans of dying men*: cf. Iliad 10.483–4: 'Terrible groans
          arose from the men as they died under his sword.'

807   *to sympathize, I think, with your sufferings*: in fact Hector is so
          vehement in his criticism of the Chorus that he does not notice
          the Charioteer in the course of his speech.

816–19   *Be sure of this . . . coward*: here Hector speaks in tyrannical vein,
          out-heroding Herod. We know him well enough, however, to be
          confident that for all his bluster he will not put his threat into
          action. See n. at 339–40.

841–2   *Paris' violation . . . allies*: Hector had welcomed the Thracians as
          his guests at 337. The guest–host relationship was of great
          importance in the Greek world—it was, in fact, watched over by
          Zeus—and the barbarian Charioteer stresses the indecent shame
          of violating it.

850   *no longer see the sunlight*: i.e. are dead. This frequently used
          Greek expression can at times seem a somewhat inert cliché, but
          it gains especial force from its use in this play with its night-time
          setting. The sun will rise, but the dead victims will never wake
          to see it.

853–4   *unless one of the gods had informed the killers*: as indeed Athena
          had at 598 ff.

856–9   *We have now had dealings . . . start with you*: in fact, in the *Iliad*,
          the allies are devastatingly critical of Hector (5.471–91,
          16.537–47, 17.142–68). They do not start being so only after
          the killing of Rhesus. See n. at 251.

866   *these Odysseuses of yours that you speak of*: Euripides was notori-
          ous for his use of sibilants. Porter (n. at 866) suggests that they
          may here suggest anger and contempt.

868–74   *You believe . . . the same theme*: stichomythia. See Introduction,
          p. xxxvi.

875–6   *My curse . . . Justice understands*: a puzzling passage in which
          there may be corruption. It could be that the Charioteer now
          feels that it is diplomatic to veil his belief that Hector is the guilty
          party in cryptic—and marginally less offensive—words.

879–80   *Priam and the elders on the wall*: in a famous episode in *Iliad* 3
          (the Teichoskopia or View from the Wall, 3.121–244) Priam
          and the Trojan elders view the Greeks from the vantage point of
          the walls of Troy.

880–1   *to bury the corpses by the public roadway*: the slaughtered
          Thracians will be accorded honourable burial among the tombs

of the Trojans near the main road out of the city. The Greek goes into further detail, specifying that the location will be be where a side-road meets that road.

893–4   *The man . . . to come*: in the *Iliad* Diomedes kills Rhesus. The Muse may believe that he did so through a stratagem of Odysseus, or she may think that Odysseus did the deed himself. She later observes, correctly, that Athena is the responsible party (938–40).

906–7   *Oeneus' grandson . . . Laertes' son*: Diomedes and Odysseus respectively.

912   *She has killed you beneath Ilium*: the Greek text is corrupt here.

916   *Thamyris, son of Philammon*: Thamyris was a mythical musician, the son of another musician. He was very beautiful, excelled both at singing and lyre-playing, and is sometimes said to have taught Homer. As Rhesus' mother relates in 917–25, he challenged the Muses to a music competition but was defeated. (Apparently he had asked, had he won, to enjoy the favours of all the Muses.) The goddesses, who had crossed the river Strymon to compete with Thamyris in Thrace, blinded him and deprived him of his musical skills.

921–2   *craggy Pangaeus where the soil is gold*: for Mt. Pangaeus see n. at 408–10. It was well known for its gold and silver mines (Herodotus, 6.46; 7.112, Thucydides, 1.100; 4.105). The *Oxford Classical Dictionary* (Oxford, 1996) observes (p.1105) that since 1981 'the Greek Geological Institute (IGME) and the Archaeological Ephorate have discovered numerous shafts, smelting furnaces, and metallurgical complexes of ancient times'. The Athenian audience would have been very conscious of these deposits—they had fought and won a war over them in *c*.465–463 BCE—and would have found the golden accoutrements of Rhesus (303–6) altogether appropriate.

941–7   *Yet we sister Muses . . . sisters*: for the Muses in Athens, cf. *Medea*, 831 ff.: '[Athens] where they say that once the nine Muses, the sacred maidens of Pieria, gave birth to golden-haired Harmony . . .' Paley (n. at 942) glosses the remaining lines (943–7) as follows: 'Orpheus too, the son of Oeagrius and Calliope, and therefore [Rhesus'] own cousin by the mother's side, introduced the mysteries to Eleusis [in Attica]; Musaeus too was from Eleusis, a deme of Athens, and was instructed by us Muses.' Phoebus Apollo was, among other things, the god of poetry and music; and Orpheus and Musaeus were pre-eminent exponents of these arts.

949   *I shall call no other to sing the dirge*: a Muse can do this for her-self. There is no need to hire professional mourners, as at *Iliad* 24.720–22.

960   *to burn with him splendid robes without number too*: the burning of clothes which cover the corpse and do it honour is a Homeric practice (*Iliad* 22.510–14).

963–4   *the bride below, the daughter of Demeter*: i.e. Persephone, the bride of Hades, god of the Underworld.

966   *the relations of Orpheus*: for Rhesus' and his mother's relation-ship to Orpheus, see n. at 941–7.

970   *this silver-bearing land*: see n. at 921–2.

972–3   *Bacchus, who lived on rocky Pangaeus*: Herodotus (7.111–12) writes of a shrine of Bacchus on Pangaeus.

975   *her son*: i.e. Achilles, whom the pro-Greek Athena will not be able to save when Paris wounds him mortally, shooting him with an arrow guided to his heel by Apollo, god of archery (977–9).

980–2   *Alas for the sufferings of mothers . . . bury them*: this pessimistic sentiment is familiar from elsewhere in Euripides, e.g. *Medea*, 1090 ff.

985   *For the day is dawning*: at last the sun rises. Despite the disas-trous events of the night Hector remains optimistic (991–2).

995–6   *Perhaps the god . . . will give us victory*: Paley, writing in 1872, saw here a possible metatheatrical allusion through which the Chorus express their hope of victory in the dramatic competition (n. at 995). However, in view of what happened to the Trojans, such a wish would sound with a decidedly ominous ring.